Penguin Books

Owning-Up

George Melly was born in Liverpool in 1926.
He has been an Able Seaman, an art-gallery
assistant and a jazz singer: now he is a writer and
critic and a professional blues singer with the
John Chilton's Feetwarmers. He has written the
scripts for two films, *Smashing Time* and *Take a
Girl Like You*; and he provided the words for the
Daily Mail 'Flook' comic strip, which was drawn
by Wally Fawkes until 1971. George Melly has
also written *Revolt into Style*, *I Flook* and *Flook
by Trog*, and the second half of his autobiography,
Rum, Bum and Concertina. He is married, with
three children.

George Melly

Owning-Up

Illustrated by Trog

Penguin Books

Penguin Books Ltd, Harmondsworth,
Middlesex, England
Penguin Books, 625 Madison Avenue,
New York, New York 10022, U.S.A.
Penguin Books Australia Ltd, Ringwood,
Victoria, Australia
Penguin Books Canada Ltd, 2801 John Street,
Markham, Ontario, Canada L3R 1B4
Penguin Books (N.Z.) Ltd, 182–190 Wairau Road,
Auckland 10, New Zealand

First published by Weidenfeld & Nicholson 1965
Published in Penguin Books 1970
Reprinted 1974 (twice), 1977, 1978

Made and printed in Great Britain by
Cox & Wyman Ltd,
London, Reading and Fakenham
Set in Intertype Plantin

For Mick then
For Diana now

Contents

1. Filthy Jazz 9
2. Good Morning, Magnolia 15
3. An Entrée in the Provinces 29
4. We're Getting Paid, You Know 38
5. The Dance Halls of Great Britain 60
6. Lovely Digs 72
7. King of the Ravers 98
8. And So the Band Folded 109
9. The Real Reason Is I Love Him 131
10. A Good Conductor 139
11. He'll Have Us All in the Bread Line 159
12. Done, Been Here and Gone 175
13. An Increasingly Dull Noise 197
14. A Bit of Fun 207
15. An Unlikely Totem 217
16. What Has Happened to the Chaps ? 240

1. Filthy Jazz

My prep-school headmaster was a fat bald brute who aimed, in the decade before the war, to turn little Liverpudlians, whose parents could afford the fees, into tiny Tom Browns.

Looking back I believe he must have been mad, or perhaps he drank. In fairness to my mother and father they had no idea what went on. He was constantly stressing that a term's notice was required, and we had seen too much of what happened to boys living through that term to complain.

'*Proditor* – masculine – a traitor,' he would mutter as he set about them, for he believed Latin prose to be the foundation of everything.

During the summer term, if a Test Match was taking place, we were expected to eat our bright pink mince and leaden jam roll in attentive silence, and listen, with real or simulated interest to the B.B.C. commentary. Any whispering, if detected, led to either a slippering or being hauled to our feet by the skin of the cheek and shaken to and fro.

'It's the pestilential day-school system, he would shout as he hammered the side of our skulls with the knuckles of his free hand.

In me he sensed a contrary spirit, and almost every day would fire questions as to who bowled the last over or was fielding at silly mid-off. As I never knew ('give me your slipper, Melly Major'), I was very relieved when rain stopped play, and even now the sentence 'and we return you to the studio' holds an irrational beauty.

Very often the announcer, in a suitably apologetic voice, would introduce a record by Ambrose and his Orchestra or Roy Fox and his Band. At this the headmaster, with the hysterical violence which characterized all his movements, would push back his chair and attempt to silence the ancient set before the first note.

If, as usually happened, the switch came off in his hand, he would drown the music, as he fumbled to replace it on its axle, by shouting 'filthy jazz!' at the top of his voice.

Sitting po-faced under a sepia photograph of giraffes in the East African bush, I would mentally add jazz to Bolshevism and the lower classes ('*Spurni profanum vulgus*'), as things I was in favour of.

As a matter of principle I began to listen to Henry Hall instead of 'Children's Hour' when I got home at night. My headmaster and I had one idea in common. We believed jazz and dance music to be interchangeable terms.

After centuries of purgatory those souls which are imperfect but not eternally damned gain the portals of heaven, and, much to the disapproval of my prep-school headmaster, I was sent to Stowe.

The great house in the landscaped park full of flaking temples and mouldering follies, the Voltarian scepticism of J. F. Roxborough, the tolerant oddness of the wartime staff were a heady mixture. I was, on the whole, very happy there.

One summer evening a friend of mine called Guy Neal, whose opinion I respected, asked me to come and hear a record, it was called 'Eccentric' and was by Muggsy Spanier. Guy explained that the three front-line instruments, trumpet, clarinet and trombone, were all playing different tunes and yet they all fitted together. We listened over and over again until it was dark. I walked across Cobham Court to my dormitory a convert.

Later that term I was passing an open study window and heard the most beautiful sound in the world. It was Louis Armstrong playing 'Drop that Sack'. I didn't know the boy who owned it, but I knocked on his door and asked if he would play it me again. I discovered that throughout the school were little cells of jazz lovers. Slowly I learnt something about the music and its history, most of it inaccurate, all of it romantic. I heard my first Bessie Smith record. It was 'Gimme a Pig-foot and a Bottle of Beer'.

All over wartime Britain, at every class level the same thing was happening. Throughout the thirties a mere handful of people had remained interested in early jazz. They corresponded with each other about the music, published transitory typewritten sheets, and spent their week-ends junk-shopping for rare records among the scratched and dusty piles of Harry Lauders. Suddenly, as if by some form of spontaneous combustion, the music exploded in all our heads.

I left Stowe and went into the Navy as an ordinary seaman. I took my gramophone and records with me, and at training camp, in Chatham barracks, and on my ship I found two or three people with the same obsession.

In the *Dido*, in the chain locker, I and a few friends gathered like early Christians in the catacombs to listen to our records. One of them told me that he had heard there was a live revivalist jazz band which played in a pub on the outskirts of London. Actually it was the George Webb Dixielanders but I never got to hear them. I didn't really believe it was possible to play this music any more. I imagined that the secret had been lost like early cubism. I knew intellectually that the Spanier ragtime sides had been recorded in the early forties, but I didn't believe it emotionally. All real jazz existed in a golden age before big bands and riffs and saxophones and commercialism had driven the jazzmen out of the garden. Even Louis wasn't the same, not with those slurpy sax sections behind him. I played my records and dreamed of New Orleans, and the river boats, and the beautiful high yellow whores shouting 'Play it Mr Jelly Lord' to Ferdinand Morton in the brothel parlour.

During this period my other interest was Surrealism. At the Naval camp in Pwllheli an old school friend called Tony Harris Reed and myself wrote poems, made collages and objects, and eventually wrote to E. L. T. Mesens, the leader of the Surrealist movement in England. We got a reply from Simon Watson Taylor, its secretary, inviting us to come and see him in London. Stationed in Chatham I took him at his word, and wasn't at all surprised to find he owned a huge collection of jazz records. Many of these were extremely rare, and the early blues singers were especially well represented. He even had Cleo Gibson's 'I've got Ford Engine Movements in My Hips', a holy grail among collectors, a title to intone over the ritualistic sharpening of the fibre needle, now of course issued like nearly everything else on an L.P.

After demob I came to London to work for E. L. T. Mesens at the newly reopened London Gallery. Although by this time there was quite a lot of live jazz to be heard nobody told me about it. In fact Humphrey Lyttelton had formed his own band and the Graham Bell Australian Jazz Band had arrived via Czechoslovakia to insist in the face of extreme opposition from the rhythm-club purists that the music could be danced to.

It was at a farewell concert for the Graham Bell Band at the Scala Theatre, Charlotte Street, that I first heard live revivalist jazz (the word 'traditional' was not at that time in use). I saw a poster for it and decided, although extremely sceptical, to risk the disappointment that I believed inevitable.

The theatre was full. The curtain rose. I don't remember

who the opening band were. It is very likely they played badly, most of the small bands did. For me that day it didn't matter. They were playing 'real' jazz, and to my cloth ears it sounded just like the records. I came out of that concert a changed person.

I had discovered too that Humphrey Lyttelton played every Saturday in a hall above the offices of the Society for the Prevention of Cruelty to Children, off Leicester Square.

You queued outside and filed slowly past the windows of the society with their big photographs of little bruised backs, beds made of rags and newspapers, the real belts studded with brass studs, and the plump and smiling children 'three months later in the arms of an officer of the society'. With painful slowness you shuffled up the staircase, paid your entrance money to one of the Wilcox brothers at a table by the door, and walked into the crowded and expectant room. It is difficult to imagine now, over fifteen years later, the atmosphere. At last Humph's great foot rose and fell to thump in the first number.

In the intervals we crammed into the big pub across the road. Like gods, Humph and Wally Fawkes drank with their peers. Beryl Bryden, covered then as now in a large floral tent, pushed her way to the bar like a giggling rhinoceros.

I began to buy the *Melody Maker*. From it I discovered there were other jazz clubs on the outskirts of London, and I set off night after night to look for obscure pubs in Clapham, to penetrate ('the 144 bus stops outside the door') that mysterious area of canals and gasworks to the east of Finsbury Park.

I began to know my fellow addicts. My appearance, eccentric enough in the rather conventional cast-off clothes of a much larger uncle plus a few *objets trouvés* like a knitted Victorian waistcoat made me easy to remember if harder to love. My violent enthusiasm, frequent drunkenness and personal manner of dancing attracted a lot of not entirely kindly amusement. Much later I discovered that Humph had christened me 'Bunny-Bum'.

Above all I had resolved to become an executant. Too lazy to learn an instrument, I had decided to sing.

2. Good Morning, Magnolia

The very first time I had gone to the Leicester Square Jazz Club I asked Beryl Bryden if I could join her in a duet. I had her cornered against the *art nouveau* ironwork of the lift shaft and didn't see how she could refuse. Actually, although I didn't realize it at the time, she used the classic evasion.

'I'd love to,' she said, 'but I'll have to ask Humph.'

My chance came a month or two later.

'Grand Jazz Band Ball,' said the *Melody Maker*'s advertising column. 'Fully licensed – Cy Laurie's Jazz Band – Eel Pie Island.'

I hadn't heard Cy Laurie at that time, but I liked the sound of Eel Pie Island. It seemed to go with 'Gut Bucket' or 'Honky Tonk'. It had the right feel to it. I found it with some difficulty. It not only sounded right. It looked right too.

Nowadays there is a bridge, but at that time one pulled oneself across in a leaking boat attached to a rope and pulley. The island is on the Thames near Richmond. Among long grass and luxuriant weeds, decaying weather-board bungalows rot silently and in the centre of the island is a large Tennessee Williams hotel. I approached it full of wonder that warm summer evening. The blistering paintwork caught the setting sun and the sound of the band playing 'My Bucket's Got A Hole In It' echoed across the water towards the Surrey shore.

There were about twenty other people at the Grand Jazz Band Ball, in those days a perfectly respectable number. After I had drunk several pints at a bar half painted to look like the window of a Spanish Hacienda, I asked Cy if I could sing. He couldn't think of any excuse so I did. 'Careless Love', the Bessie Smith version in a rough approximation of her style. The twenty people clapped, I sang several other songs, and at the end of the evening Cy asked me if I would like to join the band. I went home in a state of hysterical happiness. I was a singer in a jazz band.

Cy Laurie was a fervent admirer of the clarinet style of Johnnie Dodds, a far from unique trait. Most clarinet players were influenced by Dodds, but Cy thought he was actually his reincarnation. He had a long, sad, Jewish face which always seemed at odds to the jerky rather convulsive way he swayed his body as he played.

He lived in the East End where his parents had a jewellery business, and we rehearsed on Saturday afternoons in the dusty upper room of a pub in Bow.

After I'd locked up the gallery, I used to get on the 25 bus in Bond Street and sit, going over the words of the blues I hoped to try out, as the bus sped through the empty city towards Whitechapel.

One Saturday there was nobody there. I went round to see Cy and he told me the band had broken up. I was very upset. At Humph's that night I saw Cy's pianist, Norman Day, and he suggested that I formed a trio with him, a drummer and a banjo player. We rehearsed a few times and then he said that he had answered an advertisement to audition for someone called Mick Mulligan who was forming a band. Seeing my downcast face – I cried very easily in those days – he asked me why I didn't come along too. I said I would and we arranged to meet the following Sunday.

That Saturday at Humph's I behaved as badly as usual. Two people were watching with considerable amusement at my expense. One was Bob Dawbarn, an embryonic trombonist, the other his ex-school friend and fellow jazz enthusiast, Mick Mulligan.

Mick lived with his widowed mother in a detached house in Corringway, Ealing. The house was a surprise. I had hopes of squalor on an heroic scale. The reproduction of Cardinals toasting the Chef in the hall was an initial disappointment. Mick, however, had his own room.

It was small and mostly taken up with a piano, a sofa, a large bar and huge unsteady piles of records. There was lots of cigarette smoke, full and empty beer bottles, and a strong smell of old socks. Mick and Bob Dawbarn were listening to an Armstrong Hot Five. It was all very reassuring, althought if one looked out of the window the suburban landscape reasserted itself, and when the record was finished you could hear the whirring of a legion of Atcos.

Mick peered at me short-sightedly. He looked like an exhausted faun. I had a bad dose of impetigo contracted by shaving with a very old blade I had found stuck to its own rust on the bathroom mantelpiece, and half my face was unshaven and smeared with bright blue ointment.

'What a lecherous looking bastard,' he said, and offered me a cigarette.

The rest of the band arrived, a clarinetist, a banjo player, and a man called 'The Hermit' who played the tuba, an almost obligatory instrument in the late forties. Norman auditioned and passed. I proposed that I sing 'Darktown Strutters'. Afterwards with no encouragement I sang several other songs.

What I didn't realize was that Mick had no intention of having a singer. I just took it for granted that he wanted one, and he could think of no way of saying he didn't. The rehearsal continued. From time to time the man next door thumped on the wall.

Afterwards Mick, Bob, and I went for a drive along Western Avenue. We passed the Hoover factory, that great 1930 essay in the mock Egyptian ceramic style.

'All that,' I said, 'to suck up shit!'

Mick and Bob enjoyed this remark, and I think it decided Mick to keep me in the band.

Within a week or two we were inseparable. Mick had a car, quite a lot of money and an insatiable appetite for living it up. I, who should have been studying French at the Clapham L.C.C. night school as a help to becoming an art dealer, was only too willing to tag along. Almost every night we went to a jazz club even if it was thirty miles out of London. Afterwards we ate in a late restaurant catering to the music-hall profession, and I remember as though from a delirious dream two dwarfs on the pavement outside, both imitating Frankenstein's monster and pretending to strike each other in slow and clockwork rotation. Then we went back to Mick's place with a bottle and played records into the small hours. I often slept there and caught the tube all pale and shivering among the well-shaved pink business men from Perivale station the next morning.

My work at the gallery suffered. Even before I met Mick, I had discovered that a love of pictures is not the only thing required of an efficient employee. E.L.T. had, over the years, acquired a fanatical application to the business side of it all, which he relieved by occasional outbursts of dadaistic anti-commercial jokes. I was only too eager to contribute to these. It was the day-to-day routine that defeated me.

Now that I had met Mick, what had been vague inefficiency turned into inspired anti-commercial delirium. To keep awake during the day I discovered that a benzedrine inhaler broken under the heel yielded a wad of cotton wool which, if cut into little segments and swallowed a piece at a time, opened the eyes and enlivened the brain. What the eyes saw, however, had nothing to do with the dusting of a bookshelf or the switchboard of a telephone, and the brain, although wide awake, was receptive only to the imagery of the pictures on the walls and not to their prices or potential owners. Looking through the invitation cards, the addressing of which was my principal monthly task and the addresses on which were becoming increasingly inventive and unlikely, E.L.T. would shout in exasperation,

'Are you taking drugs?'

I would deny this accusation indignantly and frequently burst into tears. It never occurred to me that I was.

During this period the band was rehearsing for its first public appearance. Mick's neighbours had finally driven us from 90 Corringway, and we used the upper rooms of various pubs. I suppose that most of early British revivalist jazz emerged from the same womb. Rehearsal rooms existed, of course, but we never thought of hiring one at that time. They were part of the professional world of which we knew nothing.

Many of these pub rooms were temples of 'The Ancient Order of Buffaloes', that mysterious proletarian version of the 'Freemasons', and it was under dusty horns and framed nineteenth-century characters that we struggled through 'Sunset Café Stomp' or 'Miss Henny's Ball'.

Although we had not yet performed we already had a name. The fashion was for something elaborate and nostalgic. Admittedly Humph was satisfied with 'Humphrey Lyttelton and His Band' but he swam in deep water. Among the minnows, names like 'The Innebriated Seven', 'Denny Coffey and His Red Hot Beans', and 'Mike Daniel's Delta Jazzmen' were more typical. Mick decided on 'Mick Mulligan's Magnolia Jazz Band'.

This particular form of whimsy was to reappear, although for more commercial reasons, during the recent 'trad boom', but we didn't dress up. Following Humph's lead, an extreme sloppiness was *de rigueur* both on stage and off. The duffle coat was a cult object, sandles with socks a popular if repulsive fad, beards common, and bits of battle dress, often dyed navy blue, almost a uniform. The source of this was largely the post-war art schools via Humph and Wally, but there was also a strong, anti-bop element involved. This was because the two schools came at jazz from entirely different angles. The be-boppers were mostly professional musicians who discovered modern jazz by working on the Atlantic liners, and hearing the music live in New York. As trained executants they were able to understand what the great modernists were doing. As artists they were determined to preach the gospel on their return.

The revivalists began with the old records, and only learnt to play because they loved a vanished music, and wished to resurrect it. Depending on their purism, they drew a line at some arbitrary date and claimed that no jazz existed after it. The modernists did this in reverse. Nothing existed pre-Parker. Before that there was only a lot of Uncle Toms sitting on the levée strumming banjoes and crying 'yuk, yuk, yuk'.

Very slowly things changed, initially on a personal level. The two schools began to meet socially to argue and listen. Eventually some of the traditionalists became modernists or main-streamers, and others began to realize that Gillespie and Parker, Monk and Davis were not perverse iconoclasts but in the great tradition, and the modern musicians stopped imagining that bebop had sprung fully armed from the bandstand at Mintons, but had its roots in the early history of the music.

The band's first job was at the Perivale Youth Club. The audience were few in number and very young. There was no microphone, and I tried to amplify my voice by shouting into an empty biscuit tin.

The young lads listened politely. After about half an hour an even smaller boy poked his head round the door of the rec-reation room and shouted, 'Chocolate biscuits in the canteen.'

Points rationing was still in force and the whole room emptied immediately for the rest of the evening.

After a month or two Mick decided that the time had come to ask someone to hear us and give some constructive advice. He approached Jim Godbolt, who had been manager to The George Webb Dixielanders and was therefore, as far as we were concerned, a figure of great authority.

Godbolt, thin and tense, his head with its pointed features crouching between his shoulders as though emerging from its burrow into a dangerous world, his eyes as cold and watchful as those of a pike in the reeds, came and listened.

Actually Mick couldn't have chosen a less sympathetic person. Jim had been watching us for some time in the 'Blue Posts', the pub nearest to the London Jazz Club now that it had moved to 100 Oxford Street, and disliked us very much. Firstly, he had decided we were 'hoorays' – that is public-school jazz fans, an expression he himself had discovered in a short story of Damon Runyon's one anti-social Christmas – and secondly, being in those days a formidable prude, he was appalled by our language and sexual behaviour. I suspect that his motive in accepting Mick's invitation was not untinged with malice.

At the end of the session Mick and Jim went into conference. They talked for about twenty minutes while the rest of us stood some distance off, waiting for the verdict. Jim left, Mick came over. 'He says we should give up.'

We didn't though. Our belief in the music helped us over this bitter blow; we were all fighting for a despised music we *knew* to be worthwhile. It may seem incredible but at that time, before I sang, I used to appeal to Bessie Smith to inspire me. Today in the traditional world it is only Ken Colyer who has managed to keep this religious fervour burning inside him. The battle has been won and therefore lost. It's in the mainstream bands and among the modernists you still find the true spirit of non-compromise. Of course, they are less naïve about it all, and more able to mask their feelings behind a wisecracking cynicism, but then they are much older than we were. In fact some of them were us.

Musically the greatest drawback to the progress of Mick Mulligan's Magnolia Jazz Band was the amiable Bob Dawbarn. He played his trombone entirely by ear and found it impossible to learn chord structure. At the very beginning Mick did the same, but although a man of a formidable lethargy for ninety per cent of the time, Mick has always found it possible to apply himself savagely for short periods and he learnt all about chords in under a week. This meant that bridge passages and even arranged chori were now a possibility or would have been without Bob. Mick tried everything – sarcasm, threats, pleas – but Bob never learnt about chords.

Socially though – and the Mulligan band has always existed socially more than musically – Bob was an enormous asset. He had a ragged moustache, a very old mackintosh, and for no very explicable reason, for he was Ealing bred, a slight Liverpool accent. He looked far older than he was and affected the hangdog manner of someone who sells brushes from door to door. In fact he was a criminal-court reporter for an agency. He also had a middle-aged mistress. A fact I found very impressive at that time.

I was equally impressed by Mick's general success with girls. He would often leave Bob and me in his car while he went into one or another of an entire round of flats or houses, and we, having no other means of transport, had to sit there for well over an hour. Dawbarn's only revenge was to smoke as many of Mick's cigarettes as possible. Bob had little success with girls apart from his mistress. Nor did I, but I was still more interested in chaps.

Mick was convinced, and he may well have been right, that this was because I 'hadn't had enough of the other'. Although by no means puritanical about homosexuality, he thought there was less in it for all concerned and a little absurd, and he did what he could to put me on the right path.

Mick's analysis of my condition may well have been the truth. I moved slowly from homosexuality to bisexuality and from there to heterosexuality. No moral decision was involved; in my view no moral decision is involved, it just happened. I became aware of this early one Sunday morning in the bandwagon about ten years ago.

We were travelling back from some job and I woke up as we drove through the outskirts of London. Through prickling red eyeballs I watched a crowd of young cyclists from the East End pedalling past us for a day in the country. They wore shorts and T-shirts and were clean, very young, and full of energy and high spirits, the reverse in fact of the hung and exhausted group of musicians among which I sat. I looked at them with pleasure and speculative interest. I saw them, but when they had passed I suddenly realized that I had only looked at the girls. It was a moment of revelation.

For six years I lived in the top floor front of a house in Margaretta Terrace, S.W.3. It's a pretty little street with architectural detail slightly too large in scale. It was built in 1851 for prosperous tradesmen, but its elegance and proximity to Westminster made it popular with early Victorian M.P.s as a suitable place to set up their mistresses.

There are plane trees all the way down one pavement, and the harmony of leaf and peeling plaster, small house and corinthian pillar is unique and delightful.

My landlord was a man called Bill Meadmore, author and civil servant, expert on the history of the circus, chain-smoker and kindhearted ogre.

I first met him when I was still in the Navy and used to come up from Chatham to attend the meetings of the Surrealists in the Barcelona Restaurant.

Simon Watson Taylor had first lived in my room and he had made way for Sadi Cherkeshi, a young Turkish poet. When I had neglected to book a bed at 'The Union Jack Club', he used to let me snooze in a chair until it was time to catch the train back to barracks. In this way I came to meet Bill and his wife, Dumps. If I had a long pass I would sometimes stay there the whole time and eat with the family. I got to know them all well, and when I came to London to work I wrote and asked if they would have me as a P.G.

I hung my collection of Surrealist pictures on the walls, discovered what bus would take me to Bond Street, and lay on the bed, a Londoner at last.

There were two beds in my room and one of them had two mattresses on it. In consequence, after the word had spread round the jazz world, my room became a week-end dosshouse for bedless lovers, habitual last-tube-missers, provincial visitors and a hard core of friends.

Sober, I realized the absurdity of the idea, but by the time Humph had played 'Get Out Of Here And Go On Home' every Saturday night, I was convinced that between six and eight people, all of them drunk, could climb up three flights of stairs in an old house, undress, descend and ascend past Bill's open door to a lavatory difficult to locate in the dark, and even listen to a gramophone with a sock in the amplifying trumpet, without waking him up.

Bill was a light sleeper and as angry as an old bear if disturbed. On comparatively quiet nights he would wait until breakfast before complaining, but if things were right out of hand he would come up the stairs. He slept in a shirt. His hair was long and white. He would simply fling open the door with dramatic violence and glare. The sight of him standing there was enough to turn us all to stone for most of the night.

One night I heard him coming and we all pretended to be asleep. He came in, switched on the light and went from bed to bed lifting the blankets and examining the bodies feigning unconsciousness beneath. At last he stalked towards the door and turned out the light. 'George,' he said, 'what do these animals eat in the morning? Hay?'

Mick was perhaps my worst risk. In the small room next to mine slept Bill's middle daughter, Janet. She was engaged and very much in love, but always rejected Mick's lunges with tact and charm. One night Mick threw open the door of her room and hurled himself in the dark on to the approximate position of her bed. She'd moved it under the window and he landed with all his weight on the floor. I got him to bed and there was no sound of Bill getting up downstairs. Next morning I told Mick what had happened and pointed out that it might be as well if he could leave the house without actually having to meet Bill face to face. He agreed warmly but unfortunately was bursting for a piss. He crept down the stairs and looking apprehensively over his shoulder towards the door of Bill's room, opened the door of the lavatory. Bill Meadmore, an obsessive non-lavatory-door-locker, was sitting there reading the *Manchester Guardian*.

'Good morning, Magnolia,' he said quietly.

That Bill Meadmore and his wife put up with me for over six years still surprises me. His general attitude, one of affectionate exasperation, is best demonstrated by quoting in full a letter he wrote me after a particularly noisy night. Green as I was I wrote him a hurt reply. This added to his pleasure. Here is what he wrote:

> 7 Margarette Terrace,
> Chelsea, s.w.3.
> 9 August 1950

Dear Esq. George Alan Melly,

The last Mick-straw has broken my feeble but patient back. I have endured your drunken and dissolute ways, your wanton waste of light, gas fire, hot bath water, horse radish, beans, lavatory water, your assumption that my library was yours, and that you had a right to read the *New Statesman* and the Obituaries in the *World's Fair* before me. I never said an unkind word when your thick head broke the witch bowl and Dump's heart, nor when you, in your efforts to conquer Everest, pulled down the balcony next door. I tried to grin when you purloined the money from the telephone box and used my bath salts. When the house trembles at its foundations with your coughing, caused by your unchristian way of living, I do not complain, and have comforted myself with the reflection that every cough brings nearer the day of your demise.

This letter is not a grumble. I have tried to be patient and understanding of a character that is a throw-back to the stone age and who would have been a joy to Freud. Alas, I am not Freud. I never reproached you when you made this house a doss for band boys and barrow spivs, nor when you plastered the walls of a lovely room with obscenities and childish scrawls, and notwithstanding that you occasionally paid the moderate rent asked for one room, persistently regarded the whole of the house, including the two telephones and the two lavatories, as exclusively your property. And the top landing. The horde of undesirables whom you have introduced into the house have pissed over the lavatories (not into) and worn threadbare with their hobnailed boots the stair carpet. I even have not been safe from the rest of your family who roost here and make the house smell abominably of Liverpool and gin, and Gibraltar rock.

All these things I have borne with a sickly smile. My simple nature has assumed that it is proper for you to associate with such loose women as the Andys and the Irises, the Beryls, and the other flower girls. I have tried to consider that a certain amount of sexual intercourse was necessary for you, both natural and unnatural intercourse, thinking that otherwise you might find yourself in prison for loitering in public lavatories, or for rape or intercourse with birds, fishes and animals. I gloss over the noises you make, the strange, curious bursts into Zulu war cries, the din of the contrivance which you refer to as a gramophone.

I return to the LAST STRAW. Even I, the most widemined, tolerant, generous and gentle of a fair-play cricket race, cannot and will not tolerate this house becoming a common bagnio, a sponge house, a place of assignation, a pimp's brothel, or for Mick the Mulligan to bring his doxies here and perform his strange tribal rites with them in the early hours of the morning. And I strongly object that I have the next morning to straighten every picture in the house. Nor am I interested in his unflowing jabber whilst 'on the job' and his evident determination to propel bed, doxie and himself across the floor of the room. But these are things of the past, they will never happen again. The wheel of the wagon is broken and the time has come, my dear Alan, for us to part and you to find a new dump and Dumps.

We have decided that it is better to have the French girl from the Congo, so therefore, my dear Alan, please take this epistle as notice to quit. To give you plenty of time in your hopeless search for some place in Oakley Street with the same amenities as HAVE obtained here, you have been granted ONE MONTH.

THIS NOTICE IS FINAL AND IRREVOCABLE

W. S. Meadmore
BOSS

Bill's wife, Dumps, gentle and rushed, took it all in her stride. If, after finishing breakfast, I asked for a cup of tea to take upstairs, she would murmur, 'Love on a plate?' On one occasion when, believing the house empty, a girl and I were experimenting in a bath, she knocked gently on the bathroom door and pointed out in her mild way that it was not part of our agreement. Less ferocious than Bill, she was no less original. They gave me something absolutely unique, a room where I could live exactly as I chose, and a home at the same time.

On Sunday mornings in Margaretta Terrace, I made every-body get up and help clean my room. Even Mick was bullied into using a pan and brush. The rag and bone man passed shouting, 'Old lumber'.

At five to twelve we walked round to 'The Cross Keys', a public house which the revivalist jazz world held in reverence because its landlord, Billy Jones, had depped on piano with the Original Dixieland Jazz Band when they were in England in 1920 at the Hammersmith Palais de Danse. With a little persuasion he would sit down and play rags until closing time. Sometimes the musicians or aspiring musicians would bring their instruments and jam, and I would sing.

Our band began to appear in public, inevitably as a supporting group and usually in South London. Chas Wigley, a small and dapper man who wore a bow tie and worked in Covent Garden in the night, was continuously opening clubs. There was one in a garden behind a pub which, on fine summer evenings, worked a little magic, but most of them were in the upper rooms of those huge, characterless boozers in the high streets of the South London boroughs. The opening night was usually quite full, but followed by a rapid decline until the only audience was Chas' own family and our friends.

After the club shut there was a party at Chas' house in Clapham: brown ale, cheese sandwiches and jazz records late into the small hours.

Mick and I would sometimes call on Chas in the Garden, and drink among the porters until the grey dawn broke over the Endel Street clap hospital.

3. An Entrée in the Provinces

Although we had a small public, and although we knew most of
the musicians, Mick had not achieved any musical impact. Our
first success was in Acton where we played the interval spot at
the opening of a new club. The promoter and bandleader,
Doug Whitton, had gone to a great deal of trouble to make
it an important opening in the convention of the day. He had
persuaded those jazz critics who had kept the flame alight in
the dark days to come and drink at the club's expense, and,
more importantly, the Marquis of Donegall to come and open
it. This ensured that the opening would be covered in the musical Press.

Not that the Marquis was a fluent speaker. In fact he usually
managed to get the names of the bands wrong and frequently
lost his way towards the end of a sentence. It was his presence
that counted. The critics were a varied lot with only their
interest in jazz in common: Max Jones who wore a beret and
dark glasses; the enthusiastic Derrick Stewart Baxter who lived
in Brighton and whose passion for the blues could turn his great
face red; Rex Harris, saturnine, soft-spoken, elegantly bearded,
by profession an optician, by conviction a strict New Orleans

man; Jimmy Asman who had come to London from the Midlands full of jovial bonhomie and bluntness; Ernest Borneman, a German-born anthropologist and novelist; and lastly and in a way most memorably, Sinclair Traill with his protruding blue eyes, Air Force moustache, casual throw-away manner and legendary reluctance to stand a round. Sinclair was an early pet of Mick and mine. His seedy but real charm and remarkable way of getting through life in the face of every obstacle reminded us of Waugh's Captain Grimes. He was constantly in Lord Donegall's company at that time.

Later Sinclair became a friend of Gerald Lascelles, first cousin to the Queen. 'Gerald' took the place of 'Don' in Sinclair's anecdotes, and they were always together at jazz functions.

These jazz critics, most of whom hated each other, were treated with enormous respect in the jazz world at that time. No jazz concert was complete without one of them as compère. What they wrote was studied with reverent attention.

I don't remember which of them were at Acton that night, but the band's performance was described in several papers, and a photograph of me singing 'Frankie and Johnnie' appeared in a magazine called *Jazz News*.

The editor of *Jazz News* was actually Jim Godbolt, but the comment underneath the photograph was warm and even enthusiastic. Mick was decidedly impressed and even suggested changing the name of the band to 'George Melly's Magnolia Jazz Band'.

'Frankie and Johnnie' has always been my most successful number, principally because of its dramatic story line, and, as I realize now but would have denied then, what talent I have is dramatic rather than vocal. At this period my version was comparatively uncluttered with special effects. Falling down, simulating two people making love, opening a kimono, standing on tip-toe to look over an imaginary transom, firing the little forty-four, etc.; all these have gradually attached themselves to the song like barnacles to the bottom of an old ship. Even so it was always comparatively elaborate and theatrical.

Because of Acton, Mick felt ready to accept rather more ambitious jobs: not Humph's club – this he thought might kill our chances – but Cook's Ferry Inn for example.

Cook's Ferry Inn was one of London's earliest jazz clubs, and was the base of the Freddie Randall band. Freddie played a fiery trumpet, much influenced by Muggsy Spanier, and his band was decidedly 'white'. In consequence the New Orleans' purists had little time for him, but he had a large following, especially in North London. He was also one of the first Dixieland bandleaders to turn professional and go 'on the road'.

To reach the Ferry was a considerable labour. You caught the tube to Finsbury Park and then there was a long bus ride through the depressing suburbs with their chain-stores and second-hand car lots on the bomb sites. Finally there were half-hearted fields and factories making utility furniture or art metal work, and then a bridge over the canal in the style of the city of the future in the film of 'Things to Come'. The Ferry was on the far bank of this canal, a big 1935 pub in Brewers' Georgian with a hall attached. Its isolation had its advantages. The canal tow-path and the surrounding fields were suitable for knee-trembles and yet you could still hear the band.

The journey home was full of problems. For reasons either alcoholic or sexual it was always the *last* bus and its crawling progress put a terrible strain on the beer-filled bladder. On one occasion I had to stand on the bus platform and piss out into the reeling night. The god who looks after drunks stood by me, and I was neither caught by the conductor nor fell off into the road.

The central London jazz clubs in those years were all un-licensed. Jazz was the reason the audience were there. At the

Ferry the public were mostly locals who liked jazz as a background to drinking and social intercourse.

Early in the band's history, 'Hermit', the tuba player, left us and was replaced by a sousaphone player called Owen Maddock, a tall man with a beard and the abrupt manner of a Hebrew prophet who has just handed on the Lord's warning to a sinful generation. He was by profession a racing motor mechanic and designer and his hands, coat, clothes and face were always streaked with oil. His appetite was formidable. Thrusting bread and butter into his mouth with both hands he looked like the Goya of Satan devouring his children. As regards jazz he had a passion for the soprano sax of Sydney Bechet, which was so obsessive as to enter even into his erotic life. In his bedroom was an old-fashioned wind-up gramophone above which was suspended a weight through a pulley so adjusted as to lighten the pressure of the sound-arm on the record. On this antique machine he played Bechet records even while copulating. In fact the rather faded blonde with whom he was having an affair at that time told me she found it very disconcerting that, no matter what point they had reached, if the record finished, Owen would leap off and put on another. Now that there are a great many Bechet L.P.s available it must make his life easier.

Our first job out of town was on the south coast. I remember a castle on a cliff and the late sun going down over the water outside the glass wall of the dance hall. It was a perfectly ordinary job but we, having no truck or knowledge of professional ethics, carried our crates of beer on to the sand before we began to play. The manager was so amazed that he didn't even protest. It was, however, reported in the local newspaper.

Our first real success outside London was in Liverpool, and my mother was the cause.

Mick had been to Liverpool with me some months before on

a purely social visit, and it had been fairly disastrous. We had been asked to give a lift to a coloured girl, also from Liverpool, who sang with Mike Daniels. Her name was Phyllis and she wished to visit her child who lived up there with her parents. For us the whole coloured race was sacred, but Phyllis tried our faith severely. The A.A. had advised us to go via Birkenhead. Our intention was to reach home in time to hear Beryl Bryden singing on 'Radio Rhythm Club'. We had, in the car, a gramophone and a number of records mostly by Jelly Roll Morton. We picked Phyllis up in Piccadilly and set off.

Every time we went over a bridge Phyllis said, 'Eh, me tits.' Every time we saw some cows in a field Phyllis said, 'All that meat and no potatoes!'

We were only on the Chester by-pass when it was time to listen to Beryl and had to go into a pub and ask the landlord to tune in for us.

As we were driving through the Mersey Tunnel Phyllis told us she didn't like New Orleans jazz really. She 'went more for modern like'. Sensibly enough she hadn't told us before. Faced with such blasphemy we might well have made her hitchhike.

We dropped her by the Empire and drove home. My mother and Mick didn't really take to each other, although she thought him 'very attractive'. Both Mick and I have suffered throughout our whole relationship by people thinking that, in his case I was responsible for leading him astray, and, that in my case, he was responsible.

My father didn't help by saying the coffee tasted like ferret's piss. Somehow my mother thought that Mick was responsible for him saying this too. My mother was also certain we were having an affair. 'Why didn't you tell me?' she asked. I denied the whole thing, but she was by no means convinced. I can't really blame her for this. Although Mick is physically entirely hetero, he likes his men friends so much that it's an understandable fallacy.

Next morning at breakfast there was one fish-cake left over, and my mother pushed it on to my plate. Mick noticed and never forgot. The fish-cake became symbolic.

That afternoon Phyllis turned up. My mother didn't take to her either, not because she was coloured but because she was so Liverpool. She had her child with her. Both my grandmothers came to tea. They sat on each side of Phyllis as though she was a coloured Alice and they the Red and White Queens. Suddenly her child farted very loudly. Phyllis looked from one grandmother, severe and Jewish, to the other, severe and Christian. 'It wasn't me,' she said.

My mother's whole attitude towards jazz had been ambivalent. She didn't mind jazz concerts, but hated the idea of us playing in dance halls. Whenever we were near Liverpool and I went home to sleep, she would ask how the concert went. When I told her it was a dance, she would always ask, 'Did they all stop and listen when you sang?'

Mick's mother was very much the same. In later years, whenever we were playing in a particularly empty and tatty dance hall, Mick or I would suggest that Maudie and Allie (his mother's name) should really be there to share their sons' triumph.

My father, with his admirable motto, 'as long as they're happy', worried less, although he was convinced the jazz thing wouldn't last. He based this assumption on the fact he had invested in a roller-skating rink during the twenties and, shortly after, the craze had died, and he had lost quite a lot of money. He died during the trad boom in 1961, amazed that it was still going on.

Even so it was my mother who arranged our first appearance in Liverpool. She was involved with a charitable institution and, following my self-interested advice, despite the active opposition of several reactionary members of the committee, she decided to raise funds during their appeals year by organizing a jazz concert. This took place at the Stadium, a huge building usually devoted to boxing and all-in wrestling. She contacted the Liverpool jazz promoters of that period, two brothers. They agreed to help and booked Freddy Randall, other name bands, and a few local groups. She insisted we were to appear. They'd never heard of us, and wanted to put us on the side stage with the local groups. She said no. Either we appeared 'in the ring', or the whole thing was off. This is typical of my mother. She might disapprove of what her children do, but if they insist on doing it, she will fight for them like a tiger. My father called it her 'partridge defending its young' act. It is, I suppose, a very Jewish characteristic.

She won, but even so we were booked to appear early on. There was a huge audience – traditional jazz was experiencing its first boom – but no Mick. My father was very worried. 'It's a good crowd,' I told him. 'Yes,' he said, 'but that's no use if Mick doesn't turn up.' We drove to Lime Street Station and found out that the train was late due to fog outside Rugby. At last it arrived. Up the platform strode Mick and the others, Owen's tuba gleaming fitfully through the steam. We were in time to go on in the best spot and went down a bomb. On the strength of it we were booked to do a concert at the Picton Hall. We had achieved an entrée in the provinces.

Manchester was the next step. There jazz was in the hands of a man called Paddy McKeirnan. Unlike most of the promoters in those days he believed in jazz *as a business*. He didn't just run a jazz club. He was the director of 'The Lancashire Society for the Promotion of Jazz Music'. He wrote to Mick offering him a contract to appear at the Grosvenor Hotel, Manchester. It was a real contract with clauses. Mick's acceptance began: 'Dear legal-minded sod . . .'

We went down well in Manchester too. Paddy, in those days a decided puritan, was less happy about us personally. Mick asked him which of the girls fucked.

'In Manchester,' said Paddy, severely, 'we don't discuss things like that.'

Mick had stopped taking an active part in the wine business, and gone to work in a record shop in an arcade off Piccadilly.

This was a curious venture in itself. The boss was called Stephen Appleby. He had an air of languor and called everybody, 'my dear', and at first meeting you believed that he must be a homosexual of the kind who, under a vague manner, hide a formidable and ruthless sense of business. In fact he was aggressively hetero and a compulsive husband. He fell in love with girl after girl and, if the affair lasted long enough for the previous divorce to come through, married them one after another. In principle the shop should have proved a gold-mine. It had a recording studio in the basement where it was possible for Colonials to record Christmas and New Year messages on wax (there were still no tape-recorders), or the owners of talking budgies to keep a permanent record of the cleverness of their little pets. Upstairs were the stocks of records. There was, for so small a shop, a considerable staff. A recording engineer, Mick, Sinclair Traill, and a Swedish lesbian as well as Stephen himself. The social atmosphere was lively and varied, very much at the expense of the profits. Mick and Stephen spent a great deal of time in a pub in Jermyn Street, the lesbian was usually too emotionally involved with her difficult friends to pay much attention to invoices and firm orders, the recording engineer was often upstairs with various girls at the very moment he should have been recording the budgies or the Australians.

The firm also recorded revivalist jazz bands for the private label called Tempo. It was in the little studio downstairs that Mick's band and myself first made what the musical press of the time referred to as our 'début on wax'. Full of scotch and surrounded by cardboard egg-boxes nailed to the walls, we produced several lamentable sides. My own contribution was a version of Bessie Smith's 'Take Me For A Buggy Ride'. It is almost unbelievably flat and practically all on one note. It sold quite well, and was solemnly defended and attacked in Sinclair's jazz monthly. Later, in order to achieve more atmosphere, we recorded in a public hall. The records on this session at least simulated the echoing acoustics on those amateur discs of ancient New Orleans' veterans like Bunk Johnson, which had begun to reach this country.

4. We're Getting Paid, You Know

As a band, and much to E.L.T. Mesens' sorrow, we were now solidly established, and worked two or three nights a week in town and quite often played the provincial jazz clubs at weekends. Slowly, almost imperceptibly, revivalist jazz gained ground as a popular music. Humph was undoubtedly the cause, but the rest of us prospered in his shadow. In most of the big provincial cities there were now enough fans to support a local jazz club, and enough casual interest to fill a small concert hall or theatre every now and then.

It was, however, the universities and art schools which provided most of the audiences. We played Cambridge under the aegis of Jimmy Asman who had become that university's jazz critic elect. Due to their National Service, several people I had been at school with were still up. I drank gin at the beginning of the evening with Guy Neal in his rooms, and finished lying on a marble-topped pub table in a yard watching the stars spinning in the cold heavens.

At Oxford we played in a pub too, but without official sanction. The proctors raided it and the bulldogs asked Mick his name and college.

'Who,' he asked the trembling undergraduate organizer, 'are these pricks in bowler hats?'

We carried the drum kit up the marble staircase of the Royal College of Art, South Kensington, under the huge canvasses of babies in sinks and kitchen tables covered with cornflake packets and cheese graters which were *de rigueur* at that moment. Johnnie Minton, a regular at Humph's, when not engaged in fisticuffs in some corner of the room, would caper wildly in front of the bandstand, and Lucian Freud, who exhibited at the gallery, might raise a hand in greeting while staring with obsessive interest in another direction.

The music we played was more or less as before, New Orleans classics in the style of early Armstrong or Morton, and for my part blues from the Bessie Smith repertoire or the lesser singers of her period. The personnel of the band, however, began to change, mostly because the amount of work we were doing bit into working hours, and those of us who worked from nine till six found it harder to meet both our obligations.

Norman Day, the pianist who had first taken me to see Mick, had gone. His place was taken for a time by a lad from the Poly called Brian Burns. I use the word 'lad' advisedly. He was one of the world's eternal students and never to be seen, even on the hottest day, without one of those endless scarves. After he had gone Johnnie Parker joined us.

Johnnie, younger than Mick or I, had just finished his National Service. We knew him before. He used to appear in jazz clubs smiling shyly in his neat uniform, and would sit in with us or play during the interval. He specialized in rags which he handled, as their composers intended, with delicate precision.

When he left the army, he too went to the Polytechnic in Regent Street to study chemistry. His parents lived in a semi-detached in Beckenham, and he always caught the last train home. He was very small and looked younger than he was.

The jazz atmosphere took Johnnie by the collar and shook him roughly. Within the year he was a wild one. Within the year too he had dashed through every sexual stage in record time. He was almost a virgin when he left the army, and despite a rather one-sided affair with a randy N.A.A.F.I. girl, had never masturbated. This he soon corrected with fanatical zeal, even announcing his intention to indulge on railway trains en route to the provinces. Then he went mad about girls and, being both small and sexually aggressive, became extremely successful.

On drums there was first a young and very respectable boy called Norman Dodsworth, but he didn't stay long, and after him, fresh from Leeds and the Yorkshire Jazz Band, we managed to obtain the services of one of the most quietly eccentric figures of the whole jazz world. His name was Stanley Bellwood.

Leeds, that island surrounded by forty-shilling tailors, was the home of the Yorkshire Jazz Band. It was led, during its long and stormy history, by a burly half-coloured Yorkshireman called Bob Barclay. Bob lived in a cellar in a rotting elegant house near the city centre of which he was officially caretaker. The rest of the house was a small garment factory. I used to stay with him, but this had two disadvantages. For one thing you didn't get to bed until about six because Bob insisted on playing every record the Y.J.B. had ever made, and for another thing, when you did get to bed, his large boxer dog used to show how fond of you it was by leaving great snail tracks of mucus all over your face and arms.

Stan Bellwood had played for Bob. He came to London to join us bringing with him his girl-friend Doris.

Doris was a big lumbering girl who was almost handsome. Stan was much smaller than her, wore a neat moustache and punctuated every sentence with a nervous little staccato laugh. This pair descended on London in general and on the Mulligan band in particular, determined to wrest a living from jazz alone.

We were perhaps averaging six pounds a week each at that time so it was in itself a hopeless proposition. They did their best, though.

For a start they moved in on each of us in turn. Their technique was simple. They pretended to have a flat in some distant part of London, and late at night Stan would ring up (Meadmore in a rage hurling open the bedroom door and shouting, 'Telephone! Blast you!') and say they had missed their train, but happened to be round the corner. Once installed, with Doris's underwear all over the house, they were extremely hard to get rid of. They were with me, under protest, for ten days. After the whole band had shaken them off, they took to spending the night in the Charing Cross Lyons Corner House. At that time you could sit there until six for the price of a cup of tea. The clientele was both seedy and dodgy; male and female prostitutes, layabouts and mysteries, small-time tearaways. When every other door was barred to them, Stan and Doris, their eyes wide open and bright red, would sit nibbling benzedrine inhalers, for you were not allowed to sleep, until they were turned out into Trafalgar Square just as the starlings were waking up.

Due to their aristocratic disdain for work, we called them Lord and Lady Bellwood, and by extension, the Corner House, still in all its Edwardian Baroque splendour, became known as 'Bellwood Grange'.

Stan was still drummer when the band went professional, and in consequence the money got more reasonable. This did him little good however as Doris was given to the expensive whim. She would demand strawberries out of season (off a barrow), for example, so they were hardly better off.

Later Stan left the jazz world and became a public house manager.

As a band we were now completely established. Mick had lost his initial astonishment at getting into a train for an hour or so, and finding everybody at the end of the journey talking in an entirely different accent. We began to play concerts at the beginning of the fifties, and were a particular success in my native city. On my insistence, the whole band used to come home for a meal. Once I even persuaded my mother to have them to stay. I told her that other band parents did, and that anyway they weren't fussy about where they slept. She found out otherwise. Several of them demanded extra pillows and blankets. I never pressed her again. She didn't really much care for the tea performance. The moment everybody arrived they would start playing *fortissimo*, preferably on each others' instruments. At tea, in the early days of the band's history, we insisted that Owen Maddock sat at the far end of the table so that the rest of us would get a chance to have something to eat. This meant he faced my mother and she was forced to watch plateful after plateful of food vanishing into his bearded jaws. He would eat with one hand, and spread peanut butter on his next slice with the other so as to waste no time.

Our early concerts, held in a Victorian classical building in the civic centre, were perhaps, in all the band's long history, our greatest triumph. In the interval the band and my father would dash across Lime Street into 'The Legs of Man' for several quick drinks, but in fact we were intoxicated by the applause. Both my grandmothers insisted on coming. I don't know what they really made of it all. My father's mother would only say, 'I can't think what your Great Aunt Eva would have said.' My mother's mother would suggest, in a comparatively unfriendly way, 'You must hypnotize the audience to make them clap like that.' From this I took it that she, at any rate, remained unhypnotized.

Douglas Byng, an old friend of my mother's, was appearing in pantomime one Christmas and came to tea the day of a concert. As it was Sunday he also came to the concert itself. He seemed to enjoy it.

'It reminded me,' he told my mother afterwards, 'of those dear old days in Harlem.'

It was for me a sharp pleasure to see on the hoardings, in the streets of all my childhood's memories, the posters with my name in big black letters.

It was through jazz, the classless music, that I began to know Liverpudlians outside the middle-class barriers of my parents' world. Girls too. I derived iconoclastic pleasure from having it off in the public parks where fifteen years before my brother and I, neatly dressed and pedalling our tricycles, accompanied our nurse on sunny afternoons.

It was in Paddy McKeirnan's club in Manchester (in those days it was held in a hotel called the Grosvenor) that we first encountered violence. Mick had left the bandstand to go to the gents, and discovered a young thug kicking another one in the face. Mick had stopped him, told him not to be a bastard, and gone back to play. Later on he went for another piss and found him doing exactly the same thing. He'd dragged him off and the boy had pulled a razor on him. Mick relieved him of this and frog-marched him out of the building.

After the session, having no instrument to pack up, I wandered out on to the steps to breathe a little air under the Mancunian stars. The young thug and his mates surrounded me and jostled me into a dark corner. One of them had a bottle, as yet unbroken, but he had begun to tap it against the wall, gradually increasing the strength of the blows. When that breaks, I thought, he's going to push it in my face. They were swearing and lunging round me to work themselves up to what they meant to do. One of them grabbed me by the lapels and gave me the head, that is butted me with his forehead. My nose started bleeding.

I was anaesthetized by fear. I subconsciously did the only thing that might work and it did. I took out of my pocket a small book of the sound poems of the dadaist Kurt Schwitters, explained what they were, and began to read. The book was knocked out of my hand, but I bent and picked it up again, and read on:

> langerturgle pi pi pi pi pi
> langerturgle pi pi pi pi pi
> Ookar.
> langerturgle pi pi pi pi pi
> Ookar.
> Rackerterpaybee
> Rackerterpaybay
> Ookar.
> langerturgle pi pi pi pi pi
> etc.

Slowly, muttering threats, they moved off. I can't explain why it worked, but I suspect that it was because they needed a conventional response in order to give me a going over. If I'd pleaded or attempted to defend myself, or backed against the wall with my arm over my face, I think I'd have had it.

We ran into violence on very few occasions. We saw a great many punch-ups in dance halls, although none in jazz clubs, but they hardly ever involved the band.

Although it was some time before we thought to turn professional, Mick had begun to think professionally. My first intimation of this came as a great shock. We were playing a concert in Wimbledon and, prior to our stint, I was loosening my tie, pulling my shirt half out of my trousers, and messing up my hair. Mick was watching me with rising irritation.

'Smarten yourself up a bit, cock, before we go on!' he suggested crossly when I had finished my anti-toilet, 'we're getting paid, you know.'

A month or two later we had another brush. We were playing at 'The Queen Victoria', North Cheam, a regular venue of ours over the years. Mick asked me what I wanted to sing. I suggested 'Thinking Blues', one of Bessie Smith's most austere numbers. Mick blew up. 'For Christ's sake, cock,' he shouted, 'we've just got the audience going a bit.'

I walked off the stage and sulked in the bar. We had a stormy interval during the course of which I told him I'd a good mind to leave the band and join 'The Crane River'. At least Ken cared about jazz, not the bloody audience. We finished several pints later with me weeping into my beer, but won over, as usual, by Mick's charm.

As it happens, the emergence of Ken Colyer had led to a great deal of soul searching throughout the whole revivalist jazz world. I first heard him on a river-boat shuffle some years before. Like most people at that time I thought he was joking.

The early river-boat shuffles bore little relation to the twelve bands, two steamers, Margate and back 'Floating Festivals' of recent years. Everybody knew everybody. We all squeezed on to a little boat which chugged up-river to Chertsey. At the locks there was jiving on the tow-paths. Beryl Bryden swam to enthusiastic cheers. The music and the moving water, the bottled beer and the bare arms, melted into a golden haze. The last defiant chorus from the band as the ship turned in midstream before heading for the pier in the warm dusk sounded really beautiful.

There was no question of us playing that year; Mick had only just formed the band. Even so he had brought his horn, because on the way back we were to tie up for an hour at Eel Pie Island, and there was to be an open-air jam session for the second line. Ken Colyer was on board, and seeing Mick had his trumpet with him, asked if he could borrow it when we went ashore. Mick said yes, imagining that he would blow a couple of numbers and then give it him back. Not a bit of it. After about half an hour Mick asked him for it back, and Ken refused! Mick told me about this and added 'and have you heard him?'

What we expected a trumpet player to aim at was the early Louis Armstrong noise. Ken didn't sound anything like that.

His wavery vibrato and basic melodic approach was based on Bunk Johnson. He sounded, and intended to sound, like an old man who had never left New Orleans when they closed Storyville. He played traditional not revivalist jazz.

Later on he formed a band, 'The Crane River Jazz Band'. The Crane River is a muddy little stream which trickles past London airport on the road to Staines. The band played in a large hut at the side of the pub. I went to hear them and thought they were dreadful. There were no solos. Every number was ensemble throughout, and to my ears monotonous ensemble at that. The bass drum pounded away, the clarinet ran up and down the scales like a mouse in a wheel, the two cornets (Sonny Morris was Ken's partner) wavered and trembled, the trombone grunted spasmodically. To ears tuned to the Morton Red Hot Peppers it was a horrible noise.

Later, as we heard more of the Bunk Johnson and George Lewis sides, we began, slowly and reluctantly, to appreciate the qualities of Ken's approach. It was primitive but serious. It was also patently sincere. The N.O. fanatics called Ken 'The Guvnor'. With satirical intentions so did the rest of us. In time, however, it was no longer a joke. After the Crane River broke up, Ken rejoined the Merchant Navy with the intention of deserting in New Orleans. He succeeded, and got to play with the old veterans who were still alive. He got put in jail too, and came back to England an heroic figure. Chris Barber and Monty Sunshine had a band ready for him, but they had reckoned without his formidable single-mindedness. He rounded on them for attempting to dilute with commercialism the purity of New Orleans music. Chris and Monty left. The Chris Barber Jazz Band, basing its music on a tidied-up version of Ken's, moved into popular favour and sparked off the trad boom of the late fifties. A great many people made a great deal of money out of this, but not Colyer. Awkward as an old bear, often too drunk to blow properly, he has played as he wanted to since the very beginning. His band had the first skiffle group. At a recording session Ken went into the box to hear the play-backs and rejected the lot.

'You can't hear the fucking inner rhythms,' he told the astounded engineer.

Even Humph, although he has always denied it, was affected by Ken's ideas. For a month or two he turned to look over his shoulder. The ghost of Mutt Carey whispered in his ear. Then he turned away, and swam slowly and deliberately into the mainstream.

One of Humph's characteristics is to believe that what he plays at any given moment is what he has always wanted to play. He re-writes his musical history like a one-man Ministry of Truth in 1984, but the files of the musical Press remain as they were. Only the other day in an old book of press-cuttings I came across a description of Humph listening to a modern jazz record and then, when it had finished, turning away with the remark, 'Back to sanity and 1926!'

The year of the Festival of Britain, it was decided to hold a concert of British jazz at the newly opened Royal Festival Hall. The body behind this venture was the recently formed and clumsily named National Federation of Jazz Organizations, a non-profit-making body whose committee was made up of a great many jazz critics, a few of the more powerful promoters and a couple of executant players. Its President was, inevitably, the Marquis of Donegall.

At the suggestion of some of the committee, he went along, coronet in hand, to ask Princess Elizabeth if she would come ('honour the occasion by Her Gracious Presence' in more trad terms), and she, or her advisers, said yes. Before the concert started she shook hands with all the bandleaders, and the following week the musical Press was full of this or that familiar face grinning ferociously up at her from the slightly winded position, while the rest of the line waited their turn wearing that special expression of jovial despair which surrounds Royalty on every public occasion.

Mick came back behind stage in a state of quivering nerves. The two band numbers were ambitious and complicated arrangements, and sounded ragged and unconvincing. My own song was 'Rock Island Line', and according to Lady Donegall 'amused H.R.H.' but didn't mean much to the rest of the audience. The whole concert in fact was dogged by Royal Flu, and the only band which got going at all was 'The Saints' from Manchester.

Their success was, I suspect, due to the fact that the Royal Family are based in London. Like all Mancunians they were in a state of constant irritation that so much went on in the capital, whereas anybody could see that Manchester was in every way superior. They played their stint with dogged unconcern and raised the roof.

Outside the Festival Hall stood the pavilions and domes of the Festival of Britain, that gay and imaginative flyleaf dividing the grey tight-lipped puritanism of the years of austerity from the greedy affluence which was to come.

Mick was tinkering about with the band sound. He always tinkered because he was unable or unwilling to impose a musical style on any other musician. The average bandleader tells his musicians what noise he is after, and, if they refuse to play in that style, they either hand in their notice or get the sack. Mick never did this, or at least only when things got right out of hand. The periods when the band sounded quite reasonable, and the times when it was embarrassing to be connected with it, were dictated by events rather than controlled by musical policy. There were times when a trombonist played modern-tinged mainstream on his left and a traditional clarinettist doodled away on his right, a modern drummer dropped bombs behind him encouraged and supported by a right-handed piano player, while a banjo player, pissed out of his mind, hammered out a dragging two-beat half a bar behind everybody else.

Another factor which held us back was that Mick, after the

initial enthusiasm of the early days, developed a pathological hatred of rehearsal. There were times when the rest of us ganged up on him and demanded them. This made him very angry, but he usually gave in, and for two or three weeks we would rehearse. Then, using every possible excuse – lateness of musicians, double booking by the rehearsal rooms, the large number of dates the band had – he would gradually let things slide until the next explosion of musical frustration from the chaps.

When the music has become terrible the obvious thing to do is take the sound to pieces, to strip it down, and then to put it together again checking every stage. What Mick did was to add other instruments. At this time for example we had two banjo players. One was Johnny Lavender, a quiet photographer with a constant smile lurking under a half-hearted moustache. The other was a roly-poly middle-aged man called Bill Cotton who was a kind-hearted formidable pissartist.

Bill's musical speciality when drunk was to break his strings in the middle of a number. You could tell when this happened without turning round because he played at about twice the volume of Johnny Lavender, and the noise from the rhythm section almost died away. The replacement of a broken string was a comic performance in itself. He would hold the banjo about two inches from his nose and with slow glassy-eyed deliberation fail time and again to thread the new string on to the key. Eventually by the law of averages he succeeded, tuned his instrument with conscientious precision and then, often only a bar or two later, another one would snap.

Conversationally, as an evening wore on, Bill became the victim of a single idea. Cigarettes were still scarce, and he had discovered that you could always get them at an all-night café near Gunnersbury Station. If any of us ran out in a coach or train after a job, it didn't matter where we were, the outskirts of Bedford or the Essex marshes, the plump snoring figure would subconsciously sense our dilemma, jerk upright and mumble 'Gunnershby Schtathun' before collapsing again.

This ability to respond to a situation like a galvanized frog was one of his more extraordinary feats. One night, returning from a jazz club outside London in a fog, we got on to a roundabout and circled a dozen times round it trying to find the right exit. Eventually we succeeded. Bill, apparently out to the world, spoke. 'Pity,' he said, 'I was just getting fond of it.'

How he got the sack was absolutely in character. It was shortly before we turned professional, and we were to play a job for an important promoter of that period called Maurice Kinn. The night before Mick had given a party, but warned everybody that they must be on time for the coach meet at 10.00 a.m. up the side of Madame Tussaud's. At the end of the party Bill had gone round emptying all the dregs from the glasses and then staggered off home to get a clean shirt. He had, of course, fallen asleep and arrived at the meet an hour after the coach had left. Mick and I were waiting.

'Sorry, cock,' said Bill, and added in a rather pathetic attempt to justify himself, 'I've lost me voice.'

'You've lost your fucking job too,' snapped Mick, and hailed a taxi to take us to the station. Looking out of the rear window I could see Bill swaying slightly in the middle of the pavement using his banjo case to help him keep his balance. Next time I saw him, several months later, he told me that he'd had to leave the band because of his day job.

Sometime before Bill left we'd played a concert in Holland and this brought home to me yet again the difficulty of remaining a junior employee at an art gallery and becoming something of a figure in the revivalist jazz world. I had caught the earliest plane (the others were returning by boat), in the hope of getting to the gallery by ten o'clock, but I realized it was a slender chance. The plane didn't land until 9.10 and although I took a taxi, I didn't turn into Brook Street until 10.45. E.L.T. was away on the Continent, so although nervous – I had sworn I'd be back on time – I had hopes of getting away with it. Nothing doing. His wife, Sybil, who was a buyer in a big Regent Street shop, was waiting for me and *furious*. She was quite right, but I found it very hard, after an evening crowned by a lot of applause, to feel it really mattered. E.L.T. was just as angry when he got back. With the Surrealist reverence for eroticism he told me that the only valid excuse for being late was if I had been making love. Although I was usually a little late for work, it was never the direct reason. There was, however, to use a phrase of Mick's, 'a great deal of it about'.

His determination to wean me from homosexuality gradually succeeded. Perhaps the most traumatic experience was, however, none of his doing. Johnnie Parker had found an attractive if rather criminally-minded girl and lumbered her back to Margaretta Terrace for about ten days on the trot.

She was called Pat, but we called her 'Cow-Pat' because she had a distinct Gloucestershire accent, and there were a great many other Pats floating round the jazz world at that time.

I paid her no attention. I was recovering from a dose of clap, and although I had only another four days to go before being given the O.K. (three months quarantine they give you – surely this errs on the side of caution?), I had no wish to stir it into life again, and return to sitting in the long line of Cypriot waiters in dinner jackets, proud ponces and furtive junior clerks on the hard benches of the special treatment department, Endell Street. She, however, thought otherwise and climbed determinedly into my bed.

This, more than anything else, gave me heterosexual confidence, and Mick too did his best, both deliberately and by accident.

He sometimes arrived in the middle of the night with a girl, usually a night-club hostess, he had picked up, and so drunk he could do nothing about it. I was the gainer here, but usually he didn't mind because by the time I went down to breakfast he was sober enough to perform. Once though he came a cropper.

While I was eating my bacon and egg downstairs, she told him primly: 'I don't like it in the morning.'

Quite often he brought back a girl from a jazz club on his way home to Ealing, and left her there afterwards. I would sit and read while he was at it. Once he noticed that my book, a turn-of-the-century edition of *Hard Times*, was upside down.

On another occasion he was sleeping with a girl when a very jealous girl-friend of his shouted outside in the street that she knew he was up there with somebody and was on her way up. He pushed the girl he was with into my bed, flung himself down on the mattress on the floor (she was at the door) and simulated, without too much difficulty, a drunken stupor. He wasn't best pleased when I took advantage of this situation, but there was nothing he could do about it.

Later on, when we went pro, we began to lose touch with life in London because we were hardly ever there, but at this time we lived a full London life in a dozen different worlds.

Through Sinclair Traill we were asked to the houses of the rich and insecure where the ice tinkled in treble scotches.

In contrast to this uneasy world, we sometimes stayed the night with Jimmy Asman and his wife, Dot, in their tiny house in Plumstead. Jimmy, bearded and jovial, thought of himself as a no-nonsense Rabelaisian figure, but was at heart something of a prude. Because his house was so small and so full of jazzmen and their girls, he had to allow them to sleep together, but he didn't really like it. In his bedroom there was a small bed which he called 'The Grandstand' because it overlooked his bed, and he would give this to obviously randy couples in the hope that the proximity of him and Dot would restrain them. It never did, of course, and sometimes he got quite angry. He was, however, generous and warm-hearted if overfond of the idea that eight pints of beer and a loud fart were the insignia of the free spirit.

Under the aegis of the N.F.J.O. it was decided in 1950 to

hold a Jazz Band Ball at the Hammersmith Palais. The excuse for this was that it was exactly thirty years since the Original Dixieland Jazz Band had made their début there. It was in a way the apotheosis of the revivalist jazz movement. The Committee of the N.F.J.O. sat at a table in evening dress, and the groups played on alternate sides of the huge pantomime-Baroque bandstand under the revolving multi-faceted mirror-globes, while coloured spotlights combed the enormous crowds.

The size of the audience surprised the Press, they had no idea of the popularity of revivalist jazz. *Picture Post*, which covered the event in a long article, was intrigued by the day-time *persona* of the jazzmen.

'Who would believe,' it said, 'that Chris Barber is an out-of-work clerk, Mick Mulligan the Director of a firm of Wine Shippers, and George Melly a frock-coated usher in an art gallery . . .'

The frock coat was a picturesque invention, but, in the years that followed it persisted and grew in absurdity in both press reports and programme notes. I became a 'frock-coated usher at the Tate Gallery', and then 'frock-coated assistant curator at the Tate Gallery', and finally, the frock coat discarded in the face of a larger pretension, 'The Curator of the Tate Gallery'.

The night of the Hammersmith Jazz Band Ball it seemed that the whole world had gone jazz crazy. We believed it anyway, and when E. L. T. Mesens told me a week or so later that the Gallery was going to close down, and Mick suggested that we went professional, I agreed with joy and optimism.

But there were other, less idealistic people with their fingers on the jazz fans' pulse who realized that here was a huge audience temporarily excited by revivalist jazz, and a large number of bands willing to appear in front of that audience for the glory of it and very little money. What could be done about it before the moment passed? Logical conclusion: hire the largest halls available all round London, book the maximum number of bands, and run a series of Sunday concerts until the interest falls. For a month or two the huge suburban cinemas were full of jazzmen and jazz fans. Each band played for about five minutes which meant they chose their fastest, loudest numbers, 'rabble rousers' was the trade name, in the hope of making some impact on the audience.

If we'd had any foresight we would have refused to take part in these self-destructive marathons, but like the Gadarene swine we charged over the cliff, and in no time at all revivalist jazz in London was moribund.

Only Humph had the good sense and dignity to abstain. He refused to play unless he was allotted at least twenty minutes. If the rest of us had followed his lead, the slump need never have happened.

The same pattern repeated itself on a much larger scale during the trad boom, but the difference was that at least *that* time the bands made a lot of money out of it whatever the cost in musical integrity. We, poor fools, made nothing but a little beer money.

It was while the concerts were happening that Mick and I turned pro.

By the time we were completely professional the personnel of the band had changed almost completely.

There was a transitional period when I helped E.L.T. Mesens to clear up the gallery, weighing all the waste-paper in the cellar (we got thirty shillings for it), selling the books in lots to invited clients and cataloguing the pictures for an inter-directors sale. This all took several months, and by the time it was finished the revivalist boom was over, and Mick had had a good long think.

Dawbarn, our first trombonist, had gone some time before. His refusal to learn chords was the reason, and a justifiable one, but Mick had found himself unable to give him the sack quietly and reasonably, and it had all happened on Christmas Eve at Cook's Ferry when he was very drunk. Bob took this badly, and for a long time wouldn't talk to Mick at all.

In his place we had an Australian called Ian Pierce. He had played for a time with the Graham Bell Band, and was quiet, humorous, literary-minded, an Anglophile, and very highly strung. He had a beautiful ugly face functionally designed to support his huge nose. When amused he spun round and round as though in pain, holding on to his nose with one hand as if afraid suppressed laughter might blow it off. We called him Wyllie because he had been so amused by this story about a great uncle of mine.

My great uncle Bill was physically senile and would sit all day smoking Turkish cigarettes through an ivory holder in front of the fire. Behind him hung a large picture of a river bank painted in the 1870s by an Academician called Wyllie. When we were children, we would always ask my great uncle who the artist was, not because we didn't know, but because we so enjoyed watching him haul himself half out of his chair swinging his head and shoulders round to face the picture, before he answered us.

'That one?' he'd gasp.

'Yes, Uncle Bill, the river scene over the carving table.'

'It's by a feller called Wyllie,' he'd say, and fall back into his chair on the point of collapse.

This heartless anecdote so tickled Ian that he spent the whole evening repeating 'a feller called Wyllie' and then going into a nose-holding spin.

Soon after Wyllie joined us Johnnie Parker left. Humph had offered him a job. At the time I was amazed he accepted. I can't imagine why I was now. The pay was better, the prestige enormous, and the music on a completely different level. It was I suppose because I had a formidable sentimental loyalty towards Mick and the band, and imagined everybody else had too. As a result Wyllie changed from trombone to piano. This was an improvement because, although he had lovely ideas, he was so nervous that he could hardly ever pull them off on trombone, essentially an extrovert instrument, whereas on piano it was just a question of hitting the right notes.

On trombone, a boy called Roy Crimmins took over. He was a brilliant technician influenced at that time by Jack Teagarden. He hated the amateur approach of the revivalist movement, was ashamed of appearing on the same bill as professional musicians, and was very much in cahoots with Stan Bellwood who felt the same way. Between them they produced an atmosphere of near mutiny which led to increasing tension over the next couple of years.

Owen Maddock left. For a time we used Jim Bray, an ex-tuba player who had taken up double bass. Jim has lived through every development in the jazz scene. He left us to join Humph. Later he was with Chris Barber playing traditional jazz, and then joined Bruce Turner and played mainstream. Tall and balding, he is a repository of waspish anecdote, his upper lip curled in permanent amusement, his hands black with the oil of the ancient cars and motor bikes which are his passion.

He was replaced on bass by a professional called Barry Langford. Moustached and Brylcreemed, he had no particular interest in jazz, but simply played whatever he was paid to play. At one time he had worked for a comedy band and had played a bass which laid an egg and had a telephone in it.

Finally on clarinet there was Paul Simpson.

Paul has been around the jazz scene since the very beginning. He is an incredible mixture of contradictions. He can be very funny and extremely charming. He can be infuriatingly big-headed. He is given to moods of such black despair that anybody seeing him coming remembers urgent appointments and hurries away leaving their unfinished drinks on the counter.

He boasts of his excessive appetites, how much he could eat, how much he could drink, how many orgasms he could achieve in a night. We formalized this later.

'There goes Paul,' we'd say, 'off to eat three separate curries, drink twenty pints of cider, and then run round the room with a girl on the end of his cock with her legs round his shoulders.'

Musically he has some talent on almost every instrument. He can also play approximately in every idiom from New Orleans to modern; but only on piano, despite his limited technique, does he show real feeling.

Paul is tall and heavily built, but not as tall or as heavy as he imagines. He has blond hair and a red face, the traditional cider-drinker's flush, and looks rather like a bull terrier.

Mick, whose ears are as sharp as his eyes are dim, was always hearing Paul running him down as a musician. If somebody came up and requested a particular number, Paul would tell them that of course he knew it but Mick didn't. This didn't endear Paul to Mick. This then was the band at the time we went pro:

Mick Mulligan	Trumpet and leader
Paul Simpson	Clarinet
Roy Crimmins	Trombone
Ian Pierce	Piano
Johnny Lavender	Banjo doubling guitar
Barry Longford	Double bass
Stan Bellwood	Drums
George Melly	Vocals

We had a photograph taken and reproduced for publicity purposes. The photographers lined us up in profile on a series of steps. We looked young and very nervous.

Finally Mick decided we ought to have an agent and Jim Godbolt, despite early destructive advice, agreed to take us on. Jim had worked for a time with the Lyn Dutton–Humphrey Lyttelton Agency, but had decided to set up on his own. We were his first clients. Despite his irascibility, and his tendency, when angry, to hurl the telephone across the room, he became well liked in the sub-world of agents and ballroom managers, concert promoters and jazz club organizers. He and Mick were a great comic turn. There was nothing I enjoyed quite so much as Jim's accounts of Mick's devious excuses for inefficiency, or Mick's accounts of Jim's neurotic explosions. Around this thin heron-like figure a whole comic tradition of disaster has grown up.

The Christie Brothers, Keith and Ian, were an authoritative source. They used to share a room with Jim in Gloucester Place.

One night they both woke up to find Godbolt hanging from a narrow bookshelf high up the wall. He was stark naked.

Keith said, 'Look, Ian. Godbolt's having one of his nightmares.'

Godbolt said, 'Godbolt is not having one of his nightmares.'

Godbolt's own account of his co-habitation with the Christies is tinged with bitterness.

Keith's socks were famous throughout the jazz world. In fact at one time Keith was called 'The Wendigo' after a story by Algernon Blackwood about an elemental of the Canadian backwoods who took possession of trappers and forced them to leap through the wilderness twenty feet at a time shouting, 'Oh, my feet! My burning fiery feet!'

Godbolt has always been fastidious, and used to complain that when he opened the door of their room, Keith's socks would meet him, not so much as a smell, but rather as a bee-like hum.

One night Ian Christie peed in the washbasin where Godbolt, who was on one of his periodic health kicks, had left a lettuce to soak. Godbolt could never decide if he was glad or sorry to have woken up and heard him.

Later Godbolt moved into a single room in Gloucester Place. It was triangular with the bed under the window. It was also on the ground floor at the back of the house. One afternoon Godbolt was having it off with his girl-friend (the early puritanism had largely withered) when he looked up and saw the fat twelve-year-old son of the landlady leaning on the window-sill watching. Godbolt leapt up or off in a spluttering rage, and threw open the window. The landlady's son, who was standing on a dustbin, appeared unmoved. He waited until Godbolt had finished and then said quietly, 'You 'ave your fun, and I'll 'ave mine.'

We had an agent, and Mick bought uniforms, and hired coaches to take us to jobs. As a final break with the semi-pro past he changed the name of the band. 'Mick Mulligan's Magnolia Jazz Band' became 'Mick Mulligan and His Band'.

5. The Dance Halls of Great Britain

I was still living at Margaretta Terrace, the only alteration in my life being not going to the Gallery. For a month or two I spent every morning in bed, but realizing that I was becoming more and more greedy for sleep, I began to get up between nine and ten.

Mick's life had changed completely. He had left Ealing and set up house with a very pretty blonde girl called Pam Walker whom he had met on a river-boat shuffle.

The first proper tour we went on was organized by Maurice Kinn. It lasted ten days and included Dingwall, a very small town in the far north-west of the Scottish highlands.

Mr Kinn provided a manager and compère, a Jewish comedian called Michael Black. Michael was so Soho in appearance and attitude that it was difficult to imagine him as far north as Camden Town. He wore a camel-hair overcoat with enormous padded shoulders, and had a Don Ameche moustache and a permanent five o'clock shadow. He was very worldly within the confines of his own tiny world.

Michael was exactly the sort of man who is always popping in and out of Wardour Street barbers asking if Harry's been in, or what won the three-thirty or can he be fitted in for a cut and friction in about an hour and a half. He was a compulsive joke teller and kept a little book of esoteric reminders.

'Now what's this one?' he'd say. 'Jewish Bishop and pineapple chunks? Oh, yes. . . . There was this Jewish feller, very sharp dresser, lovely gold watch, cuff-links, the lot, well . . .'

He started telling jokes as the coach drove up Baker Street and didn't run out before we got back.

He also did a short cabaret act on most of the jobs. This was set material, and included imitations of such stereotyped figures as James Cagney, Humphrey Bogart and Peter Lorre.

The first job on the way up was Liverpool where we did our usual concert at the Picton Hall. Michael did his act and was not too well received by the purist jazz fans.

'What about some jazz?' they kept shouting.

They weren't too keen on the new band either.

Michael fixed the digs for us on this tour. His technique, usually unsuccessful, was to introduce himself to the landlady or hotel receptionist by smiling exaggeratedly and then announcing in a posh accent: 'I'm Michael Black of the B.B.C.'

When he had fixed the digs, he'd come out of the building, lean into the coach and tell us he'd managed to get a concession.

'Knocked her down a tosheroon,' he'd boast. Often he hadn't at all.

As we drove further and further north, Michael seemed a more and more unlikely figure. In the Scottish borders he started an absurd argument that it would only take him about ten minutes to run up and down a very large hill that would patently have taken three quarters of an hour to climb.

In Dingwall he came bursting into the hotel bar in a state of acute shock.

'My life,' he shouted, 'there's only a flock of sheep in the street already.'

When I developed a sore throat in Edinburgh he took me to a doctor. He couldn't resist inventing an elaborate lie.

'This is George Melly, the famous singer,' he told the unimpressed old practitioner. 'His throat's terrible, and he's got three broadcasts with Joe Loss, a big charity cabaret, and then he's got a film to make. Now I want you to really give him something good. No rubbish. There's thousands of pounds at stake.'

'Open your mouth wide,' said the doctor, paying no attention whatsoever.

I enjoyed everything about the tour except the jobs. For the first time we were playing mostly in dance halls. The dancers complained about our tempos, and as they passed the front of the stand would turn and look at us with cold hatred over their shoulders. Mick called them 'swivel-necks'.

The small handful of jazz fans who turned up complained on the other hand about our commercialism.

In Edinburgh we played a very tough hall at Leith. A ferocious looking man beckoned me over as I sat by the piano waiting to sing.

'Will you tell your idjits tae mak less bliddy din,' he growled.

I think we got £15 a week each for this tour, which seemed to me an enormous amount even though I didn't have any left when we got back to London.

We travelled in hired coaches at this period. Mick had bought an old van during the semi-pro days, but it had begun to fall to bits, and although perhaps it could have been repaired, he had parked it on a bomb site when it had broken down one night and never gone back for it.

Coach hire is very expensive, and in the end Mick bought a coach and added a driver to the payroll. We went rapidly through a series of mad old men. There was one who couldn't take any criticism and was always losing his way. 'Right. That settles it, guv,' he would shout at Mick when it was pointed out that, according to a signpost, we were now twenty miles further away from the job than we had been an hour before. 'Give us me cards. I'm off.'

There was another who liked to be called 'Pop', who made a habit of standing in the road by the coach steps, and helping members of the band by patting them lingeringly on the bottom as they struggled aboard with their instruments.

There was a short filthy old thing in a very long overcoat held together with a length of twine. His party trick was taking snuff. Mile after mile he crammed it into his hairy nostrils and sniffed away so juicily and loudly that we could hear him above the noise of the engine.

He had, during many years' driving, worked out an arrangement with almost every transport café in Great Britain: a coach load of people eating in the caff in exchange for a free meal in the kitchen.

We didn't mind this too much in principle. We *had* to eat in transport cafés ourselves most of the time for financial reasons, and furthermore he did know which were better value than others. What we objected to was the way he automatically swung the coach off the road about lunch time and drew up in front of one of his fry-up stations. Sometimes we would tell him that we'd rather drive on into the next town where there was more choice and we could have a beer if we fancied it. This made him very angry. Once he came with us into an A.A. hotel where we had imagined we'd be safe from his Steptoesque grumbling. When the waiter handed him the menu, he held it for some time between his snuff-stained fingers and then asked bitterly: 'Aven't yer got no working men's dinners?'

In fact, although some transport cafés are disgusting, with congealed sauce round the necks of the bottles and pools of tea on the table with crusts of bread floating in them, some are perfectly reasonable. There are gleaming juke-boxes and pin-tables and fruit-machines, and tables are clean, and the food, although standardized and limited, is at least hot and edible. In the long sour-mouthed nights on the road, where there is nothing to do but try to suffocate yourself to sleep under a blanket or watch the cat's-eyes unwinding monotonously in the headlights, the transport café is actually something to look forward to, a few minutes of light and warmth in the dark cold hours between leaving the dance hall where the old caretaker and his one-eyed dog snooze over a tiny electric fire, and climbing into bed in the London dawn, grey and shivering from lack of sleep.

We still played a few jazz clubs, mostly in the provinces, and, due to the fact that several towns still wouldn't license Sunday cinemas, there was the odd concert. Most of our jobs, however, were in dance halls.

The dance halls of Great Britain, the halls, that is, where dances are held, can be subdivided into various groups. Starting at the top are the great Palais, some, like Mecca, part of a nation-wide chain, others individually owned.

The Mecca Halls are standardized so that once you're inside you might be anywhere in the country. They are run like military organizations in which the musicians are privates. The band-rooms are full of printed rules: no alcohol to be brought on to the premises (we were actually frisked in some places), no women allowed behind stage except for band vocalists, no fraternization with the public.

The décor is usually Moorish in inspiration. There are strange bulbous ashtrays on thick stems, a forest of lights sprouting from the ceiling, bouncers with cauliflower ears circling the dance floor in evening dress, revolving stages and managers with safes in their offices and 1930 moustaches.

We never played Mecca jobs for the company but for organizations like university rag committees who hired the halls for one evening. The management were still inclined to treat us as though we were working for them, and once Mick had gained confidence, this led to innumerable rows.

'We are working for the rag committee of which this is the secretary,' he would explain icily to some officious under-manager who tapped him on the shoulder as he was drinking at the bar. Sex was another bone of contention. Once in Manchester I was caught outside the boiler house by the stoker, in my dressing-room by the manager, and finally in the bicycle shed by the caretaker. The bee-hived girl and I only made it in the end by using the band-wagon while the rest of the chaps waited patiently outside in the frosty night.

The privately-owned halls were on the whole a great improvement. Of course they very much depended on the character of the manager or owner. Some of these suffer from a Napoleon complex. The hall is their Europe, the visiting band-leader an ear which cannot refuse to listen to their grandiose schemes and delusions. Others are friendly and courteous men who ask you in for a drink after the dance and become, over the years, familiar faces in the endless repetitive nomadic round.

The décor of the dance halls outside the big chains was as varied as their owners. Some were luxurious, influenced by the Festival of Britain, given to a wall in a different colour, wall-papers of bamboo poles or grey stones, false ceilings and modern light fittings made of brass rods and candle-bulbs. Others were as bare as aeroplane hangars, or last decorated during the early picture palace era. Mick's inevitable comment as we staggered in with our cases and instruments into these was, 'What a shit-house!'

There was also a series of halls over branches of Montague Burtons and Co-ops. There were always a great many very steep steps to drag the drum kit up.

We also played for promoters whose offices were either in London or some large provincial town, but who covered a particular area and hired halls which had other day-time functions.

T–C

Territorial Halls where the floor was marked out with white lines and there were posters showing muscular young soldiers giving a thumb up in a jungle or diagrams of a machine gun with the parts painted different colours.

Corn exchanges, often rather beautiful nineteenth-century buildings with glass roofs and terrible acoustics. Round the circular walls were little wood-encased partitions with the names of cattle-food firms or grain merchants painted across the back in faded *trompe-l'oeil* Victorian lettering.

Above all the town halls, massive monuments to civic pride in St Pancras Gothic, where we played on stages big enough to seat an entire chorus and orchestra for 'The Messiah', and the young bloods of Huddersfield or Barnsley staggered green-faced from the bar in a vain attempt to make the gents, and were messily sick under a statue of Queen Victoria or the portrait of some bearded mayor hanging above the marble staircase.

The jazz clubs were moments of release and pleasure from this dismal round. We didn't have to change into uniform, we could drink and smoke on the stage, above all we knew the audience would be on our side and that we would only have to play jazz.

In London, too, we made a deliberate effort to go on playing jazz for kicks. At the beginning of the week, unless we were away on a long tour, we were usually in town, and every Tuesday we played in a cellar club which catered for French students and was called 'Le Metro'.

The club had a curved ceiling and did look rather like a tube tunnel. Behind the bandstand was painted an unconvincing metro train. The bar had Lautrec posters in it. The students, like most French students, were conceited and bloody. We did draw a small audience of our own, however. Some of the more middle-aged jazz fans who liked a drink when they were listening used to come. Also a few modernists used to drop in and even sit in, although this had a disastrous effect on Paul Simpson who immediately began to play bebop.

There was also a ballad singer originally from Liverpool. His professional name was Mike Lawrence, and he used to sing an occasional number with the band.

Mike had rather taken up with a young pretty London girl called Doreen Porter. She had one of those sulky little faces, blonde hair, and a stocky peasant's body like Maillol. Mike wasn't very interested in her but I was, and she used to come back to Margaretta Terrace sometimes and sleep in my bed, but she'd never go any further.

One night I had just finished singing a number when one of the proprietors, a Frenchman who looked like a small hawk wearing glasses, came up and told me that there was a lady and gentleman at the bar who wanted to see me.

I walked towards the bar convinced I was going to be bought a drink on the strength of my singing, and wearing my 'well thank you very much' face. In fact it was Doreen's mum and dad.

Mrs Porter was a small woman with an acid lemon-sucking face and one of those tight smiles which indicate anger rather than amusement. Her husband was a mild and bullied man who seemed very embarrassed.

'Are you George Melly?' said Mrs Porter. It wasn't a question. It was a statement of unsavoury fact.

'You've been knocking around with our Doreen,' she went on, 'and it's going to stop.'

'Now, Ethel,' said her husband nervously, 'don't upset yourself . . .'

'Be quiet,' she snapped at him, and then turned on me again.

'I know your type. Doreen has been well brought up. I don't want her getting mixed up with people like you. She had a very decent boy. Well, she's given him up. Now when she's twenty-one she can do what she wants, but she's only eighteen, and I'm telling you now that . . .'

I'd been getting quite angry during all this. I stopped her and said that if Doreen wanted to do what she wanted that was all right by me, but that if Doreen wanted to go on seeing me, I intended to go on seeing her.

She hadn't expected any answer. Years of bullying her husband had given her the idea that no man ever answered back. She tried another tack.

'I'll have you know that I shall inform the police. I shall find out where you live and . . .'

'Make an idiot of yourself,' I told her. I decided the moment had come to put an end to this conversation so I offered them a drink. Before she could stop him her husband accepted a brown ale.

'There's someone else I want to see. Another one who's been messing about with our Doreen. He's called Mike Lawrence . . .'

I could see Mike in the middle distance. What was more he saw us with drinks in our hands presumably bought by this couple, and thought it was very mean of me, a fellow singer, not to row him in. Smiling fixedly – he had very white teeth and knew it – he weaved through the jiving couples. I tried, without success, to motion him away with a hand behind my back, but he took no notice.

He came and stood by us waiting for an introduction. I didn't make it. Finally he introduced himself.

Mrs Porter turned on him. He couldn't think of anything to say. He just stood there grinning fixedly.

While Mrs Porter was attacking Mike, Mr Porter turned to me and apologized. 'She gets very 'et up does Ethel,' he explained. 'I'm a man,' he went on, 'I know our Doreen is a very attractive girl. I can see your point of view, but you must understand. A mother's feelings, that's what it is, you see . . .'

'Come on, Fred,' said Mrs Porter, 'we're going.'

'At least you've got something to say for yourself,' she snapped at me. 'Not like 'im. Grinning like a great fool.' She swept out. Mr Porter handed me his business card. He was a heating specialist.

Four minutes after they'd gone Doreen came in stoned out of her mind. She walked up to the bandstand and threw her arms round Mick and kissed him. He was obviously surprised at this because Doreen had made it quite clear that she didn't fancy him at all. He also looked very sheepish because Pam was in the bar. She saw what happened and came storming up to him and hit him as hard as she could on the head with her handbag.

'Fuck me,' he said later, 'just my luck. Hit over the head because a girl who doesn't even fancy me kisses me when she's pissed.'

I took Doreen home that night and we did it.

Doreen and I were together for some months. At first she was fascinated by the people I knew in Chelsea, but after a bit she told me that all that arty chat drove her mad.

'I only like you in bed,' she said, 'and I only like you talking when you're saying dirty things when you're coming.'

Eventually I went off for a fortnight's work in Scotland and although Doreen had said that she hoped I'd still want her when I got back, she didn't ring me up again.

Mick and Pam had left their old flat and moved into a room in a flat round the corner from me. The owners were a couple called John and Buddy. John was a very sweet shy man with glasses and a moustache who liked to play the trumpet. Buddy was a big positive woman whose charm and personal kindness just about made up for her extreme right-wing views. Even so we were always having terrible shout-ups, especially after several of the huge gin and tonics which were as much part of the ambience as the click of the backgammon counters and the placing of bets over the telephone. Buddy also had two alsatians. Mick loves dogs, especially large dogs, with a passion verging on the unbalanced. He gathers them up in his arms and licks their faces enthusiastically. He calls them 'lovely old mushes'. The near loss of an ear lobe not long ago has made no difference. I don't mind dogs providing I know them well, but I treat them with respect, and will cross the road rather than pass a chow or boxer out on its own. Buddy's dogs were mother and son. The male was a rather soppy old thing, but the mother had been trained as a police dog. She was called 'Misty Mum', and I was terrified of her. Due to her conditioning, if you shook hands with Buddy or lit a cigarette for her 'Misty Mum' would leap up and seize your wrist between her jaws. She was also a good house-dog as they say.

Mick found it hard to get up in those days, and one of my duties was to come round and tell him it was time for the band meet. I would try and get there early enough for us to catch a bus into town, but usually found that, by the time he was ready to leave, it was necessary to take a taxi. Mick thought I was very mean to only contribute the equivalent of my bus fare towards this.

One morning Pam, Buddy and John all being out, and my knocks and rings producing no signs of life, I pushed open the sitting-room window and threw a leg over the sill. I was there for an hour before the door of the room opened and Mick looked in. 'Misty's Mum's' jaws held my calf quite gently, but her low growling and the slight increase in pressure when I tried to move or cry out convinced me that it would be better to remain still and silent.

Mick and Pam weren't at Buddy and John's very long. One night after a concert they had a terrible row, and Mick gave Pam a black eye in the hall and rushed out into the night.

I was just about to eat a delicious plateful of cold roast beef in the kitchen. Buddy comforted Pam, and John asked me to go out and find Mick and tell him he mustn't come back. I put down my knife and fork and walked along the embankment. Mick was leaning on the wall staring at the oily water. I told him and said he could stay the night with me. Then I went back to see what was happening.

Pam had gone to bed. John said he realized it was nothing to do with me, and gave me a large brandy. On the table was my plate of beef, and I was starving. Even so I felt it would be heartless to suggest I eat it, so I drank the brandy and left.

For a few days Pam stayed there and said she would never go back to Mick. She did, of course, and shortly afterwards they found a flat in Lisle Street behind Leicester Square.

This street, with its electrical spare parts shops and very old whores, became so much a part of the Mulligan legend that you couldn't imagine him living anywhere else.

6. Lovely Digs

In the afternoons we used to drink in 'The Mandrake'. It had started as a chess club, but gradually it had absorbed cellar after cellar under the pavement of Meard Street. A good club is its members. The two bosses, Boris, huge and taciturn, and Teddy Turner, volatile and Jewish, accepted jazzmen as contributory. In the evenings, after the pubs were shut, we were encouraged to sit in, but it was the afternoons I liked. Under today's regulations there are far fewer afternoon drinking clubs. This deprives people of a keen anti-social pleasure; the knowledge that you are drinking and getting drunk when everybody else is working. I enjoyed the slow idiotic and repetitive conversations or arguments. The barmaids turning into goddesses, the feeling that time was not a member.

Our other stronghold was the 'A. and A. Club'. According to the yellowing rules by the entrance, 'A. and A.' stood for authors and actors, but in fact those who used the premises were mostly taxi-drivers, clip-joint hostesses, waiters, small-time criminals and jazz musicians.

The A. and A. was housed in a tall ramshackle building tucked away in an alley behind the Charing Cross Road. There were a great many stone stairs up to the club entrance and on one of them slept an old woman under a pile of newspapers. Although there was a door with a spyhole in it, unless the law was putting the pressure on it was usually open and you could walk right in. There were two rooms in use: a restaurant, and above it a billiard hall patronized for the most part by the taxi-drivers.

The restaurant was a long, cheerful, none-too-clean room with a counter at the end and a kitchen off. The food was Greek, very reasonable and surprisingly good. We usually went there when we got back into town after a job, but the atmosphere was so lively that, although we intended leaving in time to catch the next all-night bus, we often sat until the first tube in Leicester Square.

There was a juke box which held an uncharacteristic selection of good jazz and Greek music, and in the entrance to the club there was a football machine usually manipulated by seriously involved Cypriot waiters.

At one table sat an old man with a long white beard. He was an astrologer and, for a small fee, would work out your horoscope with the aid of tattered charts of the heavens. Another regular was Gypsy Larry. Larry was in his sixties but his nut-brown face, vivid black eyes, and very white teeth suggested a much younger man. He wore a brilliant red neckerchief and talked pure old-style cockney. One of his stories began: 'So this geezer went for a pony in the carsie.'

There was often a live session at the A. and A., but as there was no piano, and brass or woodwind instruments were discouraged, this was confined to guitars and banjoes. Gypsy Larry could play guitar, and 'Banjo George', a dignified grey-haired man who looked like an accountant down on his luck, usually sat in with him. Among the various jazz musicians who also contributed was Diz Disley.

Diz had come to London from Yorkshire where he had been at Leeds Art School and was also a member of the Yorkshire

Jazz Band. He wears a beard and has the face of a satyr *en route* to a cheerful orgy. He is full of talent and a real anarchist with a built-in anti-success mechanism. He sleeps through appointments with editors who would like to employ him as a cartoonist, or, if he has the job, doesn't send in his drawings on time. He became a popular compère on a B.B.C. pop programme not long ago and then missed several editions because he was in jail for contempt of an Income Tax court. He is generous with his money, and unscrupulous when he hasn't any. If reproached he simply says, 'Be fair,' and if this doesn't help adds, 'Tarrah then. Fuck off.'

What Diz has is a great feeling for style, an eye for the human comedy, and a tongue to transmit its flavour.

I saw a lot of him at this time. One day we ate in an Indian restaurant in Chelsea. There was an elderly woman at the next table talking about circuses in a loud, slightly dotty way.

'I will never go to the circus,' she told her companion, 'because of the performing animals. I should only make a scene, and it wouldn't do any good, so I don't go.'

Diz nodded in vigorous approval, his head cocked like a tom-tit on a coconut.

'The whole point is,' she went on, 'that I can't bear animals having to learn tricks. I don't mind if they do tricks naturally. Now my doggie . . .' and she patted the snuffling old hearth-rug at her feet.

'He can do lots of tricks, can't 'oo, darling. 'Es, of course 'oo can, but the point is that the tricks he can do, he's taught himself . . .'

There was a moment's silence in the restaurant while the lady drank some water. Disley completed her sentence for her quietly but clearly.

'Like fuckin' barking,' he explained amiably.

Another A. and A. *habitué* was a girl called Kinky Mavis. She was not a great beauty, but a serious eroticist with a large assortment of chains, fancy-dress (nun, schoolgirl, police-woman, etc.) and a collection of photographs she liked to spread around her bed. Outside this she seemed a friendly un-complicated girl.

Mick never went up the A. and A. much. After a couple of visits, he had decided it wasn't his atmosphere. He only liked talking to people when he was drinking and, in London at any rate, only ate when he was starving. Even then, he would usually settle for five or six pies at a stall. Like a wild animal he had established his chosen tracks through the Soho jungle and seldom deviated. He was a raver of habit.

One afternoon we had stopped for a drink at a small pub in Essex. There was a village green in front of the building, and grazing on it a tethered goat. There is something very un-English about goats. It's not only that there aren't many of them, it's their pagan eyes, either milky-blue or honey-yellow, with their elongated pupils, and their extraordinary smell, and the way their skeletons are so functional, so in evidence, with the flesh draped on the bones like heavy material.

With a glass of beer gleaming and glinting in my hand under the light-splashed East Anglian sky, I walked over the green and patted the animal's taut neck and the bulging flanks sup-ported on the neat splayed legs. Suddenly, without looking up from its grazing, the goat began to shit. Like a speeded-up film of a flower opening, its whole arse split and a formidable number of turds in clusters like black grapes emerged and fell steaming on to the grass.

I was surprised by this rather dramatic event and walked back to the band who were sitting on a long bench outside the low white clap-boarded building and attempted to describe what I had seen.

Mick listened and then asked, as though seeking information, how many points I got for seeing a goat shit. This was how the points game started.

At first it applied simply to animals shitting: two for a dog; five for the more secretive and fastidious cat; only three for a cow but an extra two if it was pissing at the same time.

I don't know at what moment 'the points system' was extended and widened to take in minor accidents and personal disasters, nor how long it was before it crystallized and became exclusively concerned with deformities, dwarfs and cripples, but eventually it did. The awarding of points became a popular band sport. A pre-sick joke.

Mick has always been concerned with the significance of certain numbers. Very soon the comparatively modest 'eighteen' became linked to points.

'At least eighteen,' he would say as we stopped to allow a hunchback with a surgical boot weave across the road in front of the band coach.

'Points' also became a noun as in the sentence: 'He is points.'

And to describe some physical handicap not immediately apparent, such as an expensive artificial leg, the word gained an adjective.

'Have you noticed?' Mick would ask out of the corner of his mouth. 'He's subtle points.'

Descriptions of athletic events on the radio were considerably enriched by the invention of the points system. Sentences like 'He has been awarded the maximum number of points' or 'I'm afraid she has lost several points there' gained a new significance.

There was in the jazz world at that time a man who was worth at least eighteen. His name was 'Little Jeff', and he was a dwarf jazz musician. He played trumpet and sang. Before the war he had worked with Nat Gonnella around the music halls. Presumably on the Johnsonian principle that why people want to see a dog walking on its hind legs or a woman preaching is not because they can do it well but because they can do it at all. It was his size and not his musical ability which had won him his livelihood. Even so he could play the trumpet quite well and was at that time lively and active.

During the bombing God had seen fit to aim a splinter of glass at little Jeff and paralyse him from the waist down. This just about doubled his points rating but didn't break his spirit. He now propelled himself in an invalid car from jazz club to jazz club and would borrow Mick's trumpet and sing and play a couple of numbers. One was 'Old Rocking Chair's Got Me'. He was not unaware of the pathos of his position; the other, 'I'm In the Mood for Love'.

The only trouble with little Jeff was that he had to be carried from his invalid car to the bandstand, and he was extremely heavy for his size.

It was here that Paul Simpson carried little Jeff in by himself. Although crimson in the face he didn't drop him, but reached the chair and walked away puffed up with pride. He hadn't gone more than a few steps when little Jeff began to shout out in pain. In his relief at being able to put him down, Paul hadn't been careful enough. Little Jeff was sitting on his balls.

In my view the points game is no worse and no better than the conventional response to deformity. When we started it may even have been better because we shocked ourselves into taking deformity into account. In time, however, our attitude hardened into convention. We simply thought 'eighteen' where most people think 'how tragic' and with as little sense of involvement.

In the early fifties the 'West End Café' in Edinburgh used to book jazz bands from London for a fortnight at a time, and eventually they got round to us. I was very excited by this because it was the band's first long engagement, and I found it possible again to relate to jazz history. Even the name of the café, in appearance a conventional Scottish tea-room, was the same as a venue in Chicago where Armstrong had played in the early twenties. Another advantage was that we could play jazz all evening with no waltzes or sambas, and that I was sure that Mick would find it essential to rehearse some new numbers as we would be facing more or less the same audience every night.

We stayed *en pension* in a boarding house. On the table at every meal were huge cake stands loaded with every sort of scone and roll. I have always been greedy and eat myself to a standstill. Until then I had been thin. Edinburgh was a watershed. I got into the coach at Baker Street a skinny lad and got out three weeks later a fat man. Mick took to calling me 'Fatso' which he shortened to 'Fat'. An incidental effect of my altered metabolism was to stop me drinking beer altogether. Consulting a calorie chart I discovered that gin was the least fattening spirit and for a long time drank it neat at a single swallow, a sight which convinced most people of my depravity.

The Edinburgh jazz musicians were divided into two cliques. There were the purists led by a clarinettist called Sandy Brown and a trumpet player called Al Fairweather. They played at that time Ken Colyer music at its most uncompromising and listened to our brand of Dixieland with glowering disapproval. Al and Sandy have the two Scottish faces: Al's is the craggy one with watch-spring eyebrows, Sandy's the long dour one with the Kilroy nose. He also wears a beard and balded early.

Their rivals played Condon music. Again there were two outstanding personalities, Alex Welsh and Archie Semple, although their band went under Archie's name. Alex was short and jolly. Archie was tall, thin, and charming in a jumpy kind of way.

The Brown–Fairweather axis and the Welsh–Semple clique hardly communicated. We became more friendly with the latter, and after finishing our Edinburgh stint went on a short tour with the Semple band. During the course of this, Archie decided to come down to London and join the Mulligan band on clarinet. Did this mean Paul Simpson left? Of course not. Mick bought him a baritone sax and yet again the band grew bigger and more unwieldy, but Archie's rather Peewee Russell flavoured style was a distinct acquisition. Mick was never against featuring soloists (it gave him time for a quick smoke in the wings), and to listen to Archie was a genuine pleasure.

Shortly afterwards two more personnel changes took place, and both replacements were Scottish. Why are there so many Scots jazz musicians, and, come to that, why so many good ones? Sandy Brown, a convinced nationalist, has a theory that it's to do with the fact that Scottish folk music is still a reality.

Johnny Lavender, the chicken-hating banjoist, left to go and practise photography in Canada. In his place, Mick took on Jimmy Currie, a convinced modernist who played amplified guitar.

Jimmy was the antithesis of the rest of us. He was a great dandy, and used to bring away on tour several suits which swayed rhythmically from side to side in their cellophane covers from a rail at the back of the band coach.

Uncomprehending and irritated we asked him why. He explained in his high-pitched Edinburgh accent: 'Well, man, you've got to look sharp for the chicks.'

For the same reason he was very concerned about his thinning hair and, to disguise this, he grew it very long at the back of his head and brushed it forward over his cranium, arranging it in little curls at the front. Although this took a long time and needed constant attention, it worked well enough in the ordinary way, but sometimes, when he was carrying his amplifier from the coach to the hall, or walking through the streets looking for somewhere to eat, a sudden gust of wind would blow the whole thing backwards leaving his head bald and a good foot of hair streaming out behind him. Later on, long after he had left the band, he, sensibly, bought an expensive toupee. Only the other day I saw him wearing a new one, completely convincing for anybody who didn't know him, in 'distinguished' grey.

He was also the first person I knew who used 'Old Spice' after-shave lotion, at that time unobtainable in this country. He told us that he 'got the fellers to bring it over on the boats'.

Jimmy worked out a cabaret act which Mick sometimes asked him to perform at concerts, mostly for our pleasure. For no self-evident reason Jimmy's act involved him pretending to be a Mexican. He opened and closed it with a chorus from 'South of the Border', and wore a sombrero liberated, I suspect, from the wardrobe of some Latin-American group he had worked with in the past. I can still remember some of the abysmal patter which he delivered in the conventional sing-song of the Cowboy film peon.

'My girl friend, she's not pretty, but then she's not ugly. She's sort of in between – pretty ugly. When I first saw her she was standing outside a pawn shop picking her teeth, so I went inside the shop and helped her pick the teeth she wanted, etc. . . .'

Our new bass player, Pat Molloy, although of Irish origin, was born in Dunfermline, a small Scottish town on the other side of the Firth of Forth from Edinburgh. He was very small, a practising Roman Catholic, and had a classic Irish face with black curly hair and a complicated mouth full of teeth. It was these which made his Irish-Scottish accent very difficult to understand.

He had been an insurance agent in Dunfermline: 'I was very, very respected in Dunfermline,' he would often tell us, but had left over a muddle with money. He was scrupulously honest, so it had been a genuine muddle mostly due, we gathered, to allowing people who couldn't pay to leave it over to next week, and marking their books as though they had paid, and then forgetting if they had or not. A muddle due to kindness in fact, for he was a very kindhearted little man.

Pat had discovered in the cheerful blasphemy of the Mulligan band, perhaps, the most worrying milieu for him. He took, as they say, 'refuge in drink', in his case Guinness. Sober he was a polite person. When drunk he began to swear, not as most people swear, in order to emphasize what they have to say, or from verbal poverty, but as though possessed. At the same time his face would alter. His eyes rolled, his nostrils distended, and his mouth grinned fixedly revealing his formidable teeth.

Pat was a virgin. He once told me that when he had been working in a sack factory a girl had pushed him back on to a pile of the finished product and 'tried to rape me, but I managed to push her off'!

He owned an enormous collection of the sort of suits you can see on men waiting for the pubs to open on Sunday mornings in Camden Town, bright blue with floppy trouser bottoms. He was also a great runner of mysterious errands involving small brown paper parcels.

Drinking and gambling so complicated his financial life that for quite a long time he was forced to live in the band coach which was parked on a piece of waste ground behind King's Cross. He washed in the nearby public baths and ate in a café. His wardrobe hung across the back of the coach, his belongings along the shelves.

But despite these economies, he was always having to approach Mick for subs and loans. Mick, although prepared to help him out, rather dreaded these moments, not only for the money involved, but because Pat insisted on giving him an hour-long explanation of just why and how his finances were in such a mess. He prefaced these sessions with a sentence that Mick learned to dread. 'I wonder,' he would say, 'if we could have a little chat?'

Pat's real obsession was his instrument. His double bass was an old one and, alone among the instruments in a jazz band, the age of a double bass would appear to add to its standing in the eyes of its owner.

During journeys it lay across the back seat of the coach, and, whenever we passed over a level-crossing or humpbacked bridge, and in consequence bounced into the air, Pat would give a loud anguished cry of 'the bass', and scurry down the coach aisle to make sure it had suffered no damage.

Musicians' reactions to their instruments vary a great deal. Clarinet players, due to the flimsy nature of the clarinet, become hardened to minor disasters, although at the same time given to irritable exasperation. Between overhauls a complicated forest of elastic bands replaces weak springs, little green pads are constantly falling off, and reeds have to be singed with matches in an attempt to harden the blowing edge.

Trombonists are very neurotic about their horns. They're usually fairly neurotic anyway, but it's impossible to say whether they become trombonists *because* they're neurotic or become neurotic *because* they're trombonists. It's easy to see why they worry about their instruments. The long slide, incredibly vulnerable and, if bent only a fraction, completely useless, which must nevertheless be temptingly pushed out over the heads of an audience, is the main cause, but also the fact that many people tend to think of the trombone as a musical joke is a contributing factor. Most trombonists alternate between pushing their technique beyond its limits and angry self-parody.

Trumpet players are musically pretty extrovert on the whole. Because it is quite hard to damage a trumpet short of jumping on it, they treat their instruments with a certain indifference.

Mick's various trumpets – he had almost as many as he had suits – were always in terrible condition, but even so they had to seize up before he cleaned them. This, in itself a distressing process for a spectator, usually took place in tiny dressing rooms when we were changing into our uniform, and it was difficult to avoid being forced to bear witness. It involved flushing out all the tubing by running hot water through under pressure, and Mick would draw our attention to anything particularly interesting as it slithered down the plug-hole.

Mick always maintained that he found it hard to blow in tune after he'd cleaned out his trumpet because he'd got used to compensating for the distortion produced by the blockages.

Once, when Mick was a member of a band which had formed to welcome Louis Armstrong at London Airport, Louis borrowed his trumpet to blow a few notes with the group for the benefit of the press photographers, and handed it back with the words: 'You want to get the saveloys out of your horn, man!'

During tours a continuous problem was finding somewhere to stay. We had an ideal in our heads; a pub where the bar was still swinging however late the job finished, where the landlady actually preferred us to have breakfast at about eleven a.m., and where a girl with a strong local accent was accepted as your wife when you got back, even though you had booked in as a single before the gig.

Here and there such places actually existed, but usually some compromise was necessary.

Some bands had their accommodation booked through their offices which meant in fact staying at A.A. hotels, but these were the prosperous organizations like the Lyttelton Band. Others kept a methodical record of everywhere they stayed and wrote off in advance. We did neither. We had a rota and tried to fix ourselves up when we arrived, taking it in turn to actually find the digs.

As we were often late, and might have as little as half an hour to spare before we were due on stage, this was a nightmare.

Of course, as time went on in most of the big towns we knew where to go. In Sheffield it was Mrs Flanagan.

She was a large, kind woman who always wore slippers and an apron. Her house, big and unbelievably shabby, was situated in the seedy area which usually surrounds provincial universities dating from the last century. An area of unlikely dogs copulating in the rain, sad Negroes and Indians, women in curlers going to shop wearing dusty maroon coats over their nightdresses, large Catholic Churches, junk shops full of rags and broken electric fires, pubs standing alone on the corners of bomb sites, bright poster hoardings, graffiti and children's street games chalked all over the pavements.

Mrs Flanagan seldom moved out of her kitchen except to answer the bell or bring in the breakfasts. Her kitchen was not large, but as well as her it contained a very old spaniel, two cats, and a budgie. It was considered advisable to ask for boiled eggs for breakfast.

In the dining-room was an old piano, a sideboard with jumbo-sized cornflakes packets on it, a looking-glass surrounded by photographs of bandleaders who had stayed there and disfigured by musicians who had worked for them. Soon after her accession, somebody stuck up a postcard of the Queen among the other photographs. On it was written 'Lovely digs, Mrs Flanagan'. It was signed 'Liz and Phil'.

Over the dining-room table with its jug of thin bluish milk, tea-stained sugar, and sliced white bread, was a remarkable lampshade which all of us for many years believed to be made of fur. One day somebody climbed on to a chair to examine it more closely, and in touching it dislodged a thick cloud of brown dust.

The beds were very damp, but once you got warm they were quite comfortable as they exuded a steamy heat due perhaps to the flannel sheets. The banisters, the walls, the handles of the knives, in fact everything in the house, felt both gritty and greasy.

Mrs Flanagan was tolerant of every kind of behaviour except sexual promiscuity.

'If yer want to go wi' a scrubber,' she'd tell us, 'there's plenty of them sort of 'otels, but don't bring 'er 'ere!'

Ken Colyer, the week before he got married, had turned up with his fiancée and persuaded Mrs Flanagan they were already man and wife. Mrs Flanagan always read the *Melody Maker* from cover to cover every Friday in her kitchen, and the following week had come across a photograph of Ken and his bride on the steps of Fulham Town Hall under the legend, 'Married Yesterday'.

She came storming into the dining-room and brought it to our attention.

'Wait 'till I see that Ken Colyer!' she shouted. 'I'll learn 'im! Coming 'ere for a bloody rehearsal!'

If you asked Mrs Flanagan to lend you anything – cards, dominoes, a clothes brush – she would hand it over with a sweet smile.

'Luke after it luv,' she'd say, and then add, after a long pause, 'It were Flanagan's.'

On the other hand, in Manchester there was never any trouble in finding a hotel where you could lumber back a scrubber. These hotels were usually converted terrace houses in which the original rooms had been split into narrow corridors and minute rooms as though bees had been building a hive in a hollow tree. They were full of half-complete innovations aimed at the American servicemen from the Cheshire airbases who stayed there with their girls on week-end passes.

'Cocktail Lounges', remnants of modern wallpapers which ran out half-way round a room, sixpence-in-the-slot electric shavers usually out of order, loudspeakers in every bedroom with a control switch marked 'Light. Home. Room Service'.

A late-night phone call to book a double room revealed in one sentence the only strict rule: ' 'Ave you got luggage, sir?'

Breakfast in the dining-room on Sunday morning was an unreal and dream-like experience due to the fact that the American servicemen's wives, club hostesses in the main, were wearing cocktail dresses.

It was perhaps because of the number of American servicemen who converged on Manchester every week-end that the city preserved a distinctly wartime atmosphere, wide-open and yet tatty, throughout most of the fifties.

Mick and I, after the jazz club session was over, sometimes went on to 'The Stork Club' which had its premises at the bottom of a dark court off Cross Street, and was run by an ex-wrestler called Billy Benny who looked rather like Henry VIII and had a slight harelip. In exchange for a song or two from me, he was prepared to set them up all night.

'Any time George will thing a thong,' he told us, 'I'll puth up a bottle of whithkey and we'll make some hap!'

He was also a fund of unsolicited but useful information about his hostesses.

'They're no good,' he'd tell us as two of them swayed past on their way to the ladies. 'Strictly platers.'

There was also in Manchester a service which until surprisingly recently existed nowhere else outside London, somewhere to eat in the small hours. All round Piccadilly were pie stalls which sold marvellous hot pies: steak and kidney, meat and potato, cheese and potato. The fierce physical pleasure of biting into one of these, a little drunk in the frosty night, is enough, even in retrospect, to fill the mouth with saliva.

There was also a very disgusting all-night restaurant where, one midnight, a drunk American speared a long thin sausage, a part of the 'Mixed Grill', and shouted at the apathetic waitress who had just banged it down in front of him: 'What do you call this for Chris' sake? A goddam dog's cock?'

But if Manchester kept alive, despite austerity, everything which was raffish and roaring about wartime night life, Birmingham preserved intact the wartime atmosphere of shortages and rudeness, the grey relish of the puritan in control. It seemed to us that the people of Birmingham were forced to bite their tongues in order to stop themselves from countering any request or demand with the whining reiteration of the sentence, 'Don't you know there's a war on?'

Alone of all the big cities, we were never able to discover in Birmingham anywhere reasonable to stay. Most of the boarding houses were run by rat-trap-mouthed women married to Poles. We seldom parted on amicable terms.

Late breakfasts were the main cause. One woman, furious that none of us had come down before half past nine, angrily switched off the wireless which I'd tuned into 'Housewives' Choice'. When she'd gone out again, I switched it back on.

She came storming into the room.

'Did you sweetch eet on when oi'd turned eet off?' she yelled.

'Yes.'

'Roight. Thet settles eet. Get owt at wonce. All of yow!'

'Not before we've eaten our breakfasts.'

'Roight. Then oi'll ring up Sergeant Green. 'E'll come reound on 'is boike and sort yow lot out! Yow'd better go at once. Are yow going?'

'No.'

'Roight. Oi'll ring up Sergeant Green roight away.'

We finished our breakfasts and left, but Sergeant Green hadn't appeared. Her husband, who took our money, apologized on her behalf. 'My wife,' he told us in his Polish-Birmingham accent, 'she is very highly strung. Very easily upset yow see.'

But on another occasion it was a Polish boarding-house keeper himself who was our protagonist.

Ever since eight o'clock he had come banging into the communal room where we were all sleeping, and shouted and yelled at us to get up. 'I wonder what he'd do,' I asked the chaps, 'if the next time he comes in we all start to imitate dogs?' We decided to find out, and had several rehearsals. Some of us barked. Some growled. Some yapped. It sounded quite impressive.

Five minutes later the man came in again. All of us funked it except Mick. His performance wasn't really up to much. Very quietly and just once he went 'Wuff'.

Why is Birmingham, the town we christened 'The Arsehole of England', so horrible a place? Perhaps it resents its proximity to London. It's never felt far enough away to develop its own personality. Its only defence is a joyless legality, a 'holier than thou' gloom.

Long before it was necessary, Birmingham had developed a complicated one-way system, simply, we felt, for the pleasure of allowing you to glimpse at the end of a no-entry street the building you were aiming for, and then forcing you to detour for another three quarters of a mile. Cafés shut earlier in Birmingham than anywhere else. Sundays are deader. The accent more hideous. The pubs more reluctant to sell proprietary brands, more inclined to impose the brewers' filthy substitutes. A bottle of local whisky once rattled about undrunk in the bottom of the band wagon *for over a month,* and it is not that we were given to Scotch advert chichi. It was simply undrinkable even when we were drunk.

The Demon Brum has, to a greater or lesser extent, possessed the whole Midlands. Leicester, Nottingham, Coventry, Wolverhampton, all these towns evoke the figure of a commissionaire exerting his authority. It is not until you reach the Potteries that cities begin to regain their confidence, to become centres, not outer suburbs.

In reaction there is a considerable violence under the surface. The audiences at Birmingham Town Hall, that surprisingly beautiful neo-classic building at the very centre of the city's hideous heart, are famous for their extremes. If they liked you they stamped for over five minutes. If they were against you they threw corporation lavatory rolls and pennies. They were inclined, throughout the whole jazz decade, to extreme revivalist conservatism. When Humph went mainstream and played a concert there with his new line-up, a whole row of the audience raised, during Bruce Turner's first alto chorus, a long banner reading 'GO HOME DIRTY BOPPER'! To execute this project reveals a fanaticism verging on the unbalanced. I can imagine no other city where it could have happened.

Another city where we spent a great deal of time was Newcastle-upon-Tyne. The City Fathers refused, long after anyone else in England, to allow cinemas to open on Sundays. In consequence, jazz concerts, held at the Essoldo, were full every week. Newcastle is the most foreign of our great cities. The Newcastle accent sounds like a Scandinavian language, and indeed there are a great many words of Norwegian origin in the local slang. We stayed at a boarding house which catered for Scandinavian seamen and there was rye bread and a smörgasbord washed down with great jugs of ice-cold milk for breakfast.

As time went on, our touring life took a certain shape. For example, Albert Kinder, a Scouse promoter who intended to tie up jazz in the North, had succeeded in organizing a regular week-end for touring bands, culminating in a concert in the 'pool. The jobs on Friday and Saturday were usually a N.A.A.F.I. dance at a R.A.F. training camp near Warrington, and a public dance held in the Territorial Drill Hall, Widnes.

The R.A.F. job was remarkable for the terrifying appearance of the two coachloads of girls imported by the authorities to dance with the trainee airmen. The whole area was still thick with U.S. air bases, and it was only natural that any fun-loving young woman of normal appearance gravitated towards them. In consequence those left over verged on the grotesque. Their eruption into the canteen where we sat waiting to play never lost its dreadful fascination.

In Widnes we were made honorary members of the Sergeants' Mess which had a bar. It also contained a very ugly but willing woman known to the sergeants as 'The Widnes Bicycle'. One night, when we were drinking after the dance, a member of the band, his judgement clouded by beer, gave her a knee tremble at the back of the building. Although keen enough on the act itself, the Widnes Bicycle was suspicious of the musician's motives.

'I know the only reason you're doing this,' she told him. He imagined that she had guessed, accurately, that it was because he was drunk enough to ignore her repulsive looks, and began to feel rather sorry for her.

He therefore said nothing, hoping she would drop the subject and spare him the necessity of lying reassuringly, but she went on.

'I know. Don't think I don't know! You're only going with me . . .'

He waited hopelessly, staring at the glowing chimneys of the chemical factories along the shores of the Mersey.

'. . . so you can go back and swank to the fellers.'

Another regular job was the Gaiety Ballroom, Grimsby. This huge hall was privately owned by an elderly Jewish gentlemen of extreme old-world courtesy, two younger Jewish brothers with a new joke each time we came, and a Scottish lady with the appearance and manner of a kindly Lowland Sunday School teacher. There was also a manager called Freddy who had played tuba in the resident band when the Gaiety first opened in 1926. There was a photograph to prove it in the office, and an old night watchman with a small corpulent dog, with one sightless eye like a white grape.

At the end of the dance, Mick and I were invited up to the table at the side of the stand where the owners sat, and the elderly gentleman congratulated us, 'Very nice show, Mick', and asked us into the office for a drink. We discussed the state of the business, listened to the two jokes from the two brothers, and drank large whiskies under the photographs of champion ballroom dancers receiving cups in the decade before the war, and the 1926 band in the evening dress of the period with a sunset painted on the huge bass drum and Freddy holding his tuba in the back row.

Then we left the hall, pausing for a minute or two to chat with the night watchman and pat his dog as they sat side by side with the long night ahead of them under a mural of Cleopatra on her barge.

The nearest pub to the Gaiety was a mile away so we became, as did all the visiting bands, automatic members of the Working Men's Club. The Gaiety, which looked from the outside like an aeroplane hangar, was built on one side of a railway cutting, the Working Men's Club occupied a large loft over some deserted stables on the other side. During the changeover waltzes, when the resident band was taking over from our rhythm section, Mick and I would charge out of the ballroom, down some steep steps to road level, under the railway bridge, and up the dark lane to the club which was a friendly place full of fat women and very old men with watery eyes wearing caps.

In fact we drank a great deal in Working Men's Clubs, Miners' Institutes and the like, especially in the North. The most magnificent of these was in Crewe, a reminder that in the nineteenth century, when it was built, the railwayman was considered the aristocrat of the working class. Marble, glass and heavy mahogany carving were there to prove it, and let into the bar were large reproductions of Pre-Raphaelite ladies.

During the summer in Grimsby, it was the custom of the management to hire bands not simply for one night, although we often did play these in winter, but for a whole week with Tuesday and Thursday off.

We stayed in a boarding house a quarter of a mile from the Gaiety. It was run by a jolly little woman called Doris who wore spectacles and usually had her hair in curlers. She always left out a huge wedge of cheese, some cream crackers and a pub-sized jar of pickled onions for us when we got in. Her husband was a dental mechanic and made his false teeth somewhere on the premises. He was a little man with a yellowish complexion. If we bumped into him on one of the landings, he would grin, as though to advertise his products, and scurry out of sight. Doris had a daughter who was a schoolgirl when we first stayed there in the very early fifties, and a school teacher when we last saw her in 1960. There was a son too who was always stretched out on the carpet of the front room (although taking up progressively more space over the years) reading comics.

The kitchen was often full of Doris's friends, middle-aged ladies in a state of infectious euphoria. Most of them worked behind the refreshment counters at the Gaiety. One of them told fortunes from tea leaves and made endless jokes about her black underwear, a decidedly unerotic concept. 'She's as nutty as a fruit cake,' Doris would say after every sally.

The first few times we stayed there Doris's father was alive, although very old and several points. Even after he died ('It were all for the best,' said Doris next time we arrived. ' 'E were past it'), we were reminded of him because at strategic points throughout the house, at the turn of the stairs, above the bath, by the side of the lavatory, were the aluminium handles which had helped him to haul himself about.

Still alive, although a little stiff in the joints on our last visit, was a large collie dog called Shaun. He was a coat fetishist, and could often be surprised rogering the mackintoshes in the hall.

Being resident at the same hall for a week at a time had its advantages sexually. We got to know a group of girls who used to stand night after night by the side of the stage and were known, according to Freddy, as 'The Grimsby Trawlers'. The bandwagon, parked throughout the week up an alley at the side of the ballroom, was comparatively comfortable.

I once asked one of the Grimsby Trawlers to come out with me on the band's night off. She stood me up, but explained why the following evening during the interval.

'I couldn't come,' she told me, and added, as though it were a perfectly adequate reason, 'You see I were asked out by . . .' and here her voice became dreamy with the grandeur of it all, 'the Mayor of Cleethorpes' son.'

I became fond of Grimsby over the years. It's a long town, lying close to the miles of fishdocks which are its *raison d'être*. Entirely undistinguished architecturally, it has nevertheless a certain picturesque quality arising from the fishing. Little shops sell ropes and nets, the pubs are full of men wearing blue jerseys with herring scales on the backs of their hands. There was (he no longer exists) a tattooist called Dusty Rhodes near the entrance to the dock. There are marvellous junk shops, and in one of them I bought for five shillings a phrenologist's head. Even in the long streets of mean red-brick terrace houses where a photographer's glass case full of weddings is an event, you can still smell the sea, and the weather too is mercantile; squalls, storms, brilliant sunshine, grey drizzle within the space of a day. Once, walking towards Doris's local with Diz Disley who was depping with us for a month or two, I tried to explain to him why I liked Grimsby. He waited until I'd finished, and then remarked quietly but firmly, 'I prefer fucking Venice.'

In the Scottish border town of Melrose there lived an ex-lawyer called Duncan McInnon. He was short and plump with an untidy off-ginger moustache and protuberant blue eyes. He dressed in wrinkled grey flannels and hairy sports coats (somehow they are always more hairy in Scotland) with large leather-covered buttons. Following his success in running Saturday-night hops all over the borders using local dance bands and small Scottish country groups, he developed larger ambitions, turned himself into a company called 'Border Dances Limited', and appointed Jim Godbolt as his London agent. It was Jim's job to book bands and send them up to play for anything between one week and three on Duncan's circuit, and in consequence from 1953 until the band folded in December 1961 we would find ourselves at least once a year working our way north.

Although several of Duncan's venues were extremely profitable he was always teetering on the edge of disaster because of his obsession with a huge white elephant in the shape of the Market Hall, Carlisle.

In itself, Carlisle is an unpleasant place, largely, I suspect, because it cannot decide if it is English or Scottish. It's the only town in England with state pubs, and an evening in one of these is enough to shake the convictions of the most doctrinaire socialist. They're like alcoholic post-offices.

The market hall is enormous with lots of permanent little shops over most of the area. There is a large concrete floor about the size of three football fields, and it was this which Duncan hoped to turn into the centre of the city's night-life. He had taken a long lease from the Council, built a stage, cut off the dance-hall area from the shops by suspending enormous dirty green tarpaulins, installed a great many heaters among the iron girders, and finally, in an attempt to suggest gaiety, had stuck thousands of little mirrors mounted on cloth around the bottom four feet of the supporting columns.

Even before the first time we went to play for Border Dances Ltd we had an idea what to expect because Jim Godbolt had gone up for the opening night. Geraldo was the bandleader and he, Jim, and, of course, Duncan had been invited by the Mayor to a dinner preceding the dance. There had been speeches including a very long one from Duncan which made up in fervour and enthusiasm what it lacked in coherence or relevance, and then the whole party made for the hall. There was a gentle incline leading down past a butcher's shop to where a gap in the

tarpaulin gave entry to the dance floor. Jim was walking behind
Duncan who was holding on to the arms of Geraldo in his im-
maculate tails. Suddenly Duncan slipped and fell, dragging
Geraldo down with him. It was an inauspicious beginning.

That first evening, according to Jim, there was at least a
decent crowd, but the night we made our début, even when the
dance was at its height, there were only about twenty people. It
was a freezing night in early spring, and the heaters, glowing
faintly some thirty feet above our heads, did nothing to remedy
this.

At about nine o'clock we came back from the state pub,
reluctantly removed our overcoats and relieved a band called
'The Mighty Redcoats'. They were a local group and Duncan
had chosen their name. He had a very nineteenth-century taste
in promotion and publicity. His posters were couched in baroque circus prose, the source of some embarrassment to Mick,
and amusement to the rest of us. Mick has always displayed an
almost ostentatious modesty, and one of Duncan's announce-
ments full of ornate superlatives was guaranteed to make his
head sink into his shoulders. I doubt 'The Mighty Redcoats'
would have chosen their name if left to themselves, but Duncan
employed them almost every night, and they had little
choice.

As the front line were blowing through their mouth pieces to
warm them up sufficiently to play in tune, Duncan himself
climbed up on the stage. We had met him only briefly in the
pub, where he had bought us a large number of double scotches,
and hadn't really taken him in.

He walked to the front of the stage, eyed the tiny audience
belligerently, and launched into a speech lasting a good half-
hour.

The gist of it was that the people of Carlisle didn't deserve
the first-rate entertainment that Border Dances were bringing
to them, but that Border Dances intended to go on doing so
nevertheless; that he, Duncan McInnon, would fight and fight

until he had made the Market Hall, Carlisle, into the greatest centre of ballroom entertainment anywhere in the North.

He concluded, as we were to discover he usually concluded his speeches, by reciting in full Kipling's 'If'. He then, with a climatic gesture, ordered Mick to play and, at the first note, jumped off the six-foot stand on to the concrete floor. He fell heavily, but leapt to his feet. The back of his coat and trousers were covered with powdered white chalk strewn there to stop the dancers from slipping. Near at hand was a young soldier with his girl. Duncan seized the girl and danced off with her into the middle distance jigging up and down in a kind of frenzy. With the exception of the pianist, who had his back to this, nobody in the band could play at all. Occasionally Mick or Roy would manage a strangled note but it would immediately degenerate into a fart of laughter.

After the dance was over, Duncan invited Mick and me into a small room where Border Dances stored their mikes and re-freshment trestle-tables during market days. He had with him a friend and a bottle of whisky. He locked the door and pocketed the key, explaining that he would refuse to let us out until Mick had agreed to change over from jazz to Irish music. Eventually he fell asleep, and we were able to remove the key and escape.

I have always enjoyed the Border Tours except for the jobs. Carlisle was in a class by itself, but even the other venues were pretty depressing. 'Hawick Drill Hall', 'The Corn Exchange', Berwick-upon-Tweed, 'The Rosewall Institute', 'The Town Hall', Galashiels: to repeat these names is to visualize bars, comparatively empty Scottish parochial halls with a row of very plain ginger-haired girls dressed in floral prints of un-fashionable length sitting along one wall, and a group of raw-boned lads huddled together in the opposite corner. The dances all started late and went on into the small hours.

Dumfries was the only exception. Duncan's dances there were held on a Saturday, and the huge hall was packed.

Furthermore, they finished early on account of the law about no dance continuing into the Sabbath. As a bonus there were always fights breaking out somewhere in the crowd, and, as the stand was high, we had an excellent view.

We stayed in hotels in strange little towns with one broad street lined with plaid-obsessed drapers and tobacconists selling Scottish novelties, fishing tackle shops, and butchers who are called 'fleshers'.

We drove past ruined abbeys and over rivers where a salmon fisherman stood waist high.

We drank in the men-only bars, experimenting with malt whisky and chasing it with 'wee heavy' beers.

We ate high tea in the shadow of laden cake stands, and pudding suppers, black, white or haggis, with bread and butter, and cups of tea poured out neat with a jug of milk on the table.

We breathed the marvellous air.

But every night we had to play a Duncan job.

7. King of the Ravers

Between 1951, when the first revivalist boom was over, and 1953, when the scene began to recover, we were on the road all the time. We tried to keep some foothold in London and we ran our own club in a rehearsal room in a Gerrard Street basement and, on the rare occasions we were in town on a Saturday night, organized all-night raves.

The word 'rave', meaning to live it up, was as far as I know a Mulligan-Godbolt invention. It took several forms. The verb as above, 'a rave' meaning a party where you raved, and 'a raver', i.e. one who raved as much as possible. An article once described Mick as 'The King of the Ravers'.

During a National Savings Drive in 1952, Mick and Jim derived a great deal of harmless amusement by ringing each other up every time they saw a new poster and reading out its message with the word 'Rave' substituted for the word 'Save' 'HELP BRITAIN THROUGH NATIONAL RAVING', 'WANTED 50,000,000 RAVERS,' etc.

Mick and I were the first people to organize all-night raves, and they were an enormous social success, but a financial loss. There were several reasons for this. For one thing the men who owned the rehearsal room insisted on half the take, and the number of tickets we were allowed to sell was limited by the fire regulations. As a result, after paying the band, printing the tickets, putting an advert in the *Melody Maker*, and buying a barrel of cider for the musicians who came along to sit in, the most we could expect was four pounds each and in fact, when it came to the share out, we were usually a pound or two out of pocket.

Anyway we didn't really run the all-nighters to make money. Although today the idea of spending a whole night in a crowded airless basement at a small loss appears extraordinary, it was very exciting then.

Forced as we were by commercial necessity to occupy most of our lives playing strict tempo music for dancing, the all-night sessions were an escape back into the jazz atmosphere of our beginnings. We could dress in shit order, fall about drunk, and tell people who criticized us or our music to get stuffed.

Of course the Mulligan band couldn't play from midnight to seven a.m. We played three one-hour sessions and relied on musicians who wanted a blow to fill in the gaps.

There was no difficulty here, in fact there was an embarrassment of riches and a confusion of musical idiom which made arranging the groups a question of great tact and firmness if the whole thing wasn't to degenerate into a huge and messy jam session.

Revivalist jazz was in the melting pot at that moment. The majority remained faithful to the Morton-Oliver-Armstrong sound, but others were moving after Humph into the mainstream or beginning to think that Ken Colyer's back-to-the-roots ideas were right. In some circles white Chicago jazz was in the ascendancy, and yet even here there were two schools of thought, the back-to-the-twenties enthusiasts and the more recent Eddie Condon Dixieland fanatics. To confuse things further a few bebop musicians would drop in. Somehow all these had to have a blow and yet be kept out of each other's hair. Mick left this to me. In fact he left most of the organization to me, and sometimes, if he was drunk enough, would even sneak back to his flat round the corner in Lisle Street and fall asleep so that I had to go and wake him up in time for our next session. He was going through a period of enormous lethargy and had made me 'band manager' at what I now consider the cynically inadequate recompense of one pound a week extra. For this I had to collect the money, pay the salaries, apologize to ballroom managers when we were late, and keep a book in which I wrote down the innumerable subs which everybody in the band seemed to need at the most inconvenient moments.

One of the revelations of our all-night parties was that there was a whole generation of jazz musicians in England who predated the revival and yet played swinging music in the Harlem style of the late thirties. Some were professionals like Lennie Felix, a small elf-like pianist influenced by Fats Waller. He played with tremendous attack, his face and body twitching and jerking in sympathy with his musical ideas. Others were amateurs, and the most remarkable of these was a timber merchant called Ian 'Spike' Macintosh who played trumpet in the style of mid-period Louis Armstrong. Small and neat, a little moustache and horn-rimmed spectacles, he looked exactly what he was, two sons down for Public School and a house in Cuffley. But inside him was a wild man in chains. He played with extreme modesty, his back to the audience, and a green beret full of holes hanging over the bell of his trumpet. In conversation he was both courteous and restrained, but he could become very aggressive if anybody suggested that there was any other trumpet player except his hero.

At parties there was a psychological moment when he would lurch towards the gramophone and take off whatever record was playing if it hadn't got a Louis on it, and substitute one that had. Another anti-social habit was his reaction when his host turned down the volume. He'd just wait until he wasn't looking and turn it up again.

He once offered Mick and me a lift home from a suburban jazz club in his car, and when we were safely inside, drove all the way out to Cuffley despite our protests. His wife was away, and he wanted us to sit up all night listening to Louis and drinking whisky. It was an enjoyable night, and didn't finish until three p.m. the following day when the local closed. It was just that we hadn't planned on it. Macintosh's friends were another hazard: huge city men in waistcoats, and pre-war musicians with patent leather hair. There was a moment when he started a jazz club in a city public house, and the guv'nor, an enormous fat man with the sensitivity of a rhinoceros, took to putting in an appearance at other clubs where we might happen to be playing. One night he staggered in to Le Metro while Joe Harriot, the West Indian alto player, was sitting in with us. As soon as the guv'nor's eyes focused enough for him to realize that it was a Negro who was taking a chorus, he leapt and capered across the front of the stand shouting, 'Walla! Walla! Walla!'

But despite Mac's party tricks and city mates, we all liked him very much. He was kind, loyal, and generous, and he could, when on form, play absolutely beautifully.

A regular at our all-night raves was Dill Jones, the Welsh jazz pianist. He would turn up with the rest of his group from the night club where they played, just as the dawn was breaking over Cambridge Circus. Dill was unique in that he could sit in with any band, whatever idiom they favoured. He loved and understood all periods and used to reproach both revivalist and modernist alike for their narrow prejudices.

'If it swings it's jazz,' he used to say, 'and if it's jazz it's all right by me, boy.'

Mick always held it against Dill that he was disinclined to pay for a round of drinks. This has always been one of Mick's real obsessions. It doesn't matter how boring somebody is, as

long as they 'stand their round' Mick will describe them enthusiastically as 'a good nut'. Personally I don't mind one way
or the other. I like some people who are mean and dislike other
people who are generous, but Mick won't have it. At one of our
all-nighters we had ordered an extra barrel of cider at Dill's
request. 'I'll be bringing down quite a lot of people,' he told us,
'so it's only fair, see. Just let me know how much.' When it
came to the crunch, Dill said he didn't have the ready on him,
but would pay us next time he saw us. He never did, and Mick
never forgave him. Although this happened in 1951, and we
bumped into Dill hundreds of times before he emigrated to
America in 1961, he always refused to hand over the two
pounds, claiming for the first year or two that he was a bit
short, and after that insisting that he had paid it. Mick, for his
part, never let slip an oportunity of mentioning it, especially
when he'd had a few.

'Hello, Dill,' he'd say, 'enjoy that cider, did you?'

At seven a.m. the band played its final number and we'd all
crawl up out of the sweat-scented cellar into the empty streets
of a Sunday morning in the West End. Hysterical with lack of
sleep, accompanied by a plump art student, her pale cheeks
smeared with the night's mascara, I'd catch the Chelsea bus
and try to read the *Observer* through prickling red eyeballs as
we swayed along Piccadilly, down Sloane Street, and into the
King's Road. Then a bath, one of those delirious fucks that
only happen on the edge of complete fatigue, and a long sleep
until it was time to get up and face the journey to Cook's Ferry
or whatever jazz club we were playing that evening.

But our periods in London were now both spasmodic and
brief. The city had become a place to collect clean shirts and
socks from. We put into it like sailors into port. Our lives there
had lost their centre.

Most of the time we were actually travelling between jobs.

We got to know the roads of Britain so well that a glance out of the coach window could tell us where we were.

The flavour of the different regional landscapes alone was enough: the flat featureless Dutch-like farmland of Lincolnshire; the honey-coloured stone and intimate scale of the West Country; the sprawling suburb of the Midlands; the hunting-print look of Cheshire and Shropshire; the kilns of the Potteries and the chimneys of the industrial north; the wild moors along the Pennines where the sheep are always black with the soot of Lancashire and Yorkshire.

Certain strange images remain. On the old A1 (there were no motorways then), thirty miles out of London was a house, the walls of which were covered with cut-out animals and faces: giraffes, seals, bears, cartoon characters. On the road to Barrow-in-Furness, which skirts the Lake District, was a small factory which manufactured something which used a great deal of bright blue dye (possibly it manufactured bright blue dye?) and the whole building, the surrounding grass and vegetation, the boulder-strewn stream which ran between the factory and the road were all bright blue. But most of it is a jogging blur of half-sleep after transport cafés' meals, the jumping print of paperbacks, the dramas of the poker school round a flat-topped tom-tom case.

Although I was interested to know parts of the country where I had never been, what I found absolutely hallucinatory was to return as a jazz singer to places I had known well as a child, Liverpool particularly, of course, but by no means exclusively.

North Wales was such an area. As a very little boy I had spent holidays in the Edwardian resorts of Llandudno and Colwyn Bay, and later, during the thirties, my father rented a farm or cottage in the Clwyd Valley to be near his uncle's fishing, and we had driven in almost every morning to swim in the baths at hideous Rhyl and gimcrack Prestatyn.

Now in my middle twenties I came back several times every summer. We usually played at Rhyl in a large dance hall, part of the same building as a cinema. One July evening we arrived there in time to see the film before the dance started, and I discovered with pleasure, keen beyond logic, that they were showing a revival of *King Kong* which I had never seen. All through that marvellous film some memory kept nagging me. There was a link between film and place, I couldn't nail it, but at the moment when Kong, mortally wounded by the machine-guns of the circling biplanes, tenderly places Fay Wray in the roof guttering of the Empire State Building before plunging to his death, it came to me. A summer afternoon of 1935. My father driving me into Rhyl from Denbigh, where he had taken a cottage, to see *King Kong*. The discovery that children under sixteen weren't allowed in. Bitter tears on the sea-front. My father telling me I would be able to see it when I was older, and me protesting 'but it won't still be on'. We played at Denbigh too. The ballroom of the County Lunatic Asylum was available for public dances when the patients were in bed, but when we arrived in the late afternoon to leave our instruments they were still wandering about.

'Men! Men!' shouted a middle-aged woman from a window before she was pulled backwards by unseen hands, and one morning walking out of the town to look at the cottage where I had stayed as a child, I was accosted by a respectable middle-aged man who asked me if I realized that Africa used to be Welsh.

'No,' I said, 'I hadn't realized that.'

'It's because she wouldn't wash,' he explained.

I remembered walking past the 'loony bin' with our nurse. If we'd been naughty she threatened to ring up for 'the van'. She used this to frighten us, not only in Wales, but when we got back to Liverpool in late September, and as I lay in bed I could hear the gangs of ragged children from Lark Lane singing in the street:

> They will dress you all in blue
> Just because you've lost a screw.

They meant Rainhill, the Merseyside Asylum, but for me they were singing about the Denbigh Institution.

In Llandudno we played to an audience of perhaps twenty old ladies and gentlemen, most of whom left in the interval. Every time I sang the manager turned off the microphone. Mick controlled himself until after 'The Queen' and then blew up. He shouted that the night before we had played to a packed and enthusiastic dance hall in Prestatyn, and that many of the audience would have come along if the concert had been properly advertised. He said it was an insult to me to turn off the mike every time I sang. He threatened to report the whole thing to the Musicians' Union. Pausing for breath he noted that the manager was smiling delightedly.

'Everybody who appears here loses his temper with me,' the man explained with great satisfaction. 'They all do it. Even the most famous.'

Another Proustian gig was the Civic Hall, Nantwich. We played there fairly regularly right through the fifties.

Outside the Parish Church, not far from the hall, was a billboard painted to resemble bricks in outline. Each brick represented five pounds of the five thousand needed for the restoration fund, and as the money was raised, the bricks were filled in with solid red paint. When we first played Nantwich, Mick and I were in our early twenties and only two or three of the bricks were red. The last time we were there, Mick's hair was grey at the sides, I had a pot belly and a bald patch, and the wall was almost filled in.

We still played concerts in Liverpool during the winter, and my mother didn't mind this. There was something possible for her about a concert. In the summer of 1952, though, we did a job which gave her considerable pain. We played in a tent for a

week as part of 'The Liverpool Show' on Wavertree Playing
Fields. Our tent was between a display of cage birds and an
exhibition of photographs showing the work of the police. We
did two shows in the afternoon and three in the evening. My
father quite enjoyed coming along after dinner to pick me up
and have a beer or two with the band in the bar tent with its
smell of crushed grass, but my mother was worried about who
would discover I was working in a side-show. As it happened,
the only time she did come she met the ex-chauffeur and
ladies' maid of a late cousin of my grandfather's, their faces
grim with disapproval.

'Good evening, Aimie. Good evening, Stanley.'

'Good evening, Mrs Tom,' said Aimie, and then added, 'I
can't think what Miss 'Olt would have thought about Master
George singing in a tent.'

In the same year, 1952, Mick's passion for dogs found practical expression. In one week he bought an alsatian puppy
when he was drunk in London, and a bull terrier puppy in
Doncaster. The bull terrier was one of a litter belonging
to a fan. Its mother had whelped in a pigsty on an allotment.
Mick bought it one afternoon after a lunchtime session in 'The
George'.

For some weeks this animal travelled in the coach. It was
Mick's intention to train it to guard the instruments and uniforms, but because it smelt so strongly of its birthplace, pissed
and shitted all over everything, and revealed, even that early in
its life, an aggressive and hysterical personality, we raised a
corporate objection, and Mick agreed to leave it behind in
town.

Doncaster was a town we never played at, but in which we
quite frequently stayed. The landlord of The George, a large
pub in the market square, had been a pro musician in the thirties
and in consequence gave bands special terms and sympathetic

treatment. On the debit side he was inclined to go on about the profession and to wake you up by shouting.

'Come on't, lad. You're due on't bandstand.'

The puppy's original owner was one of a little gang of staunch fans who used to turn up wherever we played in Yorkshire. He was a cobbler and had a skin curiously like leather of an unpleasing yellow colour. His mates were a varied lot. One was an attractive young man with a cast in one eye whose ambition was to achieve at least three knee-trembles during the course of an evening at the Palais. He usually managed at least two. I once asked him, not how he made the first girl – there is a strong tradition of promiscuity in Yorkshire – but how he got rid of her prior to chatting up the next one. He looked at me incredulously, and then told me, his voice full of 'ask a silly question' implications: 'Aye tells 'er to fook off.'

The jovial leader of this gang was a rotund man with a nervous and continuous laugh. He lived in a caravan with his pretty gypsy-like wife, and was a legitimate photographer with pornography as a side-line. As models he used local girls who wished to supplement their earnings in the mills, and some of his friends whom I imagine didn't get paid at all. He was always showing us his new sets, presumably with an eye to flogging them, but we never bit.

In the jazz world there are one or two people who have a passion for dirty snaps and collect them, but these are specialists. Mick and I were perfectly prepared to 'have a bird's eye' or 'a squint' as Mick put it, but not to actually pay out money. Besides, although these rather amateur efforts had a certain naïve charm, and suggested, which is unusual in this context, that the participants were actually enjoying themselves, they lacked the precision which is surely the essence of pornography. When Mick looked at them he demonstrated a delusion of his which he never lost. He would tilt the print at an angle as though this made it possible to see more of what was going on.

The pornographer was also something of a pimp – the two professions are often allied. He once told me that there was a female crane driver of his acquaintance who had told him that she was willing to pay 'twenty pounds for a night wi' George Melly'. The tart in me was impressed at such a generous offer; the feminine at such a masculine approach; the masochist at the idea of a *female* crane driver. I asked her pander what she was like.

'She's all right,' he told me. 'She's not a beauty like, but she's got a fair pair of bristols and muscles like an Irish bluddy navvy. By gum she can go and all.' To emphasize this he raised an arm in phallic imitation and clapped the back of his neck rapidly with his other hand. I declared myself agreeable but we never met.

One morning in the Market Hall, Doncaster, I saw an image so extraordinary and dreadful that I have never forgotten it. Mick and I had crossed the road from The George to buy him a pair of socks. Mick never washed socks on tour. He'd wait until the pair he was wearing became too stiff for comfort and then buy some more. Besides, we both liked covered markets; the mounds of glowing fruit, the carcasses of animals, the fat women holding up cheap underwear in front of their bodies to see if it was 'them'.

There was a fishing stall and, on a table in front of it, a large tin basin in which thousands of maggots, many of them dyed pink or green, writhed and boiled in the bran.

Standing with his face a few inches from this erupting mass was a child with a huge head. He was wearing a cap like most Mongolian children do, and was staring at the maggots with an almost hungry intensity.

8. And So the Band Folded

Commercial stability, a constant struggle during the first three lean years of the fifties, led Mick during 1952 to a further expansion of the personnel. Not content with a four-piece front line, a four-piece rhythm section, and a blues singer, he decided that what the band needed was some glamour, and began to look around for a female vocalist. It was Archie Semple who found her, a London girl of Italian origin called Olga Bagnaro, stage name Jo Lennard, who had begun to sing around a few of the clubs. Jo's style was simple but her pitch was good and above all she could swing like the clappers not only on up-tempo numbers but on slow ballads as well. She was a pretty girl with big brown eyes, 'well-stacked' as they say in American gangster novels, and with an insatiable appetite for car-bohydrates, particularly in the form of chips, spaghetti, and cream cakes. She spoke with the soft mid-Atlantic accent of most London girls in 'show biz', but sometimes reverted delib-erately into broad cockney when angry or happy. She lived with her parents in a tenement flat in the Elephant and Castle district, and was a strong local patriot, and proud of her work-ing-class origin. She took me once to her local, and introduced me to a gang of tearaways of her acquaintance. They were real tearaways, nothing to do with the teddy boys who were beginning to emerge at that time. These gentlemen, most of them about thirty, wore expensive, rather conservative, suits and large hats. They managed to look both relaxed and tense. They all drank brown ale.

There was a talent competition on that night, first prize five pounds, and we both decided to enter. Mick wouldn't have been too pleased if he'd known, but we weren't earning so much that we could ignore the chance to make some extra money. She sang 'Them There Eyes' beautifully, and I sang 'Frankie and Johnnie' not so well. At the end of the evening the winners were announced. Jo had won first prize and me second. This was in fact as it should have been, but even so I was rather surprised at the result because although she'd sung much better, 'Frankie and Johnnie' was a showy and eccentric number and I had won the most applause. One of the tearaways explained.

'Jo 'ad to win, you see, she's a local girl, like. 'Ope you don't mind.' I assured him I was delighted.

Although at first Jo was perfectly friendly to me, she paid me no particular attention, but after a month or two she began to sit by me in the coach, eat with me in cafés and restaurants, and drink with me in pubs. From then on we were a couple.

For some months we hesitated on the edge of marriage. I used to go and eat at her parents', huge and delicious dishes of chickens in spaghetti. I was taken to meet her rich uncle, a bookie with a flat in Kensington, all lilac wallpapers and Hollywood bed-ends, and a pretty blonde wife with a surprisingly dirty laugh. I met her grannie too, she called her Nanna – a tiny, old lady in a dark kitchen who showed me family records out of a mother-of-pearl box.

Jo's father, a hairdresser with a hairline moustache, said to me one day, 'We don't mind Olga being with a band. She enjoys it and she likes you.' He paused and then added, slowly,

'But if anything happened to her, I'd be round.' I looked at the budgerigar climbing its ladder and, as they say in Yorkshire, thought on.

Jo and I didn't get married for a number of reasons. A considerable barrier for me was the fact that she was a Roman Catholic. I was, after all, a militant atheist and the idea of marriage in the vestry of a Catholic church with a promise to bring up our children in the faith would have been a lot for me to swallow. The main reason, however, and it is, after all, a valid one, was that we were not really in love. We liked each other very much indeed, but we weren't in love.

Eight musicians and two vocalists was a large personnel for a touring band, but one day Mick announced that we were to have another addition. This was Mike Lawrence, the singer who had been given such a bollocking by Doreen Porter's mum down the Metro Club. Mick had, of course, tried to justify this – as a commercial band we needed a male commercial singer to handle ballads and waltzes, etc. – but the fact was Mike had asked Mick for a job one night when Mick was stoned.

He joined us three weeks early. We were on a short tour of Ireland, and he turned up, without any explanation, in a small market town in the west. This was a real lumber. The promoter of the tour, a young Dubliner, believed it was possible to fit eight musicians, their instruments, two vocalists, and himself at the wheel into a Volkswagen. It was *just* possible, but extremely uncomfortable. After Mike's unexpected arrival it was three vocalists and this *was* impossible. Luckily most of the time we were unconscious from lack of sleep and draught Guinness.

At the beginning of the tour Mick tried to protest to the promoter about our travelling conditions and indeed much else, but he took no notice at all. He just smiled politely as though Mick was discussing the weather. On the very first day, driving out of Dublin to a job a hundred miles away, he suddenly stopped the wagon and disappeared for over half an hour without any prior explanation. When he got back Mick asked him where he'd got to. 'To Mass,' he said and drove on. As it was the week after Easter this happened fairly often, but in a short time the agnostic section of the band learnt to head for the nearest bar which was usually the nearest building, and often, another thing which surprised us, a grocer's shop.

Most of the jobs we played were in small places, and indeed the first night we drew up in front of the hall to find the caretaker driving out some chickens with his broom. The M.C. wore evening dress which had gone green with age and was so rotted it could scarcely support the row of medals he had won in the revolution. We had, of course, rehearsed the Irish National Anthem, 'The Soldier's Song', a stirring tune of great length which, unlike 'God Save the Queen', it is impossible to cut, but this was the first time we had played it in public. Irish dances go on even longer than Scottish dances, often until three or four in the morning, but at last it was time. The M.C. announced the National Anthem and stood stiffly to attention. We began. But in the middle a patriotic but very drunk young man climbed up on the stage. We were a bit nervous. Did he consider our version lacked sufficient fervour? Did he consider it an insult that we, bloody Saxons, should play it at all? But in fact he only wished to sing the words. He started a key out, and then fell down still singing. Our first Irish dance was over.

That night we had been surprised to find a couple of crates of Guinness on the stand for the musicians. We put it down to the size and rural character of the village, but even in the larger towns it was the rule, and, after the dance was over, we usually found ourselves drinking Irish whisky with the manager until broad daylight. Throughout the tour Mick spent quite a lot of time indignantly telling people he was English, but his Irish blood, however much he denied it, showed itself in the way he launched into ferocious arguments during these drinking sessions. There was one row about birth control which would have ended in blows if everybody hadn't been too drunk. Mick raved on in defence of Durex Limited while the manager and his friend shouted him down with cries of, ' 'Tis worse than murder so it is!'

After an hour or two of this, the sessions were inclined to turn sentimental and maudlin, and various Irish gentlemen would 'oblige' with patriotic songs, many of them starting with the word 'Sure'.

In Donegal, at eleven o'clock one morning, we were stopped by a drunken policeman who leant against the car door for three-quarters of an hour expounding, while the growing line of cars honked behind us, on the beauties of the country.

In a cottage where we changed, I bought for five shillings a beautiful and old china hen which I spotted on the window ledge. The owner was delighted with the transaction, and told me that he had something I would really want although he wouldn't let it go under the pound. He disappeared leaving me to speculate on what it could be. Some treasure from 'the great house' acquired during the troubles? It was a calendar of the Taj Mahal and the water changed colour to show the weather.

On that tour we didn't only drink too much, we ate like pigs too. It was still the austere time when the greedy English rich would cross to Dublin for a week-end to gorge on steak and salmon, butter and double cream, all unobtainable in rationed Britain. We weren't rich but we were English, and even Mick stuffed himself at every opportunity.

Our last date was in 'The Four Provinces Ballroom', Dublin, a comparatively sophisticated venue. We went down well, but there were no Guinness crates on the stand. After it was over we hurried into taxis and were driven through the wet streets of the city to catch the night boat to Liverpool. It was a stormy passage, and we played cards and drank rum while Irish labourers fell about to the rhythm of the ship, using the moment's pause between the rolls to lift a bottle up to their mouths, and the potential chambermaids and hospital cleaners snored chastely by their suitcases in the saloon.

Grey with lack of sleep we docked in Liverpool in the wet, windy dawn, and I went home for breakfast. That night in Nantwich, I pulled the towel out of my case to wipe the soap out of my eyes, and the china hen fell to the floor and was smashed to bits.

Mike Lawrence, who enjoyed singing, got very little satisfaction out of his association with us. He didn't sing at all in jazz clubs and very infrequently at concerts, while even at dances, Mick's hatred of rehearsing new numbers meant that once the band had mastered about six songs from Mick's repertoire it never learnt any more, and besides, with three vocalists, none of us got an opportunity to sing much. Mick, however, insisted that we all sit together at the side of the stand during the entire evening, this was part of his 'professional' mystique, and furthermore smile broadly but remain silent. When ever we did talk, he would turn and hiss at us, 'Will the vocalists stop rabbiting?' The rest of the band called us 'the choir'. Also, at the time Mike joined us, interest in traditional jazz was just beginning to revive. We began to play more straight jazz dates, and even appeared at the London Palladium in a guest spot at one of Ted Heath's sell-out Sunday Night Concerts. We had only twenty minutes, and Mick worked out this could include two vocals at most. Poor Mike, who was very show-biz minded, and for whom the London Palladium was holy ground, was yet again rowed out. If I'd been him, I couldn't have remained as good-tempered as he did, but even so he was by nature a tense and highly-strung person, and it began to tell on him. He would get into terrible silent rages during the course of which he would flush a dark red, and then pale to an almost greenish white. He had a certain type of Liverpool face, large in area, but with small, almost feminine features arranged closely around a little nose like a parrot's beak. At the height of one of his crises his lips would compress so tightly that the mouth seemed to disappear al-together.

But although at the beginning we had several brushes – if Mick wasn't there, Mike would try and take over who sang what and when, and I wasn't having any – we got on very well. Our shared Liverpool background gave us a lot in common, and Mike had an inventive and very personal sense of humour. Together we fathered an imaginary Scouse Catholic family, and used to improvise incidents and conversations round them when the mood took us:

'You know our Bernadette? 'Er fairst Mass and she's sick right down the front of 'er lovely white frock just as she's going up to the altar,' I might start. It was Mike, however, who added the touches of wild inspiration.

'It come of 'er eating no breakfast,' he would go on, 'she's so pious like, you know. I said to 'er, "Go on. Eat your kipper. Father Riley won't know." But not 'er.'

He was a fund of Liverpool children's street songs and catches:

> Father cut the whiskers off the bread.
> There's a woman in the shit-'ouse 'alf dead!
> There's a cat upon the wall,
> And it's only got one ball.
> And it's looking for the other one on the shed.

An extraordinary adventure we shared together happened in Glasgow. After a concert in the St Andrews Hall the band was invited by a butch young man in jeans and a polo-neck sweater to be his guests at a restaurant. He didn't look as if he had a penny but it turned out that his father owned a fleet of fishing boats. Furthermore, the restaurant was, for those still frugal days, exceptional. Candles shone on greedy faces, huge steaks followed the scampi and our host had ordered a whole bottle of whisky to be placed in front of each of his guests. We'd already had quite a few in the nearest bar to St Andrews Hall, so by the time we'd finished our coffees we were all very drunk, had done nothing about finding digs, and it was two o'clock on a cold Glaswegian night.

Mick, Mike and I found ourselves reeling through the streets together. We decided to start at the top and fell into the hall of the Central Hotel. We were told by a brusque night porter that there were no rooms vacant. The same happened at the North British, St Enoch's and the Ivanhoe.

Finally we hailed a taxi, and asked the man to take us round places to stay. Down and down we went. Small hotels, boarding-houses, transport digs, doss-houses. At last we were directed into a tenement building and told there was a place which might take us 'up the stair'. Mike and I went to investigate. Mick remained in the taxi rigid with whisky.

We staggered up two flights of tiled steps and rang a bell. A young queer in the filthiest white steward coat I've ever seen came to the door, and we asked if he had a room. Drunk as I was, I could see a compliant gleam in his eye as he said yes. He showed us into a double room squalid to the point of disbelief. Two rusty bedsteads, an old sink, peeling green walls, a broken window pane mended with cardboard. I pulled back the blankets on one of the beds and pointed out that the sheets looked very much used.

'Oh, dearie me,' said the young man, 'it must have been overlooked. I'll see what I can do.'

At this point Mick, pale green in the face, loomed up in front of us and asked what the fucking hell we'd been doing and did we realize he'd been sitting in the fucking taxi freezing to fucking death for half a fucking hour. We said we'd only been up there for five minutes, but he may well have been right. The time sense, as he too has proved over and over again, entirely disappears when you're very drunk. Anyway, despite the fact that there was a bed for him, he was too angry with us to stay and stumbled down the stairs again and out into the night.

Mike and I ordered breakfast in bed in the morning, and

climbed between the filthy bed clothes. A dreadful night of
dreams! Huge insects marching in procession along the floor.
Groping awake just in time to find the sink and be violently
sick. More dreams of pustules and crab-lice, and at last a desperate awakening, eyeballs throbbing in the harsh winter light
shining through the filthy window, and an old woman smelling
of rotted knickers standing at the foot of the bed with a breakfast tray. Cracked cup, bread and marge, a pullet's egg. We
thanked her through cracked lips. She leant towards us and
whispered.

'Ye can trust me. I'm only the working lassie, but if any o'
the gairls come in tea ye, luke tae your wallets.' It was obvious,
and if we'd been less paralytic the night before we'd have cottoned on at once. We had slept in a brothel.

I got up and took my wallet out of my coat pocket and hid it
under my mattress. Mike did the same. Then we got back into
bed. A few minutes later the door opened and a quite young but
hideous whore came in wearing a filthy street coat over a
creased nightdress.

'I heard you come in last night,' she said, 'and I heard
Maggie bringing in your breakfast the noo. Can you spare a cup
of tea?'

She sat on the end of the bed to drink it. She made no pass at
us so I presume she thought we were lovers.

'That Jeanie across the stair,' she complained, 'she took a
mon all night for ten bob. It's no' right. It's letting the rest of
the lassies doon. Och, last night I was doon tae my last poond. I
bought a half bottle of whisky. I were coming up the stair and I
dropped it. It ran doon the stair sae I sat doon and keened over
it. A polis-man stopped. There I was sitting on the stair, the
gude whisky running down in a stream between ma legs and
making a wee pool on the street.

' "Have you pussed ye'sel'?" ' he asks.

'Och, I'm that unlucky if I went tae the Sahara for sand I'd
no find any.'

She talked for over an hour, and all the other girls came in and sat on the beds. I was beginning to feel better, even hysterically well with the false health of a bad hangover, and about eleven o'clock sent one of the whores out for some scotch.

At last Mike and I got dressed, and went straight to the nearest public baths before rejoining the band.

Mick, cheerful and friendly, had forgotten what had happened. He'd woken up in some respectable digs on the outskirts of the city.

A band on the road, tolerant to each other's major faults and shortcomings, are inclined to develop almost paranoiac feelings of hatred about small habits and mannerisms. For example my obsessional custom of arranging the contents of my pockets – money, keys, wallet, cheque-book – in a kind of neat collage on the top of a chest-of-drawers used to drive Mick, if he was sharing a room with me, into a state of irritation so intense that it could only be relieved by messing it up again.

A great deal of conversation, which would appear almost insane to an outsider, is taken up with describing and reiterating the faults, irritating verbal or physical peculiarities, small vanities and pretensions of any member or members of the band who aren't present. Furthermore a musician who is a friend can become an enemy, someone to be avoided at all costs, and then, a week or two later, become a friend again. As in medieval Europe the pattern of alliances is always changing.

'When the coach gets there,' whispers A to B, 'try and slip off before C notices us and tags on.'

Mick and I both liked Mike Lawrence, but we would do anything to avoid eating with him. It was not that his manners were particularly bad, although he shared with most musicians a habit which offended our middle-class prejudices, he buttered his rolls with his soup. It was simply that he based his behaviour in restaurants on a mid-Atlantic conception, complete with accent, and at the end of a meal would inevitably say to the waitress, 'Could I have the check, honey?'

He also used a great deal of tomato sauce. Not that this in itself irritated us – most of the food needed tomato sauce to make it edible – but if the bottle wasn't on the table, and in some extraordinary way it never was when we ate with Mike, he would call over the waitress and say, 'Could I have the ketchup, honey?'

Was it really because of these two sentences, one inevitable, the other well on the cards, that Mick and I would pretend we didn't want to eat and then belt off in the other direction in search of another restaurant as soon as Mike was out of sight? It seems mad, but if you ask any musician who has been on the road he tells you stories like this.

After Mike Lawrence had been with us about a year, he got an offer to sing with an All Girls Orchestra and decided to accept. It would mean after all that he got a chance to sing a bit more, to learn a few more numbers, and perhaps to get the break he was counting on. I met him a month or two later and asked him how he was getting on.

'Not too bad, Georgie,' he told me, 'but I can't bear the way their lipstick comes off on their mouth-pieces.'

He never did get his break. I don't know why. He'd a good voice in the Billy Daniels spirit, he could swing, and he knew how to project. Perhaps he wanted that break too much. Anyway after a couple of years he retired from the business altogether.

In the spring of 1953 boredom and frustration within the band produced some radical changes. Mike Lawrence had already left, now Jimmy Currie, the guitar player, followed him. He went to join a vocal group which achieved some commercial success. The night before he actually departed, Jo Lennard was made sufficiently angry by something he said to throw a cream bun at him across the dressing-room. Tension was on the increase all round.

Next Archie Semple, the clarinettist, left to join Freddy Randall. Mick knew about this offer because Freddy had, quite correctly, rung him up to warn him he was going to make it. He therefore asked Archie what he intended to do, and Archie denied he had any intention of taking it up. I suspect a certain Scottish caution lay behind this denial. He wanted it all sewn up and sealed before committing himself. Then one night, only an hour after he had yet again told Mick he definitely wasn't leaving, we heard him talking to Freddy in what he imagined was a soundproof telephone kiosk in our hotel. He was confirming the date he was to join. I had an unpleasant quarrel with him over this, not because he was going, but because he had lied.

'I suppose you think I'm a shit?' he asked me.

'Yes,' I said.

It nearly came to blows, and it was Mick who calmed us both down. Actually I suspect Mick derived some satisfaction from this shout-up.

A month or two before, Archie had come to me to say that if something wasn't done to improve the musical side of the band he was going to leave. He was entirely fed up with Mick's lack of interest. He'd tried talking to him, but all that happened was that Mick offered him a drink and changed the conversation. Could I do anything? What did I suggest?

He was perfectly right. Mick at that moment was sunk in one of his periods during which you would imagine that to play jazz was exactly the thing he disliked doing more than anything else in the world. We limped through the same programme night after night, and his only concern seemed to be drinking with the promoter during the intervals, in order to win a few minutes off our playing time.

I suggested to Archie that we approach Jim Godbolt, who, as band agent, was naturally concerned with the quality of what he had to try to sell, and see what we would work out. The outcome was that Jim asked Mick to come round to the office, and when he arrived, he found the three of us sitting like an inquisition under the map of the British Isles with its coloured flags showing all possible venues, and determined to obtain some satisfaction. We failed. Mick lost his temper and accused us of conspiracy and blackmail. He told us he intended to pay no attention to what we had to say under these conditions, and we could all get fucked. He stormed out of the office leaving us sitting there. Later he attacked Jim on his own for going behind his back, and me, on my own, for betraying our friendship. What was extraordinary was that he made us both feel real shits, and yet our intention had been to *improve his band*. This was all we wanted to do; to make the band better.

He was therefore not displeased to find Archie and me on the edge of a punch-up. He felt it proved some point.

So Archie left too.

Finally Jo Lennard got an offer to join the Ronnie Scott Big Band, and she accepted. Musically she had become very frustrated with singing the same three or four numbers night after night. Financially Ronnie's offer was an extremely tempting one, and emotionally she and I had reached a certain impasse. She told Mick of her decision and was to leave in the middle of March.

The band was again contracting.

A few days before Jo was to leave, we were playing a gig in Eastbourne and ran into real trouble. Half-way through the second set a group of yobs came in led by a tall psychopath looking for trouble. They marched up to the stand and began to pull at Jo's dress. Mick attempted to reason with them, and the leader jumped up on the stage followed by his gang and started a punch-up. In the middle of this the police burst into the hall. The gang-leader shouted a warning and the rumble stopped. Mick jumped off the stand, told the gang-leader he thought he was a bloody fool but wasn't going to take it any further, shook his hand, told the angry police sergeant he didn't intend to lodge a complaint, climbed back on the stage, announced the next number, and carried on playing. The police, after circling the hall a few times, left.

A few sets later I was singing a number called 'Send Me to the 'lectric Chair'. I was accompanied only by the rhythm section. The front line were having a quick smoke-up in the wings. I became aware that the gang-leader had climbed back on the stage and was advancing on my left. I carried on singing. When he reached me, he grabbed hold of the microphone lead and jerked it so violently that he broke the connection. There was complete silence. He then pulled a chiv out of his pocket and was holding it so that it just touched the side of my throat. He began to mutter threats in a low voice, gradually working himself up to violence. I didn't move an inch. I felt like a rabbit confronted with a stoat. Beyond fear. Somewhere else.

Behind him, out of the corner of my eye, I could see Mick creeping out of the wings, and after what seemed like a very long time indeed he sprang and pinioned the yob from behind. Then it all happened. The rest of the gang broke over the edge of the stage like a wave. Pat Molloy put his bass out of danger, and raised a chair. I saw Stan Bellwood bring down the edge of his largest cymbal which luckily just missed the head of one of the enemy. Jo had her shoe off and was using the heel. Everything was confusion, kicking, breaking chairs, shouted insults, blurred faces. Then it was all over. The gang vanished. The police were back, and the gang-leader, his arm bent behind him, was taken away. The manager told Mick to play 'The Queen'. His reaction was typical.

'We've won half an hour off our time,' he whispered triumphantly as Stan led in with the drum roll.

The police told Mick and me that we had to appear in court in a week's time to give evidence against the ringleader. Mick said that it would mean coming all the way down from the north and then travelling back again the same day. Surely there were plenty of witnesses in the audience who saw exactly what had happened and actually lived in Eastbourne? The Inspector looked severe. We were subpoenaed to appear. They'd been after this man for a long time. They needed us. There could be no excuse.

As we walked back to the digs Mick said that as we were lumbered he could at least get his coat replaced. The sleeve had been torn in the fight, and it was a Corporation dance. It would happen in Eastbourne, of course. We'd played some of the toughest towns in the British Isles, and it had to go and happen in Eastbourne where the old come to die. The next day we drove up to Grimsby to play a couple of nights at the Gaiety, followed by an American camp somewhere in Lincolnshire on the Sunday, a job in Chester on Tuesday, a day off on Wednesday (Mick and I would have to travel overnight to give our evidence), and the Denbigh Asylum job on the Thursday.

Diz had replaced Jimmy Currie on a temporary basis. Nobody, especially him, ever thought of him as a permanent replacement. His temperament was too mercurial to allow him to keep a job for long. He was with us until either we found somebody else or he got fed up.

Jo's last official job was the final night at Grimsby, but as she wasn't joining Ronnie Scott until Wednesday she decided to do the American camp as well. We were driving back to Doris's afterwards.

We did the jobs in Grimsby ('Very nice, Mick. Good show, George') and on a cold March evening drove off into Lincolnshire to find the U.S. base.

Most travelling bands at that time played a lot of bases all over the country. They were indistinguishable; a huge gum-chewing sergeant in charge of us, a sergeants' mess in a modified Hilton Hotel style, an audience which didn't want to know, a drunk who kept on asking for 'Deep in the Heart of Texas', very long hours, one-armed bandits to tempt us to throw away more than we were earning, the provoking sight of huge steaks with French fried disappearing into the faces of the crew-cutted elephantine-arsed army of occupation.

I can't remember anything special about that evening except for a notice which read: 'No lady guest will be permitted to attend open night in the Sergeants' Club with more than one member of same during any one month.'

At last we finished, and after a few drinks climbed wearily into the coach. It was freezing cold, and Jo and I sat next to each other under a rug. We felt a bit drunk and sentimental. It was our last night together. The driver climbed in and started the engine. We drove off. Soon the heater began to work, and Jo fell asleep on my shoulder.

It was about four o'clock and only twenty-five miles from Grimsby. In relation to the job in Chester the next day, Grimsby was in the wrong direction, but we'd decided to go back there because we could leave all our things, and besides it would have been hard to find digs in the middle of Lincolnshire to take us at that hour.

At six o'clock, as the first cold grey streaks of dawn were smearing the eastern sky, we were still careering through the flat countryside. Mick emerged from under a coat, and having peered at his watch asked the driver where the fuck we were.

'Och, I got a wee bit lost,' came the answer, 'but we're nearly there noo.' Grumbling but reassured, Mick crawled back under his coat. I was awake, Jo's head on my shoulder. I lit a cigarette and stared out of the window. We seemed to be approaching a town of some size. It must be Grimsby. The driver seeing a town on the flat horizon, and an apparently straight road ahead of him, put his foot down; but the town was not Grimsby, and the road was not straight.

We were on the outskirts of Boston fifty miles from our destination. We knew the town well as we had often played at a hall called 'The Gliderdrome', famous for its white-hot stoves, a unique and dangerous method of heating which effectually prevented brawling, and also for an eccentric member of the public, a young man who appeared in full evening dress, stood in front of the bandstand, bowed to the audience and then raised a baton he had been presented with by Joe Loss, and conducted us throughout the evening.

We had even considered staying in Boston that night, but had decided against it because it was a hard place to find digs. We had memories of a night when we had been forced, by lack of accommodation at any price, to sleep in the coach, taking occasional little walks through the freezing streets to try to get warm.

If all had gone well, in a few minutes we would have drawn up in the main street, recognized the 'Stump', the famous church spire so popular with suicides, and rounded on the driver, but the road was not straight.

Three quarters of a mile out of Boston it suddenly bent, and at the same time crossed a bridge over one of those canals which irrigate the flat fields of Lincolnshire and are called 'ditches'. The driver had his foot down. He didn't see the bend in the road until it was too late. He braked. We skidded across the road towards the low stone wall of the bridge. I was awake and saw it happening. I felt entirely detached, almost a spectator. I seemed to see it all from outside and from various angles, as if I were watching a film.

We crashed through the side of the bridge and out into the void beyond. The coach turned over in the air. Splinters of glass, luggage, instruments and bodies obeyed the law of gravity, but almost indolently, almost outside time. I remember shouting, 'Here we go', and thinking 'this is probably my lot'. Then the coach hit the water twenty feet below.

In the ordinary way, they told us later, the ditch would have been twelve foot deep so we would have drowned. Later in the year, they pointed out, it often became little more than a trickle so we would have been smashed to pieces. As it was, after a moment or two watching myself struggling under water, I was able to stand up in four feet of water and look about.

The coach was on its side, so that above us through the broken windows we could see the cold grey sky. We counted each other and we were all there. Paul Simpson had a badly cut hand, and I had a cut under one eye and a bleeding finger. Everybody else seemed all right. I began to shiver.

Jo was crying and we all patted her on the back to cheer her up. This was the worst thing we could have done, because several long splinters of glass had punctured her back and lung cavity.

Diz Disley climbed out through the emergency door and waded ashore. He came back in a few minutes with a ladder. 'Me bling ladder,' he explained in a Chinese accent. He used it to make a bridge between bank and coach and some of us climbed across it. The others waded to the opposite bank and scrambled up it. In two small parties we advanced on the two houses at each end of the bridge. The noise of the crash had woken them and their lights were on.

The house which Disley, Jo, Paul and I were soon to disrupt was a villa belonging to the local photographer. It was of modernistic tendency and had petrol blue tiles. The photographer's wife seemed very kind. She put Jo, who by this time was feeling very ill, to lie down on the sofa in the lounge, and rang up for an ambulance. She showed the rest of us up to her bathroom and went to make some tea. Diz and I shared a steaming hot bath giggling with hysteria. As my finger was still bleeding badly, I decided to go to the hospital in the ambulance. Jo was on a stretcher. Paul had convinced himself that he had cut a tendon in his hand and would never be able to play again.

When we got to the hospital they rushed Jo in for an examination and left Paul and me sitting on a bench in the emergency waiting-room. I had got the chats, and made lots of jokes while they were stitching up my finger. The sister didn't smile. When she'd finished she said that she was surprised I could make jokes when the girl who was with me was quite likely to die. They were going to operate immediately, but there wasn't much hope. I hadn't realized she was even seriously hurt, and asked if I could wait while they operated.

While I was sitting there, a priest hurried past into the theatre. He had come to hear Jo's confession and give her the sacraments.

They took two hours operating. When they'd finished, the sister, who by now could see how upset I was, came and told me that, as she was a strong girl, the surgeons thought she had a fifty-fifty chance. They wheeled Jo past on a trolley. She had no colour at all. I took a taxi and went back to the band.

By this time the photographer's wife had largely recovered from her attack of warm-heartedness. You couldn't exactly blame her. Half the mud from the ditch was all over her fitted carpets, and her lounge was full of jazzmen dropping ash all over everything and making a terrible noise. Mick was in the hall on the phone to Godbolt, and it was all getting too much for her.

Even so the couple in the small house on the other side of the bridge, although they had no bathroom and no telephone and he was a farm labourer, couldn't do too much for their contingent.

Mick saw me come in ('Would you mind wiping your feet,' said the photographer's wife) and asked me how Jo was. He asked, of course, quite casually, imagining as I had that she was suffering from shock. I told him they thought she had a fifty-fifty chance. He put the phone down on the table – I could hear Godbolt's voice barking irritably – and I told him what I knew. He picked up the phone again and told Jim to let her parents know.

He finished talking to Jim and rang up the hospital ('I hope you're keeping an account of all those phone calls,' said the photographer's wife) and asked how Jo was. No worse, they told him, but of course it was too early to say anything definite.

Mick sent the rest of the band home by train, and he and I moved into a pub in the town. We drank about a bottle of rum a day for the next two days and never got drunk. We had settled on rum as 'comforting'.

We salvaged what we could from the coach. The instruments were all right although of course they had to be dried and greased to stop them rusting. We took the uniforms to a cleaners. They would be needed again in three days, the longest Jim thought we could cancel our engagements.

Jo's parents arrived and with them her Uncle George. When we were getting the stuff out of the coach, the two men were measuring the skidmarks on the bridge above us. They looked stern and speculative.

I spent a lot of time at the hospital and was allowed to see Jo. She was on the mend. My mother sent her freesias. I'd rung her immediately after the accident as I guessed it would be in the papers.

Finally Mick and I sent the uniforms and instruments by train to Denbigh for our next date, and travelled down overnight to give our evidence at the trial of the psychopathic yob in Eastbourne.

We broke the journey in London and rushed home to change into suits. We met at Victoria Station at 8.30. Mick had his Uncle Jim with him who had insisted on coming along to 'lend moral support' as he put it.

Mick's Uncle Jim wore a beard and a beret and looked rather like an artist in a cartoon in *Punch circa* 1903. He was not an unkind man, but very reactionary and given to great self-dramatization. We could have done without him that day.

We gave our evidence. The magistrate, once he had understood that we were jazz musicians, seemed inclined to treat us as if we were the accused. Admittedly, my appearance didn't help. The unhealed cut under my eye give me a very villainous appearance, but even so I feel it was our profession which made him so unpleasant. He was particularly incensed over the fact that Mick had shaken hands with the yob after the first fracas.

'You shook hands with this man?' he queried in a voice like a creaking gate. 'Now why did you do this?' Mick explained that he wished to show he had no ill feelings, and had imagined that the whole incident was closed.

'And yet it was not,' said the magistrate. 'It does appear to me the most extraordinary behaviour.'

When it came to my turn, 'Is this man also a jazz musician?' – it was explained to the bench that I had cut my eye in an accident and not during the fight.

The yob had a long list of convictions for causing or attempting to cause bodily harm and was sent down for six months.

We walked out of court to be met by Uncle Jim in a state of near hysteria. He had been sitting in the public gallery and had overheard the yob's mates muttering threats and writing down our home addresses.

'Officer,' shouted Uncle Jim at the policeman on duty, 'get these men out of town.'

Mick and I refused to take any notice of him, and went into the local for a much needed drink before catching the train.

Later Mick wrote to the town clerk to ask if the Municipal Authorities would pay for his coat. He got a brusque refusal citing that the coat had been torn *after* he had shaken hands with the man, and that therefore it was his responsibility.

That night we played the first job since the crash.

I went up to Boston to see Jo while she was getting better. Her back looked like a railway junction. Eventually she sued Mick and won. The Corporation also sued for the repairs to their bridge, and they won too.

This shouldn't have mattered in the ordinary way as Mick's Insurance Company would have paid, but it was discovered that the driver had lied in filling in his qualifications, and had claimed to hold a licence which he hadn't got. What was so aggravating was that there was no need for him to have this licence anyway – it was for something like driving public transport – but because he'd claimed he'd got it, the Insurance Company didn't have to cough up a penny.

Afterwards, whenever we crossed that bridge, we would ask Mick if it belonged to him. He never really liked that joke. 'Very fucking amusing,' he would mutter.

When Jo was all right again she joined Harry Gold's Pieces of Eight (Ronnie Scott had found another vocalist), but after a bit she got married and left the business.

A month or two later Mick, who was fed up with everything anyway, decided to give up the band altogether.

He put it to me that I could go solo. Jazz was on the up again, and there was plenty of club work. He would be my manager, and I ought to be able to make out pretty well.

He told the rest of the band one night when we were playing a South London jazz club. Nobody seemed either upset or surprised. During the interval I heard Stan Bellwood and Roy Crimmins making plans to form a band of their own.

'And I've got a great gimmick,' said Stan, 'we'll call it, well it doesn't matter, "The Crimmins-Bellwood Allstars", something like that, and then, on the posters, under the name, in big letters in Day-Glo, we'll 'ave the words "SELLING EXCITE-MENT"!'

And so the band folded. Wyllie took his wife and child back to Australia and a job in a Melbourne bookshop. The others gigged around or joined other bands, and Stan, despite his ambition to sell excitement, sold his drums instead and became, as I said earlier, a publican.

9. *The Real Reason Is I Love Him*

Towards the end of 1953 and during the opening months of
1954, there was indeed a great deal happening in the jazz
world. I refer here to our jazz world. The modernists lived
their own life which touched on ours as little as if they had been
vets or haberdashers.

Ken Colyer came back from New Orleans like Moses
coming down from Mount Sinai with the tablets of the Law.
Chris Barber and Monty Sunshine had a band waiting for him.
To the growing number of New Orleans purists he trailed
clouds of glory, and every note he blew was sacred.

Humph was in full revolt against his revivalist past. For
some time he experimented wildly, dropping the trombone altogether and trying such far-out combinations as a West Indian
rhythm section. His monthly newsletter was a masterpiece of
dialectical justification.

Finally he settled for mainstream, the small-band jazz of the
late thirties and early forties, the music to which he has remained faithful ever since.

Alex Welsh decided to come down from Scotland and form a
band to play white Dixieland jazz, similar in character to the

music produced by various American groups under the direction of the guitar-playing professional whisky-drinker, Eddie Condon.

The great success of that time, however, was the band which had attracted and held all Humph's disappointed revivalist fans, and which won the adherence of the recently self-styled Beatniks (until that year they had called themselves existentialists), Soho layabouts and the art-school students, and was led by my first boss, Cy Laurie.

His cellar-club, an enormous basement in Windmill Street just off Piccadilly, was jammed, and his all-night raves, based very much on our earlier efforts but financially tenable, in his larger premises, merited a shocked article in the *People* with photographs of necking couples lying on the floor and a wealth of salacious moralizing.

It was at Cy's that I first got to know David Litvinoff, an extraordinary person on the fringe of a dozen worlds. The fastest talker I have ever met, full of outrageous stories, at least half of which turn out to be true, a dandy of squalor, a face either beautiful or ugly, I could never decide which, but certainly one hundred per cent Jewish, a self-propelled catalyst who didn't mind getting hurt as long as he made something happen, a sacred monster, first class.

David can only breathe in London. We once went to the country to deliver some furniture to somebody's mother. He was appalled at the waste, at the lack of human activity. 'All that grass. All those trees . . .' he speculated irritably. 'They must be worth something to somebody.'

His hatred of nature is so intense that he refuses to acknowledge that there are any separate species of bird. He calls them all, even sparrows, ducks.

Cy Laurie's success was very largely due to his manager, a plump, middle-aged man with grey hair brushed back over his head in wirelike strands. He realized that national, as opposed to local, fame was the product of publicity, and to this end employed a publicity agent called Les Perrin. At this time such tactics were unheard of in the jazz world, and they certainly paid off.

Les Perrin, a tiny cockney sparrow, was a dynamo of ideas. He would distribute pamphlets from a helicopter, fire bullets through a band coach window and, in Cy's case, build up a fanatical following whose identification with the band was hysterical rather than musical.

A little later, with the ascent of Chris Barber, Cy's star began to wane. Always a prey to self-doubt, and given to fanatical solutions and mystical enthusiasm, Cy broke up the band and went to India to study, so it was said, under a guru.

The National Federation of Jazz Organizations was attempting during this period to keep the growing enthusiasm for the music under some kind of control. This was to avoid the over-exposure which had all but killed off the interest during the earlier boom in 1950. The only trouble was that the elected committee was so divided by differences of opinion as to what jazz was, and so split by personal animosities, that it had a difficult job keeping itself under control. During the year 1953–4 I served on this committee. I had been proposed as a kind of joke at the General Meeting but somebody seconded me and I was elected. While the band was still in existence I had never been able to attend a meeting, but after it broke up I used to go along every other Tuesday to The Three Brewers, Seven Dials, and put in what Mick would call 'my two penn'orth'. It was during my term of office that Big Bill Broonzy came over under the auspices of the N.F.J.O. to do a series of concerts. This was a very big deal indeed. He was the first American jazzman to play in England since the war. The Musicians' Union, in a hopelessly parochial way, refused to allow Americans in although it was obvious that in fact the interest they would arouse would *create* work for British musicians on the same bill. They only let Broonzy in because he was a folk singer.

For me the idea of hearing an American Negro singing the blues was almost unbearably exciting. I went along to his first concert at the Conway Hall in a state of tense anticipation. Alan Lomax introduced him at great length while Bill stood patiently at his side. I found Lomax extremely paternalistic. I knew he'd done a great deal for the blues, got Leadbelly out of prison, recorded work songs in prison camps, and rediscovered many forgotten and obscure artists – for all this we owe him a great deal – but I got the impression that he felt he owned them. The southern voice droned on and on. Finally it got too much even for Bill, an extremely well-mannered and equable man.

'. . . and ah am sho,' said Lomax, 'that when yo' heah Big Bill . . .' 'If they ever gets the chance,' said Broonzy resignedly and there was a round of applause which had the effect of hurrying up the introduction.

I won't describe how I felt listening to Bill that summer evening. This was the first live blues I'd ever heard in my life, the music I loved, and love above any other, sung by a great artist.

His whole visit was a splendour. There were sessions that lasted all night long, the most memorable at Jimmy Asman's tiny house in Plumstead, where Bill would drink a whole bottle of whisky and talk over quiet chords on his guitar, lie outrageously about things he had seen and done, and sing the blues until the dawn broke over Woolwich.

The N.F.J.O. promoted a series of concerts in the provinces for Bill, but delegated the responsibility to various promoters. We decided that it would be as well to appoint some representative of the federation to watch our interests in each town and for the Liverpool concert I proposed my father. He was delighted, took his duties very seriously, and wrote us a long report which ended: 'Mr Broonzy was received with prolonged and enthusiastic applause, and declared himself willing, if only it were possible, to continue to sing all night, a statement I am prepared to believe.'

Bill stayed with my parents and told my mother that this was the first place he had stayed in England where you didn't have to put money in a meter for the gas fire. He ate an enormous breakfast: two plates of corn flakes, two helpings of bacon and eggs, and about a loaf and a half of toast. My father was so fascinated he was very late for the office.

Broonzy came over four or five times before he died. I got to know him well and loved him very much. He helped to create the taste for Mississippi-style blues, and opened the way for all the singers who came here later.

Dressed in a black shirt, black trousers, black socks, black shoes, a very expensive black sweater from Simpsons, and a white silk tie, I embarked on my solo career.

Mick managed to arrange several little tours of the provincial jazz clubs at a fee of ten pounds a night. As I'd only been getting three with the band this seemed an enormous amount. What I failed to take into account was that I had travelled free in the coach, and now I had to pay my own train fares. Also I had to pay Mick commission so I was in fact no better off.

I would have been actually worse off if it hadn't been for Alex Welsh coming down to London from Edinburgh to form a band. Alex realized that whereas he was still comparatively unknown outside Scotland, I had a certain reputation. He therefore used me a great deal, encouraged by Mick who was for a short time his manager as well, and could draw commission from both of us. Then Mick began to itch to get back in the business. There were several reasons for this. The improvement of the situation financially was certainly one, not to mention the fact that a bandleader earns considerably more than an agent to a modestly-paid singer and a newly-formed band; but it was not only this. He was after all only twenty-six, and had known applause and enthusiasm. You don't go into the jazz business simply to earn money. There is a wish to play in front of an audience. There is some element, although Mick hid it better than anyone I have ever met, of exhibitionism. At all events slowly, so slowly you could hardly see it happen, Mick began to play again.

At first he didn't even form a band of his own. He just used Alex's. While Alex was still finding his feet this suited him too, but as he became better known the situation got impossible. The promotor of a jazz club could not be expected to be best pleased if he booked Mick Mulligan one week and Alex Welsh the next and found himself landed with virtually the same group plus or minus Mick. Furthermore, Alex became established in his own right, was approached by a serious agent and saw no reason to spend his evenings blowing away for Mick's benefit when he could be doing it for his own. There came a time early in 1955 when Mick had to re-form a band. He asked me to join it and, despite an offer from Alex, I did.

Many people would have said I was mad. Alex took his responsibilities very seriously. He rehearsed. He was determined to succeed. Mick, as I well knew, alternated between bursts of enthusiasm and complete apathy from which nothing could shift him. He drank a great deal in those days and in consequence often played extremely badly, whereas Alex was still a teetotaller – a failing he made ample amends for later – and was known in a not entirely kindly spirit, as 'The Lemonade King'.

Of course I also drank and quite often sang disgracefully because of it, but I never took that into account when thinking of Mick's lapses. In fact Mick and I discovered later that whenever one of us was describing to the other some drunken shout-up with a third party, we inevitably made our enemy talk in the slurred voice of the Music Hall inebriate whereas we, in retelling our triumphant and cutting role in the argument, always assumed a sober and rational voice.

Furthermore, my own status had improved out of recognition. An appearance with Alex at the Festival Hall in one of the N.J.F.'s festivals of British Jazz had been recorded, and my version of 'Frankie and Johnnie' was actually selling quite well. I had been cheered for three minutes, and about thirty seconds of this intoxicating noise is at the end of the record to prove it. Fame, that dangerous bird, brushed my cheek. Several offers came from agents to manage me as a solo artist, and then I joined Mick, a bandleader without a band.

The real reason is I love him. Two stories to show why. One night we played an R.A.F. camp and, unable to finds digs, were kindly offered a billet by the Wing Commander. His only condition was that we were quiet, a not unreasonable request as it was by this time two o'clock in the morning and we were next door to airmen who had to be up at six. Mick stayed behind for a final drink, and the rest of us, stoned out of our heads, staggered along the neat paths to find our hut.

After crashing, despite detailed instructions, into several sock-scented billets full of sleepily angry personnel, we eventually found our own quarters and began to shout, scream, pillow-fight, fall about, and finally managed to push over a wardrobe. At this moment the door burst open and there stood Mick absolutely livid with rage. For three minutes he gave us a perfectly justifiable bollocking. We took it with the masochistic repentance of the very drunk. We were ashamed of ourselves. Mick was perfectly right. We hung our heads. Then, in full spate, he stopped and looked at the flimsy wardrobe at his feet.

'What the fuck,' he shouted joyfully, and jumping into the air landed on top of it, splintering it to match-wood.

The other story I heard only the other day from Ian Christie. Mick was very drunk and playing a solo. His control was minimal, his head entirely empty of any constructive musical ideas.

His timing gone. All he could do was blow unbearably loudly, his neck swollen, his eyeballs popping with effort. Ian listened with embarrassed irritation. When somebody is playing as badly as that it reflects on everybody in the band. Finally Mick finished his thirty-two bars of nothing, and waved his bell in the direction of the trombonist to tell him to take the next chorus. He turned to Ian, his face running with sweat:

'All the noise and vulgarity of Freddy Randall,' he said, 'with none of the technique.'

I stayed with Mick, despite periods of exasperation and occasional tempting offers, for the next seven years.

10. A Good Conductor

Most people who decide to form a band go about it like this:
they approach any musicians they want and, if they are already
with another group, make a financial offer. They advertise in
the musical press and hold auditions. They get around the
smaller clubs to see if there is any potential talent in the semi-
pro bands. They brief spies to keep their ears open in the provinces.

Mick did none of these things. He let it get about he was
reforming and then sat on his arse. Being Mick he was about
twice as lucky as anyone else would have been. For a start
disagreements within the newly-formed Alex Welsh Band shot
three musicians into his lap: they were Ian Christie (clarinet),
Pete Appleby (drums), and Frank Thompson (double
bass).

Ian Christie was already well known in revivalist circles
before he joined Mick. He had played second clarinet with
Humph, and had co-led, with his brother Keith on trombone, a
band called 'The Christie Brothers Stompers'. This had two
distinct periods: the first when Ken Colyer on trumpet had a
decidedly purist flavour, the second with Dickie Hawdon,

basically and progressively modern. Ian, unlike his brother, was the opposite of eclectic, and the band broke up.

Keith's modernist tendencies led him into the Ted Heath Band. Ian's musical conservatism held him faithful to revivalist jazz. Even within this field he was extremely dogmatic. All he really liked at that time were the late Louis Armstrong, Condon music and, outside this pattern but with extreme fervour, the Mississippi blues singers like Broonzy.

His own playing was accomplished but limited. His principal influences were the New Orleans clarinettists, Edmond Hall and Albert Nicholas. Neither are dramatic players. They are both lyricists. Their effect on Ian was to lead him to play a continuous string of notes at approximately the same volume from the first bar of a number to the coda. As a result his solos, when on form, were often beautiful in an unpretentious and restrained way, but in ensemble, because he didn't listen to what the rest of the front line were up to, had no give and take. He just played, as if he were taking a solo. Furthermore he had a bad memory for arrangements. This suited Mick very well, as it gave him a perfect excuse not to hold rehearsals.

'What's the use, cock?' he would ask. 'Ian can never remember new numbers.'

It was this difficulty which had led to his departure from the Alex Welsh Band. Alex and Roy Crimmins were after an arranged sound, and Ian was continuously holding them up. I attended several rehearsals, and could see that the extreme politeness with which Roy and Ian treated each other, masked exasperation and near enmity. When Archie Semple left Freddy Randall and offered to rejoin his old Edinburgh friend and musical sidekick, it was a foregone conclusion that Ian would go.

Ian is small, almost mouse-like in appearance, and wears horn-rimmed spectacles. His movements are neat and precise, his vocabulary enormous, his accent Lancastrian. His father, a piano tuner by profession, was Scottish, but his mother came from Blackpool where Ian and Keith were brought up.

Ian had qualified as a photographer before coming south, and until it became possible for him to earn his living as a full-time musician, had worked in the photography department of Harrods. The idea of him asking debs to smile was not without irony, as his considerable talent for hatred, his powers of invective, his whole reserve of malice were directed night and day, drunk or sober, at the upper classes (short 'a'). The word 'hurray', Jim Godbolt's happy synonym, became in Ian's mouth a deadly insult. Collectively he referred to Hurrays as 'the enemy', and to a typically hurray face, either of the chinless, slack-mouthed variety, or of the florid small-eyed strain, as 'an enemy face'.

To work himself up yet further he had only to say the words 'public school'. The phrase 'public-school hurray' was enough to produce a psychosomatic state not far removed from apoplexy.

One fine winter morning at about eleven o'clock we were driving through the West Country, and were forced to stop by a hunt crossing the road. It was a pretty, if absurd, spectacle, and the rest of use were inclined to watch it pass with tolerant pleasure. Not so Ian. He lowered his window and subjected the entire charade, from the leading hound to the last velvet-capped child on a pony, to a blistering stream of insults. Mick was amazed. 'I thought he was going to pass out,' he told me later.

Ian and I frequently engaged in violent political rows. Most of these took place late at night in the wagon when we were both rather drunk and, whatever the subject, followed an identical course. Ian was on the extreme left bordering, although he never joined the party, on the edge of official Communism. I took the anarchist position, holding that ends never justify means, and that authority, whether on the left or right, is always wrong. Ian usually finished up by accusing me of talking a load of liberal humanist shit. There was one memorable incident in these otherwise identical and fruitless arguments, and this was due to a misunderstanding. Ian had been stressing that all my thought patterns were the result of my middle-class background. I agreed that this might be true but that it was after all an accident where any of us were *dropped from the womb*.

'Don't try and confuse the issue with that Surrealist bollocks,' shouted Ian. I was puzzled, and asked what he found Surrealist in what I'd been saying. It turned out he'd thought I'd said, 'lopped off the moon'.

In general the rest of the band ignored these shout-ups, preferring to sleep unless there was a bottle circulating, but Mick would occasionally enter the lists only to find himself, like a passer-by intervening in a fight between man and wife, turned on by the pair of us. Mick's political ideas are extremely reactionary although he is the opposite of pragmatic in day to day life.

Ian's political viewpoint forced him to consider Mick, in his role as bandleader, as a representative of the boss class. He was always pressing for a change of structure. He wanted the band put on a cooperative basis with Mick taking a double share. Mick refused to countenance this idea. He *liked* being bandleader, and besides it was probably true that he did make, when things were going well, considerably more money than a double share. I was against it because I preferred a straight screw with none of the responsibility for breakdowns and broken contracts, and the rest of the band didn't want to know either.

Until he got married Ian was usually involved in some intense affair. It was only occasionally he was able to treat sex on a light level, and he was not very adept at the quick chat-up followed by a knee tremble. He had a habit if he saw one of us getting on well with a girl he fancied of sailing in with a cry of 'Is this man annoying you?', but it never worked. Besides, if it had, he wouldn't really have enjoyed it much. He was an extreme romantic. Just by chance most of his pre-marital affairs were with upper-class girls.

Some days before his wedding, Ian's father gave him as a joke a vulgar rubber toy. It was about six inches long and turned one way represented a girl wearing a shawl over her head, but turned the other way it became an erect penis. The next evening, during the interval of a seaside dance, I was leaning on the esplanade and became aware of Ian standing below me on the shingle at the edge of the incoming sea. Suddenly he raised his arm and threw the phallic pun as far as he could. Being rubber it floated, and the waves deposited it again at his feet. It was a very Freudian moment for a Marxist.

Some months ago a dreadful game went the rounds. All it consisted of was deciding whom among your friends and acquaintances were 'winners' and who were 'losers'. Likeable characteristics had nothing to do with the decision – many losers are extremely likeable – but neither did material success guarantee you to be a winner. Paul Getty for example is a proto-type loser. The distinction, and it is a very hard one to make in a great many cases, is that the loser gives off an aura of defeat and possible disaster, whereas the winner emanates a justified confidence in the inability of things to go wrong. It was no less shaming to be judged a winner than a loser. Only the players derive any satisfaction from it, and that based on extremely suspect motives. One thing is certain, however, and that is that if the game had been invented at the time everybody in the band would have judged the drummer, Pete Appleby, a one hundred per cent winner.

Pete Appleby, small but wiry, is one of those people who seem to have no past history. His childhood, a period of which even the most non-Proustian is unable to prevent some impression forming over a period of years, remained a complete mystery to us. We did meet his father once for a few moments, because the band-wagon was passing his house and Pete had something to tell him, but apart from the fact he looked exactly like a slightly older version of Pete and wore a bow tie, we learned little from this encounter. His mother, whom we gathered was separated from his father, we never saw. The only concrete fact I can recall about Pete's early years was that during the war he had been evacuated to Bedford and gone to school there.

His later career was equally sketchy, although it was certain that he was in the Navy. Pete was even prepared to talk about this period of his life occasionally, but the trouble was that, being one of nature's Walter Mittys, he frequently promoted himself. If any of the band pointed out that he appeared to have risen in rank since the last time he told us a particular story, he would give the answer with which he always refuted any accusation of inconsistency. Moving his padded shoulders rapidly about, his inevitable response to emotional stimuli, he would tell us with emphatic confidence, 'I never said that.'

Most of Pete's naval stories were to remind us of the fact that he had served under Prince Philip, and that they were like 'that'. In the course of these stories Philip would call Pete 'Pete' and Pete would call Philip 'Phil'. Actually if they were like 'that' it is on the cards that Pete did call Philip 'Phil' because he had a horror of calling anybody by their full name and would shorten it if possible. If it was a two-syllable name like 'Gerry' there was no problem. Pete could call its owner 'Ger', but if it was a name of only one syllable like 'Mick', Pete would prefer to shorten the surname, and usually called Mick 'Mul'. He invariably referred to himself as 'Apps'.

For a long time none of us could decide why Pete was so different from the rest of us, almost as if he belonged to a different species. I forget the exact moment of revelation, but after it the problem no longer existed. What made Pete so different was simply the fact that he came from, lived in, and was loyal to, South London.

The problem no longer existed, but there was still a linguistic block. We had for some time no adjective to describe South London in general and Pete Appleby in particular. We could and did say that Pete's clothes, for example, were typical of South London, or that he had a very South London approach to driving the band-wagon, but we knew there must be a word for it, and at last I found it.

I was reading Mayhew's *The London Underworld* in the wagon and came upon a description of a gentleman who had crossed Waterloo Bridge and entered 'a transpontine brothel'. From then on Pete's clothes were transpontine clothes. Pete's driving was transpontine. Pete himself was transpontine.

Of course he had a come-back. Once he had understood that the word meant nothing more than 'across the bridge' (and yet for the rest of us how much more) he pointed out that to him 'All you cunts is transpontine.' He had logic on his side, but he knew it didn't work.

Pete didn't drink and had a fantastic reserve of energy. It was natural, therefore, that during the five years he was with the band, he put in most of the driving. He was paid for it at so much a mile, but although this certainly influenced him, it wasn't the only reason he drove so much. He genuinely had a feeling for driving, and also enjoyed the power it gave him over the rest of the band. The times he liked best were when he was the only driver in the band. Very often the bass player was also a driver, and towards the end Mick raised the energy to reapply for his own licence, but there was a year or two when Pete alone was legally entitled to take the wheel.

During this period, if he was angry with the rest of us for hanging on at the end of a dance or jazz club to drink when he wanted to drive home, he would wait until we were on the outskirts of London and then pull into a layby for an hour's sleep. On two occasions during rows with Mick he found himself in the happy position of handing in his notice, and then giving Mick the keys to the wagon knowing full well that he would have to be placated, persuaded to take them back, and drive on. To remember his cry of ' 'oo's the driver then?' is still sufficient to stimulate my adrenalin glands.

As a driver he was a natural, although given to taking considerable liberties. He was always very polite to lorries, making the accepted signals, and flicking his lights on and off, but he couldn't bear being overtaken by a private car and when this happened would chase it mile after mile. If anybody irritated him he would lean out of his window and shout, 'Where did you learn to drive?' or, if there wasn't time for the whole sentence, he would make do with 'Cunt!'

There were times when a gentleman so addressed would take advantage of the traffic lights turning red at the next intersection to jump out of his car and threaten Pete with physical violence. When this happened Pete would point over his shoulder with his thumb to where the rest of us sat unaggressively in the back of the wagon and explain laconically, 'There's seven of us.'

Cars were Pete's god, and the garage, pronounced 'garidge' in the accepted transpontine manner, his church. He was always driving up to the meet in a new second-hand model, and spent a lot of time on long journeys explaining the complicated deals he was engaged on with various used-car firms. Needless to say he was always the winner in these transactions.

Pete, despite this one extravagance, always seemed to have plenty of money. As I said he didn't drink. 'Don't see no point in it,' he explained. 'Pissing all you get up against a wall and making cunts of yourselves.' On the other hand he gambled, but unlike the rest of us, won consistently. Here his non-drinking certainly helped. During the long smoky nights in hotel lounges or boarding-house bedrooms, while the rest of us became more and more befuddled as the bottle passed, Pete, clear-eyed and obsessed with the will to win, played us like a matador plays a bull. He was a brilliant bluffer, and knew how to needle us into exasperating raising, and frighten us into throwing in good hands when he had nothing. When he pulled off a coup,

'Packed 'ave yer? Beaten a Queen 'igh could yer? Thought so,' his shoulders would gyrate in such an ecstasy of glee as to suggest that he might at any moment leave the ground. As well as being a good player, he was also diabolically lucky.

Drummers have an enormous sexual potential for a certain type of girl, and Pete, although small and no beauty, had considerable charm. He looked not unlike Frank Sinatra. His reaction to being told this was in fact typical of his own special line of mock-modesty. 'Funny you should say that,' he would tell the girl as he packed up his drum kit at the end of a dance with a special puzzled frown on his face. 'Several girls *'ave* said it. Don't see it meself though.'

What is perhaps missing from this description is how likeable Pete was. His very outrageousness worked in his favour. His self-dependence and absence of self-pity commanded a certain respect. He had one very comical delusion, namely that everybody was blind outside the band. Time after time he would be caught pulling faces, and if anybody struck him as particularly ridiculous, he would hold up his open palm and jab at them from behind it with the forefinger of the other hand convinced that they wouldn't see what he was doing.

I was glad to hear recently that his cheek, his outrageous poise, remains unimpaired. Not long ago the Chris Barber Band booked in at an hotel and saw in the register that the Donegan group were staying there too, and that Mr and Mrs Appleby were in room eight. They crept up in a body and threw open the door hoping to catch Pete in some embarrassing situation or at least to discomfort him.

' 'Ullo boys,' he said getting out of bed in his immaculate pale blue silk pyjamas. A mound of bedclothes showed where 'Mrs Appleby' lay concealed. Pete grinned and with a quick movement whisked the clothes off the bed revealing a naked young lady looking none too pleased. ' 'Ow bad!' said Pete Appleby.

Like Ian Christie and Pete Appleby, Frank Thompson

joined us from Alex Welsh. He had from Mick's point of view a great advantage. He owned a station wagon and was prepared to rent it to the band for a very modest sum per week. This seemed to solve the transport problem. With Pete and Frank both able to drive, we could travel overnight, and accept bookings hundreds of miles apart on consecutive dates, a necessary lumber during the period we were re-establishing ourselves. Furthermore, the cheapness of the wagon meant that Mick could take jobs at a much lower rate than was possible in the grandiose days of coach hire. However, as with so much to do with Frank Thompson, it only *seemed* to solve it. His station wagon was so old, and broke down so often, that Mick was always having to hire fleets of taxis or take the whole band by train, so that in the end it worked out as a very expensive form of economy.

Inside Frank Thompson's head a permanent fairy godmother waved her wand. All pumpkins were coaches. All rats were coachmen. His wagon was a case in point. Whatever went wrong with it, as far as he was concerned it remained a new and efficient machine.

Frank's appearance was against him. He was short and yet gangling. His hair, although heavily Brylcreemed, fell down in a lank cow's lick over his forehead, and stuck up in spikes on the crown. His complexion was yellow, his skin rough and en-grained with grease from repairing his vehicle, and his teeth were green and furry. His most memorable feature was his nose, a Cyrano-type organ, enormous and snub.

He didn't drink alcohol, but in pubs would order a pint of orange squash. This going down was an unattractive sight. The same applied to his consumption on every possible occasion of large and squashy cream cakes.

Perhaps his best cabaret, and it lost nothing from daily re-petition, happened when the van stalled. There was no question of a self-starter, and Frank had to get out and crank it into life with the starting handle. This seldom took less than nine or ten attempts, but it was his timing which, if he had been a comedian, gave the performance its distinction. He was out of sight behind the bonnet for a count of nine, and then on the ten his face in agonized profile would shoot up in front of us to an accompanying lifeless cough from the engine. Very often the handle kicked back, and Frank would stagger about the road in a dramatic fashion clasping his wrist.

I believe it was Ian who first pointed out that this scene had very much the flavour of *Monsieur Hulot's Holiday*, a film most of us had seen, and we took to chanting the name 'Hulot' every time Frank cranked up the handle. We prolonged the first syllable on a rising note while he remained invisible and then shouted the second syllable as loudly as we could as he sprang into view. By about the sixth repetition he very often lost his temper and used to pace off and sulk round a corner for a minute or two.

We also called him 'Hulot' as a nickname, although after a time this got to be pronounced 'Youlow' in imitation of Pete Appleby. Pete, of course, hadn't the faintest idea who the original Monsieur Hulot was. He never took in anything outside his own interests however much it was talked about in the wagon, but he was delighted with the name, and was even willing to overlook that it contained two syllables.

Frank Thompson's delusions extended far outside the confines of his van, but what was so extraordinary about him was that he never seemed to mind our being able to compare what he said with the reality. He told us for instance that he had a flat in town and a house in the country and this turned out to be a single room with a sink and the use of the bathroom in a small terrace house in Clapham, and his mother's identical house three miles further out into the suburbs.

Like the rest of us he was frequently in a financial mess but he found it necessary to tell us: 'You know it's an extraordinary thing. Whenever I get into money difficulties another legacy falls into my lap.'

He was not a bad-hearted person at all but, like the boy at school who is always bullied, he managed to bring out the worst in us all.

He eventually got engaged and on tour he used to put a large photograph of his fiancée by his bedside. In Scotland Paul Simpson, who was with us during one of our tromboneless moments, pencilled in a moustache on the young lady's upper lip. Frank was furious, although he couldn't find out who'd done it, and actually suspected his main persecutors, Ian Christie or Pete. It wasn't of course a kind thing to do, but then Frank's reaction was so typical as to alienate any potential sympathy.

'I've rubbed out the moustache,' he told us as we loaded up the wagon next morning, 'and I forgive whoever did it, but . . .' he paused to give what he had to say its full weight, 'if they'd have drawn in breasts I'd have killed them.'

Mick had decided to make it a small band this time, so with clarinet, drums and bass fixed up, he'd only a piano player and trombonist to find. Our first pianist, they were always changing, was a tall Glaswegian called Angus Bell.

The first time I met Angus 'Miff' Bell we nearly had a fight. It was several years before he joined the band and just after he'd come down to London to earn his living as a pianist. It took place in Henekey's Cider Bar in Kingly Street, a favourite fall-about station for the musical profession at that time.

We were introduced by a mutual acquaintance. I was at my fattest and was wearing, Miff told me later, a red waistcoat obviously dating from my slimmer days. He took an instant dislike to me, and I to him.

After some minutes' conversation I began to realize from certain remarks of his that he was a Scottish nationalist, and I had the audacity to disagree with him. . . . I knew, of course, that Scottish nationalists existed but never imagined that I might meet one, particularly in the jazz world, and thought that a few words would convert this tall dour Scot from his convictions. Miff, much to my surprise, told me to get stuffed.

By the time he joined the band he'd turned against these ideas and indeed like all 'ex-people' — ex-Catholics, ex-Communists, etc. — had turned against his previous convictions with a special violence. What he hadn't lost, indeed what had probably attracted him to fascism in the first place, was a constant manic rage, only now it's found outlet, to my continued pleasure over six years, in ferocious black humour.

Miff's daemon demanded a considerable quantity of drink in order to materialize. He remained faithful to malt whisky, a taste acquired in his Scottish nationalist days, and he became very anti-Sassenach when he couldn't get it. Although he no longer rooted actively for the King over the water, he remained in this, and much else, a convinced patriot. Every time we crossed the border into Scotland he would sing 'Speed Bonny Boat' in that curiously exaggerated 'rrrolling' tenor deriving from the late Sir Harry Lauder. When he was really raving Miff would begin to caper around doing what he called his 'bits and pieces'.

'Finger in bum. Finger in mouth,' he would shout in his distinct brogue, suiting the action to the words, and then, after a few more seconds of 'leaping aboot', he would yell, 'CHANGE FINGERS!'

His imitation of the Pope was another speciality. As this had to be performed sitting down it was usually given in the wagon. It was a generalized picture of the head of Christendom rather than a portrait of any particular prelate. I deduce this because it didn't alter at the death of Pius and the election of John. It consisted of puffing out his thin face until it turned crimson from lack of breath and at the same time squinting at his nose. Then, raising two fingers in benediction, he would slowly lean backwards on his seat until his legs, bent at the knee, rose into the air presenting his bottom to the spectators.

Miff's mother-in-law, she was a lowlander and very anglicized so he called her 'Mummy', gave him an old fur coat to wear in the wagon on cold winter nights. This did him good service for some years, although the sight of his ginger hair and freckled snub nose emerging from the shabby but feminine collar was a distinctly comic sight. At length he decided that the coat had to go and waited for a suitably symbolic occasion.

This materialized in Scotland while we were touring the Highlands. Although Miff had been brought up in Glasgow he had in fact been born in a market town in the Western Highlands, and one morning as we passed very near it, Miff asked Pete to stop the wagon. There was a signpost pointing down the road towards the village. On it was written: 'To the Free Kirk. One mile.' The 'Wee Free', that most narrow of all churches, still dominates large stretches of the Highlands with its joyless hellfire puritanism. Miff hung his coat on the signpost and pinned a note saying: 'A present from Angus Bell to his native village.' At his suggestion Mick got out his trumpet and blew the 'Last Post' while the rest of us stood in a circle at the base of the signpost and pissed on the coat in the cold bright morning light.

For six months we had no permanent trombonist and Mick's block against doing anything until the last possible moment meant that he never tried to fix a temporary until the morning of a job. When, as quite often happened, he couldn't find one at all, he substituted a different front-line instrument, usually Paul Simpson on baritone sax.

He did try out two trombone players as possible fixtures but neither stayed very long.

The first was Harry Brown who, although ex-Lyttelton band, was a convinced modernist by this time and very unhappy playing Dixieland so eventually he had to go.

It was Harry, however, who found Mick his nickname. Apparently, he had been waiting for the last tube one night, and had been drawn into conversation by one of those near-tramps who haunt platforms and bus-shelters late at night. He asked Harry what he did. Harry admitted he was a musician. The man said that was a very rewarding profession as long as you had a good conductor. That was what made all the difference, a good conductor. He asked Harry what his conductor was like. Harry told him he was all right. Next day he told us about this encounter, and the name stuck. From then on Mick was 'the conductor'.

The other try-out was another Scotsman called Davie Keir. Like Pat Malloy, the Irish-Scottish bass player, he too came from Dunfermline. He shared with Miff an interest in Scottish nationalism which he tried to synthesize with certain Communist ideas. He was also drawn towards fascism, but as he was a kind person whom I cannot imagine performing a physical act of cruelty, the attraction was based on naïve and credulous premises. In fact, Davie's fascism had a Nietzschean origin. He believed in the superman and he believed he was a superman.

He could believe anything, and the more impossible the easier he found it. He reminded me of the White Queen who told Alice that she could sometimes believe as many as six impossible things before breakfast. The last time I saw him he was on the edge of a conversion to Catholicism based, as far as I could make out, on a book by Group Captain Cheshire about Christ's shroud.

When Davie had saved up a few pounds he left us, as he left every band he played with, to form a band of his own.

Eventually Mick found his trombonist. He came from Liverpool and his name was Frank Parr. We had known him for a long time. He had played for many years with his local, semi-pro band, the Merseysippi, and used to come round the back of the Picton Hall to see us in the days when we'd played concerts there.

He was a professional cricketer, and although this meant nothing to me – I have had a block against all team games since my preparatory school – Mick was very impressed.

The summer before he joined us, Frank kept wicket for Lancashire and quite often going round to Lisle Street I would find Mick slumped immovably in a chair in front of his newly acquired television set, watching a tiny grey Frank crouched behind the stumps. Mick told me he was brilliant and would probably play for England the next season.

It might therefore appear extraordinary that, far from playing cricket for England, the following summer found Frank touring with a jazz band. The reason had nothing to do with Frank's wicket-keeping, but it had a lot to do with Frank. From what I can gather, although the 'gentlemen' and 'players' labels have disappeared, the attitude of the cricketing establishment remains firmly entrenched. The professional cricketer is not just a man who plays cricket for money. He has a social role. He is expected to behave within certain defined limits. He can be a 'rough diamond', even 'a bit of a character', but he must know his place. If he smells of sweat, it must be fresh sweat. He must dress neatly and acceptably. His drinking habits must be under control. He must know when to say 'sir'.

Frank, we were soon to discover, had none of these qualifications. He was an extreme social risk, a complicated rebel whose world swarmed with demons and Jack O'Lanterns, and was treacherous with bogs and quicksands. He concealed a formidable and well-read intelligence behind a stylized oafishness. He used every weapon to alienate acceptance. Even within the jazz world, that natural refuge for the anti-social, Frank stood out as an exception. We never knew the reason for his quarrel with the Captain of Lancashire, but after a month or two in his company we realized it must have been inevitable.

Frank had a rather fine head set on a long but muscular neck. In repose his face resembled one of Nevinson's pastels of gallant N.C.O.s which achieved such popularity during the last war, but it was seldom in repose. A family of grimaces and ticks were usually in residence, the most spectacular of which was a gum-baring similar to the rictus of a sudden and painful death.

Frank used to go through his repertoire of 'mushes' as Mick called them at any time, but it was catching the sight of himself in a mirror which inevitably provoked the whole series. Dressing-room, boarding-house bedroom, Victorian public house, the staircases of dance halls, wherever a sheet of glass threw back his image, Frank's urge to play Caliban took over.

He had the hard, spare, useful body of the professional athlete. Its only failing proportionately was that the legs were a little short in relation to the length of the waist. This would have been unnoticeable if he'd had his clothes made or even altered, but what clothes he did buy were off the peg; the legs of the trousers were an inch too long, and the excess material gathered below the buttocks in a series of sagging folds like the backside of an elephant.

Frank's attitude to clothes, like his attitude to so much else, was to use them to make his personality less easy to accept, as yet another barrier between himself and the others. He would, of course, deny this, and make out that he didn't care, but this simply wasn't true. His clothes were not just shabby or old – they were anti-clothes.

His mac was famous, but personally I always found his sweaters more extraordinary. Under the arms, the perspiration had eaten into the dye in such a way as to produce a series of rainbow-like rings, the darker colours at the centre nearest the glands. Frank's sweat was in any case unique and he was very proud of it. It didn't smell of sweat at all for a start. The nearest I can get to it is the smell in the hallway of a cat-infested slum. Somebody once discovered written in the lavatory of a Soho drinking club the words, 'It's always summer under the armpits', and Frank, whose obsession with formalized linguistic concepts remained constant, always used the word 'summer' to describe the state of his armpits. Several times a day, with the stylized gestures of a Japanese actor, Frank would lean slightly backwards, bring his arm round in a wide curve in front of his body, and plunge the hand through his shirt opening and under his arm. There would then be a pause during which you could count four slowly. Then the hand was withdrawn with the same hieratic deliberation, and carried up to the nose where Frank would sniff it, emit an 'ah' of great satisfaction, and announce 'Going a bit!' in the voice of a man at peace.

The same phrase he applied to his socks on hot days, but there was nothing unique about the smell of his feet, and in this department Mick ran him close. To be fair Mick wasn't very keen on washing either in those days, and, in justification, used to say that too much soap and water destroyed the natural juices, but the point was that Mick didn't bath much out of indolence, Frank *because* it made him smell.

Frank never washed any of his clothing. He used to save it up, wearing anything in rotation, until we did a job in Liverpool when he took it all home for his mother. This was not laziness. It was part of his Liverpool mania. Liverpool was for Frank the Golden City and the Good Place. Towards the end of the band's history he began to accept London as a possible town to live, but for the first few years he went about as though he had just been expelled from the Garden of Eden. If we drove along behind a lorry with the word 'Liverpool' written on its tailboard, Frank would shout it aloud. The sight of a Liverpool face galvanized him as though he had touched a live wire. Everything in London, tea, people, the air itself, was compared to its detriment with the Liverpool equivalent. It's true that all ex-Liverpudlians are hysterical patriots – even the other day I found myself calling the town 'home' and I haven't lived there for seventeen years – but Frank was exceptional in his fervour.

Food and drink were the other weapons in Frank's armoury.

He was extremely limited in what he would eat for a start. Fried food, especially bacon and eggs, headed the list, then came cold meat and salad, and that was about the lot. Any other food, soup for instance or cheese, came under the heading of 'pretentious bollocks', but even in the case of the food he *did* like, his attitude was decidedly odd. He would crouch over his plate, knife and fork at the ready in his clenched fists, and glare down at the harmless egg and inoffensive bacon enunciating, as though it were part of some barbarous and sadistic ritual, the words, 'I'll murder it.' What followed, a mixture of jabbing, tearing, stuffing, grinding and gulping, was a distressing spectacle.

In relation to drink he was more victim than murderer. He drank either gin and tonic or whisky and, once past the point of no return, would throw doubles into himself with astonishing rapidity, banging the empty glass down on the counter and immediately ordering another with a prolonged hiss on the word, 'please'. He passed through the classic stages of drunkenness in record time, wild humour, self-pity, and unconsciousness, all well-seasoned with the famous Parr grimaces. His actual fall had a monumental simplicity. One moment he was perpendicular, the next horizontal. The only warning we had of his collapse was that, just before it happened, Frank announced that he was 'only fit for the human scrap heap' and this allowed us time to move any glasses, tables, chairs or instruments out of the way.

Frank's spectacular raves didn't stop him looking censorious when anyone else was 'going a bit' – he used the same phrase for socks or drunkenness – but then we were all like that.

If I think of him I can see certain gestures; his habit of rapidly shifting his cigarette around between his fingers, his slow tiger-like pacing, his manner of playing feet apart, body leaning stiffly backwards to balance the weight of his instrument.

His music was aimed beyond his technique. Sometimes a

very beautiful idea came off, more often you were aware of a beautiful idea which existed in Frank's head. In an article on Mick in the *Sunday Times*, Frank was quoted as saying, 'All jazzmen are kicking against something, and it comes out when they blow.'

This was a remarkably open statement for Frank who, during a wagon discussion on our personal mental quirks and peculiarities, had once told us that he was the only normal person in the band.

This gained him his nickname, 'Mr Norm', and any exceptionally Parr-like behaviour would provoke the conductor into saying, 'Hello Frank. Feeling normal then?'

11. He'll Have Us All in the Bread Line

Once the band had re-formed, once the days of deps and fill-ins were behind us, touring continued much as before. Such changes as took place in the kind of jobs available or the popularity of the music were due to other, more ambitious spirits than the conductor's. In one way, it was more difficult for a band on the road to know what was going on than for the most cloth-eared member of a provincial jazz club who could at least hear a different group each week. Except for the occasional big concert or jazz festival we hardly got a chance to listen to other bands, and only Frank Parr, who neither knew nor wished to know anybody outside the jazz world, was prepared to spend our rare nights off cruising round the London clubs to remedy this. Even so we were aware of the radical change taking place. It was just that Mick, the least commercial of men if it meant hard work, had decided to ignore it.

He theorized that it was better to stay in the second rank. You could be sure then, he argued, of a modest but steady living. You didn't price yourself out of the clubs and smaller dance halls during your hey-day only to discover that during your decline you could get no work at all. You went on, fatter in the booms, leaner in the slumps, but at least available for what jobs there were. In consequence the rise of Chris Barber during 1954–5, and the resulting swing away from revivalist jazz towards traditional, made no difference to the Mulligan band whatsoever.

Mick was not alone in his failure or refusal to jump on this particular band-wagon. Humph played mainstream from reasons of conviction. Alex Welsh remained faithful to Dixieland. Sandy Brown and Al Fairweather, both recently down from Edinburgh, moved against the current with strict historical logic, from their early championship of the most uncompromising traditionalism towards a brilliant and individual paraphrase of the Armstrong Hot Five.

Mick continued to play a loose approximation to the later Armstrong-cum-Condon sound, not from any burning integrity, although it is certainly true that he preferred this sort of music, but because to have changed would have meant a lot of sweat and many hours of rehearsal.

What was the difference between revivalist and traditional jazz? Revivalist jazz was based on the Negro jazz of the twenties as it can be heard on recordings of that period. It was played (the original, not the revival) by musicians who, for the most part, had come from New Orleans and had been in at the birth of jazz in the brothels and cabarets, in the street parades and funerals during the early years of the century; they had moved north after the naval authorities closed down Storyville in 1917, and had developed the music further (ruined it according to the traditionalists) during the next decade.

What the revivalists thought of as 'New Orleans Jazz' was the music of Armstrong, Morton and Oliver – New Orleans musicians but based on, and recorded in, Chicago during the Prohibition era.

What the traditionalists meant by New Orleans Jazz – for both schools claimed the same name – was the music played by musicians who had never left the city, and whose style was presumed to have remained unaltered since the first decade of the century. The basic difference between the two sounds is that revivalist jazz includes arranged passages, solos, and considerable emphasis on the individual musician, whereas traditional jazz is *all* ensemble. There are of course many other differences, but this is the most obvious.

The revivalists accused the traditionalists of sentimentality, of basing their music on the recordings of very old men past their prime, for it was not until the early forties that the surviving veterans were rediscovered and recorded, and they claimed furthermore that those musicians who *had* stayed in New Orleans had done so only because they were inferior in the first place, and that the music had reached its golden age in the hands of those who had been good enough to go to Chicago, and inventive enough to take the music a step further.

The traditionalists put forward no such reasoned arguments. Like most fundamentalists they just knew they were right. Real New Orleans Jazz had never left New Orleans. Everything which had followed was less pure, less moving. The very genius of men like Armstrong had betrayed and ruined the music from which they sprang. 'Back,' as Ken Colyer put it, 'to the roots.'

Modern jazz was of course outside this dispute. Modern jazz was like the Roman Catholic Church at the time of the Reformation. It had developed historically from the origins of jazz but had, in the eyes of the early revivalists, become decadent and it was time to return to the source. The revivalists represent in this parallel the Church of England. Later the traditionalists arose, like the non-conformist sects, to accuse the revivalists themselves of decadence, of meaningless ritual, of elaboration. Back to the Bible – jazz from New Orleans; Away with Cope and Mitre – solos and arrangements; Down with the Bishops – Armstrong and Oliver.

Ken Colyer was initially responsible for this revolution. It was he who established the totems and taboos of traditional jazz, the pianoless rhythm section, the relentless four to the bar banjo, the loud but soggy thump of the bass drum. Even so Ken by himself would never have effected the trad boom. He was too uncompromising, too much a purist. Picasso, accused of ugliness, pointed out that the inventor is always ugly because he has had to make something which wasn't there before, but that afterwards others can come along and make what he had invented beautiful. It was rather like this. Ken invented British traditional jazz. It wasn't exactly ugly, on the contrary it was quite often touchingly beautiful, but it was clumsy. It needed prettifying before it could catch on. Chris Barber was there to perform this function.

Chris Barber had been around for a long time. He had a great love of jazz, but towards it as towards everything else, his approach was pedantic in the older and less critical meaning of the word. He was a record collector who knew the matrix number, personnel, and date of recording of every record in his immaculately filed collection. He had studied trombone at the Royal College of Music. His other interest was fast cars, and he carried over into jazz a somewhat mechanistic approach to the music. He also possessed a formidable will to succeed, and a complete belief in his ability to do so.

During the early days of the revival, Chris had a band which was based exactly, even to the presence of two cornets, on the King Oliver sound. He was converted to fundamentalism by Ken Colyer, and when that holy fool returned from New Orleans in 1953, it was Chris Barber who had a band ready for him. Within a month or two Ken sacked the whole band, or the whole band resigned – both versions were about, depending on who was telling the story – and Chris added Pat Halcox on trumpet and became, for the second time, a bandleader in his own right. The formation of the Barber Band in 1954 seemed to us at that time of purely parochial interest. Later it was proved to have been a watershed.

It is a temptation to look backwards, to select those events which showed the way things were going, and imagine that they appeared significant at the time. This is just not true. During the same months in which the Colyer–Barber schism was taking place, a whole new world was in the process of being born, and we were entirely unaware of it. I can't remember the first time I heard the word 'teenager'. I don't know at what point I began to take in the teenage thing. I doubt many other people can either.

It was certainly through its musical aspect that we did begin to realize what was happening. We had heard the Bill Haley record of 'Rock Around the Clock', and decided that it was a drag. I can remember asking who was the white blues singer somebody had put on the gramophone at a party, and learning with some surprise that it was Elvis Presley. When Haley's film was shown, we naturally read in the papers about fans rioting, and had taken in that the ten records which were selling best in any one week were being printed in the *Melody Maker* in order of popularity. But at first none of these seemed very different from what we were used to. Fans were nothing new. Dickie Valentine for example had a fan club which held an annual reunion at the Hammersmith Palais. Hit records were a fact. We never bought them, but we knew they existed. What we failed to understand was the *age* of the new audience. Dickie Valentine's fans were between eighteen and twenty-five. The records of Donald Peers or 'Winnie' Atwell were bought by Mums and Dads, but the new audience, the multitude outside, the secret society preparing a revolution in 'the Two I's', Old Compton Street, were sixteen or less. There had, of course, always been young jazz fans, but they'd just liked jazz and happened to be young. What was different about the teenagers was that they were young first and foremost, and everything they did and said, everything they liked or rejected, was useful in that it identified them *as a group*. At that time the boys were faced with conscription. This meant that they knew their 'real life' as adults was not in question. Between leaving school and going into the army, they could live out a fantasy life, their pockets full of money from a dead-end job. Circling round them and quick to move in were various interested adults: agents, record companies, clothing manufacturers, concert promoters, but the invention of the teenage thing was initially the work of the teenagers themselves. It was they who chose Haley and Presley as their heroes, and it was from their ranks that they threw up and deified their first British idol, Tommy Steele, *né* Hicks.

It was through Tommy that I first began to understand it all. Following the modest success of my recording of 'Frankie and Johnnie', I had been put under contract by Decca. As whatever fans I did have were jazz fans and had presumably bought my record for that reason, I suppose it was inevitable that the company decided I should record more commercial material. My first attempt to conquer the pop market was a Dixieland version of 'Kingdom Coming', the American civil war song. I substituted the word 'Brothers' for the word 'Darkies' throughout, and Mick added a tuba and flute to the instrumentation, but despite our efforts to compromise it only sold about a hundred copies. My next shot was a comic song of the twenties called 'My Canary's Got Circles Under His Eyes', and this too was a complete failure. It was due to its release that I came to meet Tommy Steele.

Television, still confined to one channel and furthermore considered an essentially working-class entertainment, provided the occasion. The Birmingham studio, in advance of its time, had a weekly programme featuring the new releases and illustrating them visually by what was then an unheard of innovation; the artists themselves miming to their own records. The week that 'Canary' was issued, Tommy Steele had a new one out too. It was called, as far as I can remember, 'Rock with the Cavemen' and wasn't to become one of his great hits, but he'd already recorded 'Singing the Blues' and was a very big deal indeed. The only thing was I'd never heard of him. I didn't listen to pop music at all in those days except by accident, and although I'm sure there must have been a lot about him in the *Melody Maker*, I didn't read the pop pages there either. He, in his turn, hadn't heard of me. I don't know which of us was the more surprised to discover that neither of us were aware of the other's existence.

After we'd finished the first run-through, I thought it would be friendly to ask this fresh-faced lad across the road for a drink. His manager, a very astute young man called John Kennedy, came with us. Tommy drank orangeade. John Kennedy said he'd have a beer. 'Pint?' I asked. He accepted, and was told off by Tommy whose Dad had told him it was common to drink pints. Tommy asked me if it was my first record. I said it wasn't, and asked him if it was his. He told me it wasn't either. He then suggested that if I was to be a success in show biz it would be as well to dress a bit more sharp. He put this to me with such charm that I couldn't take offence. He asked me what sort of car I had. I told him I hadn't got one. He looked at me with the sort of pity usually reserved for the badly deformed and offered to run me back to town after the show. We were at the Ferry that night, and I accepted immediately. We did the transmission and were back in London in just over two hours, a rather terrifying experience in those pre-M1 days.

Sitting next to Tommy in his powerful open car, aware of his heavy gold watch, his strange but immaculate clothing, his complete confidence in himself, his cocky innocence, I found myself puzzled and fascinated by him. When I got to the Ferry, I tried to explain about him to the rest of the band, but they hadn't heard of him either. It was a good session. The place was full and enthusiastic. We all drank quite a lot, and in the second interval I had a knee tremble under the canal bridge. By the end of the evening I had forgotten about Tommy Steele.

But not for long. During the next few weeks I saw his name

everywhere. This always seems to happen. You hear of somebody for the first time, and from then on can't open a newspaper without seeing their name. It's a kind of magic.

A month later we shared a concert bill with Tommy in a cinema somewhere on the southern outskirts of London. We did the first half, and nothing happened at all, even Pete's drum solo won no more than token applause. The audience was not hostile. It was just that we didn't seem to be there. We were rather puzzled and a bit hurt. I saw Tommy in the interval. He was very friendly.

' 'Ow's "Canary" going then?' he asked.

One of the band knew the alto player in his group. He was a modernist playing rock and roll for the money. This he felt entitled him to a good moan-up.

'I used to be a musician,' he told us in the pub, 'but now I'm just a fucking acrobat!'

I was curious enough to go back behind stage to watch the opening of the second half. I saw that the ex-musical acrobat stepped, by mistake, on the plug connecting Tommy's guitar with the amplifier. He didn't own up, and when Tommy switched on his instrument, it didn't work.

' 'Ere, me guitar's broke!' he cried in anguish.

The interval was extended a further five minutes while it was mended. During this delay a low continuous hum began to rise from the auditorium. It was like a swarm of bees getting ready to swarm. I looked through the peep-hole and saw with some surprise how young the audience were. Furthermore most of them were girls.

The moment the curtain went up a high-pitched squeaking and shrieking started. I was absolutely amazed. After a couple of numbers I left and went back to the pub. The band was playing darts and Frank Parr was getting quite drunk. The orgiastic cries of worship inside the cinema were perfectly audible, and this moved him to prophesy.

'You hear that!' he announced as he swayed about, 'that's the death of jazz. We've had it. In six months we'll all be in the bread line!'

When the concert finished, thousands of girls streamed out of the cinema and clustered round the stage door. Frank leaned against the door of the saloon bar and watched this spectacle.

'The death of jazz,' he reiterated, 'rock and roll, the beginning of the end, and he'll have us all in the bread line!'

Frank's pessimism was exaggerated, but there was no doubt that rock and roll did give traditional jazz a hammering from which it took a year to recover. The big Festival Hall concerts came to an end, and so did the fortnightly concerts in the smaller recital hall in the same building. These, held under the auspices of the N.J.F., came under various headings based on the musical style of the groups involved. 'Back to New Orleans' featured either Ken or Chris; 'Dixieland Revisited' either Alex or ourselves, and there was also a less well patronized 'Modern Jazz Workshop'. Rock and roll put an end to all this. Modern jazz had a small, if perceptive and faithful, audience anyway, and its exponents were resentfully accustomed to neglect. It was the rest of us who felt betrayed, and the Mulligan band began to suspect, as they copied down in their diaries the increasingly empty date-sheet for those months, that perhaps Frank had been right after all.

But we didn't starve, and we didn't have to give up. The jazz-club audiences, older at that time than during the trad boom of the early sixties, remained faithful enough to give us some work in town, and we found ourselves booked in again at some of the venues we used to play in our very early days. Furthermore, the north of England, always resistant to fads which they thought of as originating in the south, continued to support jazz on a comparatively generous scale. We still played The Bodega regularly for Paddy, and, sometimes the whole band, sometimes

Mick and I as guest artists, were featured on the bill of some
extremely successful concerts which he promoted in Manchester and elsewhere under the all-embracing title of 'Jazz
Unlimited'. Finally most of the dance halls found it uneco-
nomic to employ rock groups except as an occasional gimmick.
They could only play for twenty minutes at a time, and they
drew in a young audience who alienated the regular ballroom
dancers, so we won out there.

A sign of the times were the large notices: 'NO JIVING. NO
ROCK AND ROLL.' which appeared prominently displayed
in the various dance-halls up and down the country.

Even at the height of its popularity, rock and roll was not
unchallenged. There was also skiffle, a bastardized rather folk-
sie music with a strong country and western flavour and a pref-
erence for the material of the great Negro folk singer, Huddie
Leadbeater.

Its history is typical of the kind of *accident* which seems to
operate in the popular field, and is the opposite of the imaginary Machiavellian manipulation of taste which most people
think of as the way it works. Of course when something does
become popular there is any amount of exploitation, but that is
rather different.

Skiffle: first the word. Originally it was used to describe a
kind of sub-jazz in which kazoos, tea-chest and broom-handle
basses, seven-gallon jugs, and empty suitcases replaced the
more conventional musical instruments. Presumably in the first
place these improvised instruments were the invention of poor
Negroes unable to afford the proper thing, but during the
twenties skiffle music caught on as a novelty, and in particular a
white group called 'The Mound City Blue Blowers' achieved
considerable vogue. By 1953 the public had naturally enough
forgotten about skiffle, and only the serious jazz-record collector knew what the word meant.

Like so much else, the skiffle boom originated with Ken

Colyer. In order to provide a contrast to an evening's diet of undiluted New Orleans ensemble, he introduced a short vocal session of Negro folk music with himself and his banjo player, Lonnie Donegan on guitars, and Chris Barber on bass. Ken himself sang most of the numbers, helped out from time to time by Lonnie. He called these interludes 'Skiffle Sessions', to differentiate them from the more serious activity of playing blues, rags, stomps and marches, and they achieved great, if localized, popularity among the band's followers. In choosing the word skiffle, Ken was, of course, consciously misapplying it. It was as trumpet player that he would wish to be judged, skiffle had a light-weight almost flippant sound to it, but I feel that his version of these old songs was surprisingly moving and authentic, a case of what the folknics would call 'identification'.

When Ken's band broke up and Chris picked up the pieces, he naturally retained the skiffle-session idea. Lonnie Donegan took over the singing and became very popular round the clubs, although personally I always found his country and western nasal whine rather unpleasant. His version of 'Rock Island Line', originally part of a Chris Barber in Concert L.P., was requested so often on the radio that it was put out as a single and rose to be top of the Hit Parade. Lonnie left Chris and formed his own group. He became a big star, the first member of the jazz world to do so, and was widely imitated.

By historical irony some of the smaller groups, unable to afford proper instruments over and above the leader's guitar, began to use washboards and kazoos and especially tea-chest basses with broomstick handles. Gypsie Larrie owned one of these and could produce from it a remarkably accomplished noise.

The skiffle craze had its own radio programme on Saturday mornings. It was called 'Skiffle Club' and was the direct fore-runner of 'Saturday Club' even to the extent of having Brian

Matthew as compère. I was invited to appear occasionally on this show and formed within the Mulligan Band a group I called 'The Bubbling Over Five' after an obscure band on a record from the collection of Simon Watson Taylor. There was Miff, Appleby, Diz on guitar, and on bass a newcomer called Alan Duddington. We always seemed to be having new bass players. Unlike other musicians connected with the band, they had a high turnover.

Alan came from Lancaster. He was younger than the rest of us, still in his early twenties, a neat precise person, a bit of an old maid, with a very slight Lancashire accent. His features were a little on the weak side, but redeemed from mediocrity by a large and noble nose similar in character to that of the first Duke of Wellington.

He was proud to be a musician, but not proud to be in the Mulligan Band. Everything about it distressed him – the music, our attitudes, the way we dressed – and it was very surprising how long he stayed, especially as he was teased unmercifully and without a moment's respite.

Why did we tease him? There were in fact two reasons. For one thing he reacted so splendidly, concealing his mounting exasperation under a tight-mouthed, straight-backed indifference with only an occasional low sigh, or at most, a quiet if terse 'Very amusing' to show we were getting through, but the real reason was that he *knew* he was right about everything. There was no question of doubt. There was no possibility that any alternatives existed, or that some things were a matter of personal taste. On every subject, at every level, Alan Duddington was right. If anyone disagreed with him, he didn't shout or even try and argue. He just repeated his own opinion in a quiet but firm voice until whoever was trying to contradict him gave up.

Alan was a perfectionist. He had certain standards, certain things he expected to happen. However far short reality fell from his expectations, it never affected his optimism. However often he didn't get what he wanted, it never occurred to him to lower his sights.

Opposite the Town Hall, Huddersfield, is a small public house called 'The County'. It's a friendly little pub, but as regards food anybody could tell at a glance what you could expect: crisps, nuts, possibly a pie or a sandwich. One evening we arrived in Huddersfield rather late and Mick told us we hadn't got time to go and eat, but perhaps we could grab a sandwich in the nearest boozer. Duddington looked at him coolly.

'I presume there's no objection if I have a crab salad instead,' he asked.

'No, cock,' said Mick, 'but where?'

'In the public house,' explained Duddington as though to an idiot child. We took it for granted that he didn't know the pub, and that once he saw it, he would realize there wasn't a chance, but that wasn't Alan. He marched in, and ordered a small strong ale and a crab salad. The old girl said they didn't do a crab salad. Alan looked hurt and surprised.

He was very fussy about his small strong ales too. He would first look along the bottles of beer until he had spotted what he wanted – barley wine, Stingo, whatever the local brewery supplied – and then order it by name. Very few people drink these small and potent ales, and quite often the barmaid would spend a long time searching the shelves for it, and even come back to Alan to tell him she didn't think they had any. She would find him standing up as stiff as a ramrod and pointing at the bottle he'd asked for.

It was his nose and personal fads which provided us with most of our ammunition, and the wagon was our usual theatre of cruelty.

His nose. How we went on about it! If he fell asleep, somebody, usually Frank Parr, would trace out a tiny head with a huge hooter on the steamed-up window so that it was the first thing he saw when he woke up. ('Very amusing.') Whatever came up in conversation was, if it was in any way possible, altered to include a reference to noses, e.g. 'Cat on a hot tin nose'. ('Very fucking amusing.')

His habit of opening his suitcase at frequent intervals and producing a bar of chocolate which he unwrapped and ate with the formality which characterized all his movements was another moment in the day we never allowed to pass unremarked. There was an obscene limerick we all knew about an old girl of Silesia. Its last line was: 'If Jimmy the tapeworm don't seize yer!', and we pretended to believe that Alan's perpetual chocolate eating was because he had a tapeworm.

'Jimmy-time, Alan?' Frank would ask politely every time Alan opened his suitcase.

He tried to defeat us by forestalling this question.

'What time is it, Frank?' he'd ask as he reached for his suitcase.

'Jimmy-time,' said Frank in a matter-of-fact voice.

Even when he had left us, we didn't allow him to escape. We discovered that he was appearing at the Metropolitan Music Hall in the Edgware Road with a country and western group and hatched a plan.

We all of us went to a joke shop one afternoon and bought enormous false noses. That evening we took a box at the Met as near as possible to the stage. We had previously got in touch with another member of the group whom we knew, and put him up to telling Duddington that he had met a beautiful girl who had told him that she was mad about Alan, and would be sitting in a box that evening hoping that he would smile at her.

Just before Alan's turn was due, we hid below the level of the front of the box and put on our noses. As the curtains drew we slowly rose to our feet. Alan was staring at the box. Instead of a girl, there was the whole Mulligan band in their false noses.

What was nice about Alan was that he never bore any grudges. Despite our rotten teasing, despite even this final malevolent prank, he has always, on the few occasions we have met since, greeted me in an open and warm way. I doubt the rest of us could have claimed as much.

Skiffle was never a real threat to jazz, but even rock provided us with occasional employment. From time to time we appeared on 'Six Five Special', the prototype teenage show. It had a live audience, and two compères, Pete Murray and Jo Douglas, while outside the Riverside Studios in Hammersmith a little group of young girls used to cluster and shriek their love. At the time it appeared madness, but I imagine a re-showing of a programme picked at random would seem both staid and droll.

During one appearance on this show we met Wee Willie Harris, a small and frantic rock singer and piano player, who lacking the sex-appeal of Tommy or Terry Dene, dyed his hair pink or green. We discovered that he was already known to us. As 'Fingers' Harris, he used to play interval piano at the Wimbledon Jazz Club. We bumped into him again a little later at Mrs Flanagan's for, unlike most of the artists who 'made it', he had the foresight to avoid big hotel suites and save against his decline. One morning, looking out of the window of Mrs Flanagan's dining-room, I watched him setting off for some appointment in the pouring rain, the collar of his raincoat stained pink from dye which had run from his hair.

Tommy Steele grew too old for his audience and became what all rock singers claimed they wished to become, 'an all-round entertainer'. Poor Terry Dene went into the army, an event which the authorities attempted to use, *vide* Presley, as a boost for that increasingly unpopular interruption to civilian life, and was straightway released on psychological grounds, a circumstance which gave rise to an outcry of rage from filthy Blimps of both sexes and the newspaper you'd expect. The rock and roll stars themselves became younger and younger until it came to an end due to the difficulty of recording while still in the womb. Before this happened there were two tiny ones who achieved success: Laurie London who, it was reported in an interview, wrote his God-bothering hit, 'He's Got the Whole World in His Hands', while sitting on the lavatory, and Jackie Dennis who gyrated in a kilt. At a large charity dance where the band appeared, I had the pleasure of watching with Mick a screaming row between these two mites because only one of them, Jackie Dennis as far as I can remember, was included in that part of the evening which was to be broadcast. 'I'm a bigger star than you, and if I'm not on I won't appear at all,' piped one. 'I'm higher up the hit parade than you anyway,' squeaked the other. Above their heads, their managerial fathers were engaged in similar, if less high-pitched, argument.

Skiffle faded, rock and roll eroded, and Chris Barber, his band now including a remarkable Northern Irish ex-art teacher called Ottilie Patterson who sang in uncanny resemblance to Bessie Smith, began to attract a larger and larger audience. Although a few purists, faithful to the Ken Colyer line, found Chris's music overcommercial, it was fresh and well played. Chris, convinced of his own worth, brought a serious, rather dignified approach to his music and presentation. His audience likewise were appreciative but unhysterical. It is hard to remember that out of these gay if formal occasions was to sprout the grotesque and funny-hatted excesses of the Trad Fad.

12. Done, Been Here and Gone

In 1955 I'd got married. This took place in Scotland because my wife's parents were Roman Catholic converts and, as she was under twenty-one, we were forced to elope. Our decision dovetailed in with a Duncan tour of the Borders, and a guest appearance with Freddy Randall at Birmingham Town Hall on the way up, allowed us to feel justified in travelling by train instead of squashing into the bandwagon.

We registered for the obligatory period into a small hotel in Leith Walk, Edinburgh. Every day I set off for the job but getting back in the small hours was more of a problem. Later I discovered that I needn't have been quite so conscientious. Most people simply booked in, informed the Lord Provost of their intentions, left a suitcase and a few clothes to imply residency, and came back in time for the ceremony. As it was, obsessed by the idea of something going wrong, I somehow or other struggled through the Scottish night and into my pyjamas before it was time to get up for breakfast. Quite often it was necessary to leave almost immediately for the next gig. I can still hear through waves of sleep the elderly waitress asking in her precise Edinburgh accent if I would prefer 'porridge or fruit-juice?' The name of the town 'Berwick-upon-Tweed' evokes a rainstorm of some five hours' duration during which I huddled in a shop doorway until they opened the station for the first train. When the job was nearer Edinburgh the problem was less acute. Frank Thompson was still with us on bass at that time, and for a small bribe and a bed booked into our hotel was willing to drive me back. Furthermore the whole project appealed to his romantic nature.

'I'll get you married if it's the last thing I do!' he would mutter through clenched teeth as we tore along the dark country roads with unnecessary urgency. What made this odd was that like my future in-laws, Frank Thompson was a Roman Catholic.

These drives through the small hours were not without other manifestations of his imaginative temperament. Sometimes when we were so nearly there that the lights of Auld Reekie glowed tantalizingly in the sky, Frank would start swerving about, shouting that he could see lorries bearing down on us. He would draw into the side of the road, cradle his head in his arms on the steering wheel and, for a good three quarters of an hour, complain of hallucinatory fatigue. There was nothing I could do about it. I had to pretend to believe every word he said.

During an elopement, once your three weeks' Scottish residency is established, you are allowed to go away for a week, the banns yellowing in the window of the Registrar the while, and return on the morning of the actual ceremony. At the end of the tour I travelled back to London in the band-wagon to do some jobs, and Victoria went to stay with my mother in Liverpool.

The convenient way the Scottish tour coincided with our elopement may suggest a bit of luck bordering on the uncanny. In fact the truth is more prosaic. Victoria and I had known each other for some time, and were able to arrange our elopement to fit in with the Scottish tour, although the Randall concert in Birmingham did appear as a last-minute bonus.

Before our marriage we'd found a flat. The room in Margaretta Terrace was too small and I'd discovered that an old school friend of mine, the painter Tim Whidbourne, had bought a large house down the unfashionable end of Cheyne Walk, and sub-divided it. In the rather damp basement was a young man called Andy Garnett who was a business-efficiency expert. He told Tim that he found the rent rather too high and would be willing to share the place with us. We'd have our own bedroom, and he'd sleep in the communal sitting-room. There was a bathroom and a kitchen adjoining the Thames. The half-share of the rent was within my means, and despite objections from Victoria I took it.

Andy was one of the original members of the Chelsea Set. He was hysterically inventive, curious about everything, mercurial, sensitive, an obsessive raconteur with an especially rich vein in frantic obscenity. Despite the fact he had been to Eton, even Ian Christie took an immediate liking to him, although he compensated by calling him 'My favourite hurray', to Andy's slight irritation. Victoria on the other hand didn't get on with him a bit.

She would lie in bed keeping up a stream of whispered rage while the unsuspecting Andy had a rather noisy shit in the bathroom and blundered about the sitting-room. After years of band life, I couldn't see why she minded us sharing our first flat with somebody else.

It was Andy, yet another R.C., who was responsible for me getting to the Registry Office in Edinburgh on time. The night before I was married I was to give a lecture at the Institute of Contemporary Arts in Dover Street on the subject of 'Erotic Imagery in the Blues', and then catch the midnight up from King's Cross. Using Simon's collection of early blues records as a basis, I had prepared a serious theme dividing my subject under various headings: 'The Machine as a Sexual Image', 'Animal Symbolism in Erotic Blues', 'Sexual Metaphors in Rural and Urban Blues', etc. In the Chair were two jazz critics, Vic Bellerby and Charles Fox. Quite a large number of I.C.A. regulars turned up and so did a great many of my friends. What divided the Chair and the I.C.A. regulars from my friends was that the former had no idea I was getting married the next morning, while the latter knew it very well. While the Chairmen were introducing me, Mick Mulligan came up and handed me a glass. I nervously swallowed it in one. It contained four neat gins.

When the Chair had finished David Litvinoff rose with a question. Was it, he asked politely, permitted for the audience to wank during the recital? There was a pained silence from the bulk of the audience and an ominous shriek of laughter from my contingent. I began my talk.

At the beginning I stuck to my text although, under the effect of Mick's perpetually renewed gins, I understand I threw back my head and joined in several of the records. Ian Christie snored quietly in the front row, but woke up to ask when he was going to hear some jazz. As there was a Bessie Smith record playing at the time, I took this very badly and threatened to throw him down the stairs.

After the interval I put aside my subject altogether, and delivered a comparatively incoherent attack on the I.C.A. itself referring to it throughout, with a certain lack of originality, as 'the Institute of Contemporary Farts', occasionally relieving the tedium even I felt arising from constant repetition by offering an alternative version, 'the Institute of Contemporary Arseholes'. When the Chairmen attempted to close down the meeting David Litvinoff pushed them both off the platform and took over. During this struggle he apparently sang his own version of Bessie's, 'You've Been a Good Old Wagon, But You Done Broke Down' with the word 'Chairman' substituted for 'Wagon'.

The evening finished badly with the staff of the I.C.A. stacking up the chairs and the friends of the bridegroom unstacking them. A sculpture in sponge and burnt cork by Dubuffet was destroyed. I was insensible.

Andy Garnett got me down the stairs, into a sports car, and on to the train at King's Cross. I didn't wake until we crossed the border. I was in clean blankets but with a terrible head and a mouth like a gym mistress's armpits. 'Thank God I wasn't sick,' I told my companion, a Scottish merchant seaman. 'You weren't sick!' he said. 'You was sick three times, Jock! Your mate told the guard you were getting married and slipped him a quid when he got youse on the train. You've had three sets of blankets. I'd slip him another quid if I was you.'

I got up and shaved. I looked dreadful, and my appearance wasn't helped by the rather bright blue ill-fitting suit I'd bought at a second-hand outfitters ('Entire Wardrobes purchased. West End Misfits, etc.') in the Charing Cross Road, or by the pink carnation I bought on the way to pick up Victoria from our hotel in Edinburgh. At the Registry Office she was handed a large bouquet from the Glasgow Jazz Club. It was of daffodils and iris.

The aftermath of the I.C.A. lecture filled the correspondence columns of the *Melody Maker* for several weeks. One I.C.A. member said that he would have left 'except I was frightened to pass the group of teddy boys near the door'. Mick Mulligan was one of them as it happened.

I wrote in defence citing Dada and Rimbaud, but leaving out Messrs Gordon and Booth which was perhaps unfair. Simon also wrote:

Bessie Smith – and Clara and Trixie too – would have been on the side of the 'riotious' element among which I am glad to include myself ...

But the masterpiece was a dead pan 'attack' on the whole evening by Chas Robson, a regular from Cook's Ferry with an impenetrable Geordie accent and a compensatory obsession with Wittgenstein. A typical paragraph read:

The unfortunate young man who gave the lecture, and the 'despicable minority' appeared, quite happily and sincerely to accept and proclaim a gutter morality based on sex and jazz – a case of 'publish and be damned' – but if Mr Wheeler (my principle critic G.M. wishes to retain his responsibility then I beg of him to heed the dangers of accidental contamination inherent in his asymtotic approach to the heart of jazz by eschewing all further contacts with the music . . .

Actually Chas had been involved with the I.C.A. before. He had brought to the attention of the staff at a Jazz Social that a young man was removing some of the huge photographs by Cartier Bresson which were on exhibition at the time with the words, 'Eh, Mister, someone's pinching your fucking snaps!'

After our marriage Victoria and I returned to Cheyne Walk. We wrote to her parents who were very angry but soon forgave us. They were pleased, when they came to see us, to discover that Andy was a descendant of Blessed Saint Adrian Fortescu, an Elizabethan Catholic Martyr. They admired English Catholic Martyrs.

In under a year our marriage was in a very bad way. It's difficult to say now whose fault it was, if indeed it was anybody's, but I was certainly as unhappy as she was, and when Simon Watson Taylor offered me a room in his flat, I accepted and moved out. Victoria was away for the week-end so I pedantically divided our wedding presents and Pete Appleby came over in the bandwagon one afternoon and, for a quid or two, helped me to move. There were a few things that wouldn't fit into the wagon in one load, and these I wheeled over later in a handcart belonging to 'orace. It wasn't too far – up Blantyre Street, across the King's Road, up Park Walk, right along the Fulham Road, up Redcliffe Gardens and into Tregunter Road.

Simon, who works for B.O.A.C., was in America the day I arrived. By the time he got back, I'd all my pictures hung, my books and clothes put away, my furniture and objects arranged.

Victoria became a model and sometime later she went to Rome on spec and stayed there, working for the fashion houses for over three years. We wrote each other chatty and friendly letters and I sent her my new records.

Although a lot of people in the jazz world knew our marriage was breaking up – for one thing Monty Sunshine's girl friend had a room in Tim's house – nobody said anything. This was always a sympathetic part of our code. In relation to personal troubles we never interfered unless the person involved wished to discuss it. Behind his back, my back in this case, there was undoubtedly a great deal of highly enjoyable speculation and gossip, but while I was actually present it was taken for granted that I would prefer to be treated as if everything was O.K. In the ordinary way Mick was as punctilious as anybody in observing this civilized rule, but one evening, very drunk, circumstances forced him into such a corner that his only defence was to be as unpleasant as possible. This was by no means a unique instance but it was the most extreme.

After a pub crawl, we had finished up in a cellar club in the Fulham Road. It was called 'La Fiesta' and was run by a small ginger-haired anarchist called Gus. In its favour was an open fire, cheap food and wine. Against it, bullfighting posters, a Spanish guitarist, and cries of 'Olé' from some of the clientele. But it was open late and we often used it if we'd been drinking in Finch's and got 'the taste'.

Sitting there that night, Mick discovered that he had no cigarettes and called over the waitress, an elderly, amiable woman dressed as an Andalusian peasant. She told him they'd run out, but that there was a machine over the road, and that if he gave her a florin she'd go and get him some. Mick had no change and gave her a pound. She took it without any objection and a few minutes later came back with the cigarettes and the change. Mick, without thanking her, picked up both the change and the cigarettes and put them in his coat pocket.

Sometime later as she was passing, Mick asked her in a sarcastic voice if she had got his snout yet. She didn't hear, imagined he was thanking her for her help, smiled, and hurried past with her order. On her way back he said he hoped she'd enjoy spending the pound. She looked puzzled. I told him that she had in fact brought him both the cigarettes and the change. He gave me a look to suggest I was somehow in on the racket. For the next twenty minutes or so he subjected the poor woman to unpleasant remarks every time she came within earshot, and at last I could stand it no longer. I leant over, took the cigarettes and the change out of his pocket, and put them in front of him on the table.

He looked at them for some time, checked the change twice, and put it in his trouser pocket. Then he looked for a long time at me, his eyes swimming about like goldfish. Finally he spoke. 'How's your married life going, cock?' he asked me.

While I was still at Cheyne Walk, at the very moment I was at my most miserable, a marvellous thing happened. The Musicians' Union finally reached an exchange agreement with its American counterpart and the Louis Armstrong All-Stars came over to this country.

They played for ten nights in London on a revolving stage at the Empress Hall, Earl's Court, an absurd choice in every way, far too big and acoustically lamentable.

Furthermore, somebody at the American end, unaware that it was an interest in jazz which would make people want to go and hear Louis, and that if a whole evening's blowing was too much for the old man, there were plenty of other jazzmen, many of them far from overworked, we'd have been delighted to hear too, filled up the first half of the bill with a series of vaudeville acts including a Mr Peg-Leg Bates who danced in a surprisingly agile manner on his single artificial limb, and of course scored a great many points but was not exactly full of high jazz content.

In consequence, during the first half of every evening, the bar became a 'Who's Who' of British jazz, and the critics, whose enthusiasm for the local product had rather naturally cooled over the years, reappeared, their mutual enmity in no way impaired by the passage of time.

Among the musicians, Humph's great height emerged from the surrounding animation, while from the general hubbub, the voice of Diz Disley, a fanatical Louis enthusiast, could be heard peppering his lyrical monologue with his favourite adjective.

We were out of town for the opening and it was several evenings later before I was able to leave the dusty and empty flat, and walk up Blantyre Street in the direction of Earl's Court. It was very sunny, and even the railings of the Gents at the World's End seemed made of gold. I walked all the way to the Empress Hall repeating to myself, over and over again, 'I'm going to hear Louis Armstrong.' That extraordinary hunger in the pit of the stomach, a sensation which even the idea of jazz had been able to induce in me in the early days, came back again. Louis Armstrong, who had been brought up in New Orleans, played with Oliver, accompanied Bessie Smith.

Jazz is an impure art. There's a great deal of romantic nostalgia involved. Even the early British bop musicians who used to sneer at our sentimentality have fallen into the trap. Minton's has become their Storyville, Parker their Buddy Bolden.

After the interval the All-Stars, each to his own round of applause, climbed on to the platform and tuned up. The crackling American voice over the amplifying system requested our attention. The house lights died. A spotlight picked out the curtained entrance from which the boxers usually emerge on their way to the ring, and out stepped a small, surprisingly plump, Negro in evening dress who, accompanied by discreet chording from the distant band, advanced slowly down the gangway playing the opening chorus from 'Sleepy Time Down South'. It was the most moving sound I ever heard in my life.

Later, of course, after I'd heard Armstrong several times both in London and the provinces, it was possible to make several criticisms: a very limited repertoire, too many vocals from Velma Middleton, a singer who made up in bulk what she lacked in swing, the 'show-biz' insincerity of some of Louis' mugging, but nothing could destroy the magic of those first few phrases. How after all those years a man of his age could blow with such freshness, excitement and invention, and at the same time impose on every note his own inimitable stamp is beyond explanation. Furthermore, the fact that for at least thirty years he has had no real life, no centre, only a series of hotel rooms, planes, ships, concert halls, recording studios, and yet can evoke, night after night, a whole way of life that vanished before the end of the First World War seems little short of miraculous, unless, as André Breton suggested, music is the most stupid of the arts.

I wasn't at the London Jazz Club the night Louis sat in with whatever band was playing, but somebody who was there stood next to Ken Colyer during the session and was naturally interested to hear what Ken, for whom Louis Armstrong was *the* enemy, the traitor who had left New Orleans and changed the course of the music, would have to say when he'd finished.

Armstrong blew his final coda, and stepped off the stage to a roar of applause and a flutter of autograph hunters. Ken turned to make his way back to the 'Blue Posts'.

'He'll do,' he said laconically.

One of the band myths, relating in this case to Ian Christie, was that if at a party he asked, 'Who's that hurray cunt by the mantelpiece?' and then discovered it was a literary or artistic figure of some eminence, he would scarcely allow time to mutter, 'Oh, really,' before scampering across the room to engage him in conversation. This story which Ian always emphatically denied, and which in consequence the rest of us produced at every possible occasion, may have been true or untrue, or as is most likely, a gross exaggeration of the truth, but Ian was no more a lion hunter than the rest of us. Like most people, we were all keen to meet someone we admired for one reason or another; it was just that most of the band only wanted to meet jazzmen, who were seldom if ever hurrays. We were all inclined to concentrate on approaching those who played the same instrument, or in my case, sang. This was natural enough, as not only were we most likely to admire someone who could do magnificently what we did less well, but also we had a ready-made subject for conversation. It was therefore quite understandable that Mick should have gone to some trouble to meet Louis Armstrong, the man he had most admired since his adolescence, and during Louis' London engagement, he spent a fair amount of time in his hotel suite. There he had the childish but none the less real satisfaction of answering, at Louis' request, the telephone, and recognizing the excited stutter of Chris Barber, already the most successful British bandleader and well aware of it too, asking deferentially if he might speak to Mr Armstrong.

'Oh, hello, Chris,' said Mick, 'Mick Mulligan here. I'll just ask Louis. Hang on, cock.'

The rest of the band followed the pattern. Ian saw most of Edmund Hall, Frank of Trummy Young, and as for Pete, he actually moved in on Barret Deems for a day or two, where, drummers being what they are the whole world over, I've no doubt that they enjoyed an entirely satisfactory relationship based on the technical intricacies of the drum kit and a willingness to listen to each other boasting about their percussive abilities. When Louis went on tour in the provinces, the organizers sent the rest of the bill home and employed local jazz bands. This, although by no means an ideal solution, was certainly an improvement and no doubt helped to draw in, on the grounds of local patriotism, many of the audience who might otherwise have been put off by the exorbitant, but no doubt necessary, price of seats.

Having a night off in Grimsby when Louis was playing in Newcastle-upon-Tyne, we drove up to hear him, and went to both concerts. Between the shows, using Mick's prior acquaintanceship, Ian, Frank and I accompanied him back stage and spent a long time in Louis' dressing-room. He was kind and friendly and accepted a token whisky from the bottle we'd taken round, but I felt we weren't really there. This is by no means a criticism; travelling year in and year out all over the world and meeting hundreds of admirers daily how could it be otherwise. What was so surprising was the number of people here he did remember, but what was significant was that he had known them all before the war when interest in jazz was still a comparatively minority affair. Sinclair, for instance, 'my man, Sinclair' as he called him, and Nat Gonella. From his post-war visits I wonder if he remembers more than a handful of people – Humph and Chris certainly, Mick perhaps, and almost without doubt due to their continuous attendance on the band, Diz and Beryl Bryden. Beryl in fact was so devoted in her pursuit that she would be there to wave off the coach when it left London for the provinces and be waiting to welcome it when it arrived at the other end.

Louis' dressing-room manner was an extension of his stage personality. He was willing to talk about the early days, 'King Oliver, he was my man,' and more than keen to impress on us, as he did on everybody, the importance of inner cleanliness, and the efficaciousness to this end of a product called 'Swiss Kriss'. It was all, however, in my view, on the surface, and it was only when he discovered that one of his entourage had neglected to book a seat on a plane for his wife, Lucille, to go to London to get her hair 'fixed', and for a moment lost his temper, that the real man showed through. Within a few seconds he had recovered himself, the 'red beans and rice' mask was back in place, and he was telling Mick, as he rubbed white ointment all over his astounding lips, pitted and cratered like a photograph of the moon, how essential it was for him, as a trumpet player, to 'look after your chops heh heh heh!' I met Louis several times over the next six years, but never tried to remind him that we'd met before.

In the years that followed most of the great American bands and a great many solo performers came over under the new arrangement. We met those of them we particularly wanted to, worked with some of them, listened to most of them. After a time, although we admired their work and envied their ability much as ever, we gradually lost that sense of awe, the feeling that the gods had come down to walk the earth. Respect replaced idolatry, and in the case of the Condon band visit in 1956, imitation resulted in temporary disaster.

The Condon band were famous for their tough, hot jazz, and equally for the amount they drank. It was, I suppose, natural that Mick should be over-excited by their visit. Not only did he admire their music, but, in Eddie Condon's ability to swallow the hard stuff and yet continue to run a band over so many years, he saw the justification of his own periodic excesses.

The day these drunken, middle-aged delinquents arrived, Eddie's first official engagement was to sign copies of his famous autobiography and drinking-primer, *We Called It Music*, at a jazz book and record shop in Charing Cross Road. A great deal of whisky was provided by the thoughtful management. Mick, Ian and Frank were among the guests. After the official junketing, during the course of which Mr Condon signed such copies of his memoirs as was necessary with a wide selection of names including on occasion his own, the whole party moved to a nearby drinking club called 'The Cottage'.

Here the photographer from the *Melody Maker* took several shots of Mick and Eddie with their arms round each other's shoulders, a gesture which could be interpreted as affectionate respect or mutual physical support. An article in the same paper had recently crowned Mick 'King of the Ravers', and it was felt that a record of this, his first meeting with his American counterpart, was worthy of publication. Eventually Condon, Wild Bill Davidson, George Wettling and company retired to their hotel, and Mick, Frank and Ian, far too late to arrive in time, set out for Barnet where the band had an evening engagement.

I forget now why I hadn't been at the afternoon's seance, perhaps I hadn't been asked, but I was in consequence completely sober. This meant I had the difficult and indeed hopeless job of attempting to divert the promoter's attention from how late it was getting before they arrived, and the painful recognition, acquired from a single glance at Mick's swimming eyeballs, Frank's manic grin, and Ian's puppet-like animation, that it was going to be a bumpy evening.

Barnet Jazz Club, which held its weekly meetings in a Trade Union hut, was typical of the suburban and dormitory town clubs which had begun to open within a thirty-mile radius of the Charing Cross Road, in order to cater for the growing interest in traditional jazz, which the success of the Chris Barber band had sparked off. What usually happened was that a promoter would examine a map, settle for an area as yet virgin territory, and open two or three clubs with common membership on different nights of the week about ten miles apart. During the height of the trad boom in 1960–61 these clubs sprang up and proliferated like weeds on a bomb site, but Barnet, and its sister club in St Albans, were in advance of the trend. They were founded by Ken Lindsay, an old-time jazz enthusiast from the Asman-George Webb era.

It was the Alex Welsh band who christened these new-style clubs 'The Milk Round'. Although they didn't pay very well they provided regular work during the early part of the week. The official definition of 'The Milk Round' was, that to qualify, a club had to be near enough for the band to get back in time for a drink at The Cottage which closed at midnight.

The difference between these clubs and the older places like Cook's Ferry and Wood Green, was that the audience were not jazz fans who liked a drink and a little live jazz. They were much younger, knew nothing about the history of jazz, wanted 'the trad sound' as a background to jiving and that was all.

The Mulligan band was not very popular on this circuit. It had no banjo for a start, and was inclined to stretch its intervals. Its appearance on the stand that evening, three quarters of an hour late and with the whole front line obviously extremely drunk, was calculated to displease the new puritans who had paid to come in. Their irritation mounted when Ian fell asleep on a chair during a trombone solo, nor were they in any way placated when Mick launched into a long apology, almost incomprehensible even to me, who at least knew what he was on about, but pure gibberish to the audience who had certainly never heard of Eddie Condon, the main justification of his argument. There were a great many complaints, several demands for money back, and, despite Ken Lindsay's affection for Mick, it was some time before we worked for him again.

There were several equal disasters during the Condon Band's British stay. Quite often the conductor didn't appear at all, and in some ways this was better as we could tell the promoter that we knew he'd been complaining of imminent 'flu, but more often he *did* appear, late and drunk, with no greater excuse than a favourite sentence of his in these circumstances:

'There comes a time when you say, "fuck it".'

A lunch-time drink with Wild Bill Davidson, Condon's trumpet player, was where the eggs of these dreadful evenings were laid, and the Cottage Club the incubator in which they were hatched. The Cottage had taken over from The Mandrake as the trad-world club. It justified its name by a thatched roof over the bar, a false window on one of the walls, through which a naïve but sentimental picture of a country lane failed to achieve the intended *trompe l'oeil*, and a large number of horse brasses. The afternoon clientele was made up of those jazzmen who had got 'the taste', in Mick's phrase, in a lunch-time pub, and a small but regular coterie of elderly music-hall artistes who appeared to be permanently 'resting', but at night it was entirely taken over by trad-jazz musicians, and to burst in there just before midnight after a milk-round job was to discover our whole world crammed into one room.

In the basement, for the main bar was on street level, there was a piano available for rehearsal during the day, much to the rage of the music hall clique, and for impromptu sessions at night. The manager we called 'Cottage Al', and there were, among the regulars, several of those kind, plump, promiscuous girls who occupy an underrated and therapeutic position in this frequently lonely and often desperate life.

During the visit of the Condon Band, 'The Cottage' really came into its own as a falling-about centre. Professionally, however, the tour was not a success. Like Mick, Eddie was inclined to launch into the stream of consciousness in front of an audience, a large proportion of which would have preferred to hear more music. I only saw them perform once, a late-night concert at the Festival Hall. The organizer had conceived the idea of arranging a series of tables round the edge of the platform to produce an intimate club atmosphere. I was amused to see the conductor as one of the extras. Although I was sitting in the circle, I could tell without any bother at all that he was in the same condition as the band.

Finally the Condon mob, to the grief of 'Cottage Al', returned to the States, and Mick to comparative sobriety. Wild Bill and Condon from their end and Mick from his took to ringing each other up in the small hours when the mood took them, an operation complicated by the difference in time between the two continents. The telephone has always proved a temptation to Mick in his cups. He once took a great liking to Joe Loss, the bandleader, when we played a dance with him at Leeds University. After it was over, and we'd travelled back to London in the band-wagon, I went up to Mick's flat to finish off a bottle of whisky. He was going on about what a 'good nut' Joe Loss was, and it was all I could do to prevent him ringing him up for a chat there and then at five fifteen in the morning.

The Kansas City Blues singer, Jimmy Rushing, became my own particular mate among the regular visitors. Jimmy, the original 'Mr Five by Five', had influenced my style for some time before he actually came over to sing with Humph, and I very much wanted to meet him. When I did we became immediate friends. He was, as the song says, 'five foot high and five feet wide', but Jimmy's bulk, and its attendant problems, getting in and out of cars for example, appeared irrelevant except to give his movements a deliberation, an almost balletic adjustment of weight in relation to gravity, which suggested his inner calm. His slow smile, the controlled lyricism of his singing, his anecdotal ability, every story built like a blues with repeated lines, are all more evocative of Jimmy Rushing than his twenty stone.

Jimmy doesn't drink much, but he loves parties, and it was a pleasure to watch him sitting there taking in, with sardonic yet kindly amusement, the mounting absurdity washing up against him like the sea against a rock. At one party I gave for him at Tregunter Road I'd asked all the band except for Frank Parr, not out of nastiness but because Simon, who was in town, had just bought a new carpet, and it is Frank's habit when drunk to stub out his cigarettes under foot. In the end, of course, I relented, but warned him about the new carpet. Inevitably he forgot and Simon threw him out. Half an hour later he was back to apologize. Simon declared himself bored and indifferent to what he had to say, but was on the point of giving in when Frank, in the very middle of his tearful repentance, took the cigarette out of his mouth and ground it into the carpet with his heel. I shall never forget the expression of mock pain which spread over the face of Jimmy Rushing at that moment.

Jimmy saw me perform on several occasions and was very complimentary, not about my voice, but about my showmanship. This was reassuring. The general feeling in the band was that my poncing about had become a bit much. Ian Christie, for example, while acknowledging that whatever popularity we retained with the public was due to me, resented the way this allowed Mick to pay the minimum attention to the musical side.

'It's not very bringing up,' said Ian, 'for a musician to feel he only gets work because you can imitate a monkey.'

He was referring in particular to my practice on 'Organ Grinder' of swinging about the stage, scratching myself and examining the conductor for fleas during the band chori, but his criticism was intended generally, and I did to some extent share it.

Jimmy wouldn't have any of it. 'We're entertainers,' he insisted, and told me by way of practical emphasis about a producer of 'them big Harlem shows I was in during the thirties'. It was this gentleman's custom to line up the chorus, 'Them beautiful high yellow girls', at the front of the stage on the first day of rehearsal and tell them: 'I don't care if you've been fucking all night, when the show starts, I want you to get out there and *show them teeth*.'

Jimmy had one small and rather endearing vanity. He liked to hear his own records. His way of achieving this, for most people imagine that the last thing an artist wants is to hear himself, was to ask if you had such and such a record of his because 'the arrangement is so pretty and I haven't heard it for some time'.

I was always sad to see him go, and sometimes went to Waterloo Station to wave good-bye when he caught the train to Southampton, for he refused to fly anywhere. He would walk a little down the platform and then swing round on one foot to wave, holding his grey trilby in place with his other hand, his brilliant red shirt catching the light. I would always remember his adaptation of the traditional way the old itinerant blues singers finished their songs:

'If anybody asked you who done sung this song,

Just tell 'em little Jimmy Rushing done been here and gone.'

The practice of using a British group on the same bill as a visiting American band became, after the Armstrong All-Stars provincial tour, pretty widespread. In the case of solo artists the accompanying group was selected if possible because they played in the same idiom. Jimmy Rushing naturally sang with Humph whose brand of mainstream was approximately the same vintage as pre-war Basie with whom Jimmy had made his name. The New Orleans veterans on the other hand usually played with Ken Colyer.

Chris Barber carried this a stage farther by actually importing, for admirably altruistic reasons, as his own band at that time could fill the largest concert halls in the country, a series of old and forgotten blues singers.

Some of these have since achieved international stature through the present boom in rhythm and blues, others, kindly old gentlemen who had been working in obscurity since the early twenties and beyond, enjoyed their temporary share of the limelight and retired again into the shadows. I am thinking in particular of 'Speckled Red', an elderly piano player and blues singer of great charm who was so delighted with his reception here that he contemplated staying and opening a school of ragtime.

He was an Albino Negro with just a few spots of pigmentation, hence his name. He was also very short-sighted and between numbers would remove a list from his breast pocket, peer at it closely and, having reached a decision, announce with great courtesy: 'My next selection is a song called, "You Got the Right String But You're Playing with the Wrong Yo-Yo". I thank you for your attention.'

He dressed like a Southern Colonel in a rye whisky ad, and his life, which had been hard, had failed to embitter his patiently sweet character.

The Mulligan band, never an automatic choice to accompany American visitors, did occasionally get in on the act. This only happened when the bigger names weren't available, but was none the less rewarding for that.

We did one tour with Big Bill Broonzy and a younger Gospel singer called Brother John Sellers. Apart from the pleasure of hearing and being with Bill for a week, there was the additional if less kindly interest of watching the interplay of two entirely dissimilar characters.

Brother John obviously considered Bill as something of a has-been. He was furious when Max Jones, reviewing their first London concert together, made it clear that he found Broonzy the finer artist. Not that Max was particularly strong in what he had to say; he simply suggested that, although Brother John could swing adequately enough, for those who preferred a more authentic blues style, Broonzy was of greater interest. This however was quite sufficient to infuriate Sellers. He slammed down the *Melody Maker* and hissed through his teeth: 'Why! That lil' bol' head man!'

His habit of shaving with depilatory wax, a painful and lengthy process, was another facet of his behaviour which Bill found endlessly amusing, and he would mime the operation with surprising accuracy for a man so different in build and temperament. It's true that superficially Broonzy appeared a far more naïve character, almost illiterate, and, due to his age and background, a walking compendium of stock 'Uncle Tom' mannerisms, even going so far as scratching his head forward from the back, but it was all on the surface. As Mick said so often: 'There's a lot going on in that old nut.'

When Bill died we were sent some rather harrowing photographs of his funeral. Brother John officiated in religious drag, and Broonzy lay in the open casket – the excuse for what was clearly a big emotional deal.

We could imagine what he would have said.

The other major tour we did was with Sister Rosetta Tharp, another Gospel singer. I was rather nervous about this. I admired her as an artist, but had always understood that the Gospel singers, although full of jazz feeling, were an ostentatiously pious lot. The blues singers certainly did nothing to dispel this idea. Broonzy was once booked to appear at the Albert Hall on the same bill as the magnificent Mahalia Jackson, and was terribly worried about what the Baptists would have to say about it when he got back to the States.

'They think the blues is sinful music,' he told us.

He was also inclined to believe it himself. His criticism of Ray Charles, 'He's singing the blues sanctified, and that ain't right' (a reference to the obvious gospel-influence on Charles' style), showed that he accepted the moral superiority of the hot gospeller.

I wasn't, of course, over-concerned about the Baptists back in the States, but I thought we might be in for a tiresome and God-bothering ten days.

In fact it was a rave. It's true that Sister Rosetta, who could, as we discovered at a private session, belt out a marvellous blues, would never do so in public, but that was about her only strict rule. One of her numbers was called 'God don't like it', and the words were aimed at most pleasurable human activities. It became clear to us within the first two days that if she believed in what she was singing, she must realize that she was causing the Almighty almost nonstop displeasure, but that there was no sign it bothered her at all.

On stage her performance was splendid, although we all found her introductions a bit strong. The sentimental piety of these was, however, in part relieved by the outrageous way she managed to plug her recordings in the same breath as the love of Jesus. When she actually started singing though, her formidable bottom swinging like a metronome in time to her wailing voice and emphatic guitar, it was pure delight. She wore on stage a series of brilliant dresses with plunging necklines, and a great deal of chunky jewellery. She asked me whether I approved of these and I told her yes, emphatically. They reflected the larger-than-life theatricality of her personality to perfection. She seemed pleased.

'Lot's of people has criticized me because I don't wear robes like Mahalia do!' she explained. 'Well what I says is robes suits Mahalia and they don't suit me. The Lord is beautiful, and I dress pretty to praise the Lord.'

The only member of the band who couldn't take Sister was Miff Bell. This dated from our very first concert with her. During the course of one number she decided to play a few chori at the piano, and not only failed to signal her intention, but simply backed towards the instrument still singing and smiling at the audience with her usual manic expression of piety, but having made contact with the piano stool, she gave a kind of controlled twitch with her monumental backside and shot Miff into the outer darkness. She did the same every night.

'The old black coo!' Miff used to mutter with rage, as she sat hammering the keyboard.

The day she left England, Mick and I went round to say good-bye to her at her hotel off the Edgware Road. She flung her arms round us and tried hard, although obviously feeling no pain at all, to make herself weep.

13. An Increasingly Dull Noise

Several years before Ian Christie joined the band, Mick and I bumped into him one Monday evening in a pub in South Kensington called 'The Hoop and Toy'. We drank together until closing time and enjoyed each other's company very much. As we swayed about on the pavement outside before going our separate ways, Mick, with the serious optimism of the convivial drunk, suggested that we made it a regular Monday date.

Needless to say neither Ian, Mick nor I ever looked in at The Hoop and Toy again, not even the following Monday, and when Ian finally joined the band we often referred to the incident; if we had a job on a Monday, Mick would apologize to Ian for having to forego the pleasure of our weekly reunion. The satisfactory element in this simple joke was that it somehow exemplified a general truth. It was rare, once the days of semi-pro enthusiasm were over, for a musician to form a proper friendship outside the confines of his own band. We all knew each other, but it was very much on the 'Hello, man. How's it going?' level. The reason for this was that, being on the road most of the time, it was difficult to meet except on a casual or accidental basis. It was almost like being a member of a ship's company. It was therefore with some surprise that answering the telephone quite early one morning shortly after I had moved to Tregunter Road, I discovered it was Wally Fawkes.

I'd known Wally for a long time, but very much on the Hoop and Toy level, first as a hero of my early Humph club days, later as someone I was always happy to see at a party or in a pub. Several years before I'd done a gig for him, a twenty-first birthday in the Home Counties where I'd nearly had a fight with the burly bearded academician, Ruskin Spear, who was attacking Max Ernst, and whose own paintings I described in my rage at this blasphemy, as 'Sickert's wet dreams'. What I remembered best about that evening was the presence, for want of a revivalist, of a bomb-dropping bop drummer called Dave Smallman whose only vocal contribution was the phrase, 'Crazy shit, man!'

I'd also been round to Wally's place a couple of times, but none of this was enough to suggest that his telephone call that Thursday morning in 1956 was purely social. In fact what he wanted to ask me was, would I be interested in writing the dialogue for 'Flook' in the *Daily Mail*, and if so could I come round and discuss it in the office that afternoon. I said yes to both questions, put the phone down, picked it up again and rang up my father in Liverpool because he was a great Flook fan and I knew he'd be knocked out.

At the *Mail* that afternoon I wished I'd waited a bit before telling him. The art editor, Julian Phipps, warned me I mightn't make the grade, or that if I did, it might be necessary to use me as one of a team. However, with a lot of initial help from Wal, I managed to coast over the first few weeks and today, almost a decade later, I'm still writing 'Flook' under his critical but entirely constructive surveillance.

In restrospect that telephone call entirely changed the direction of my life, and yet, if I'd been on tour or even out shopping, Wally would have had to ring up somebody else. The stock-pile was only three days ahead of the paper instead of the statutory three weeks, and Humph, who was scriptwriter at that time, was out on the road. Wally had recently left the Lyttelton band whose increasing professional commitments had led to this decision, and Humph was, in his fashion, returning the compliment. That morning Wal and Julian, faced with the strip grinding to a halt, had reached the conclusion that a new scriptwriter had to be found at once. I found out later it was Jim Godbolt who had suggested me.

The immediate effect of writing Flook was financial – even at the comparatively modest salary of my trial period it more than doubled my income – but it also had a disastrous effect on my ego. Here the deflationary tradition of the Mulligan band came in useful. On the first tour following my change of fortune Mick, irritated by my pseudo-casual proffering of the *Daily Mail* every morning, and my anxious hovering about until I was sure that he had read my contribution, remarked quietly but acidly that it was very good of me to let Wally draw my strip. This was the opening shot in the campaign to cut me down to size, but it was only a beginning. The band never let anything go if they could avoid it. An early and shame-making attempt to hammer out some script in the Cottage Club one quiet afternoon was frequently resurrected. My newspaper order to night porters in hotels, my pre-breakfast expeditions to newsagents when in digs, seldom passed without comment, and none of this did me any harm at all, but I was not going to be laughed out of actually getting my script written. I brought my typewriter (it became known as the 'Flook machine') away with me on tour, and if at dances there was a suitable room near the bandstand I would sit and work between songs. 'Office satisfactory?' the conductor would inquire with sardonic politeness as he passed on his way to play the opening number.

Inside the band the Flook money altered my life very little. I was able to buy more whisky and ate better on the road, and I took to travelling up to the first job of a tour by rail, but that was about all. Mick usually came with me on the train. It meant we could leave London much later than the wagon, and of course it was also more comfortable. Only Frank Parr, to whom the wagon was a holy place, seemed to resent our defection to British Railways. With typical verbal ingenuity he took to calling us the B.T.C.s, initials standing for both British Transport Commission and Big Time Cunts.

It was in London that my life changed and I very quickly found the way to jack up my standard of living a little above my new-won prosperity. There were drinking sessions with Wally and a circle of Fleet Street acquaintances in El Vino's after our weekly conference at the *Mail*. A girl-friend of sophisticated appetites told me she saw no reason, with what I was earning, to continue eating in cheap cafés, and made me take her to Wheelers, the Ivy, and the new and expensive little restaurants that were beginning to spring up round the King's Road, a habit which, even after our affair was over, I saw no reason to drop. I began to go to the theatre too. *Look Back in Anger* coincided with my apprenticeship to Flook, and from then on I saw almost every production at the Court and The Arts. It was Ian Christie who first persuaded me to go. 'It's a play about the chaps,' he told me enthusiastically. I began to buy pictures again, and less constructively was for a short but disastrous period involved in the private chemmy parties which were held each night in a different studio or flat somewhere in SW1 or 3. On the credit side all this experience came in useful in keeping the strip topical – 'Flook meat' was Wally's phrase for it – but then so did my other life with the band.

From 1955 until the band folded at the end of 1961, there was very little change professionally. The music remained static and so for the most part did the personnel. We played less concerts and more jazz clubs. We covered and re-covered the roads of Britain from Wick, a mile or two south of John o' Groat's, to Redruth, a similar distance from Land's End.

Except for the occasional evening when one or more of us was too drunk, we usually gave satisfaction. It was an increasingly dull noise we made but comparatively professional, and during the last twenty minutes or so we pulled out all the stops and for the most part succeeded in stirring up the audience to some effect. This last burst had become, like everything else to do with the music, completely predictable. It was known as 'the show', and during the second half Mick would keep us informed with increasing satisfaction of how long there was to go before it was time for it. 'Bracket of waltzes, bracket of slows, and then the show,' he would mutter out of the corner of his mouth after an elaborately sly glance at his watch.

The show consisted of three numbers. First Pete's drum solo which was set into the framework of 'Didn't He Ramble', an old New Orleans funeral march. During the opening bars, which were at a very slow tempo, I used to walk on carrying a trombone case as though it were a coffin, a piece of 'business' originally conceived in high spirits which had become a fixture. Then, after two vocal and two instrumental chori, I would pick up 'the coffin' again and march slowly off stage followed by all the band except Pete. At the last moment the front line would turn and blow three introductory chords before diving into the wings to light up, and Pete would then hammer away for a variable but always satisfactory length of time. At the beginning it had been necessary for Mick to listen throughout as the brief prearranged patterns of thumps and crashes which told him it was time to lead the band back on for the final chords was dependent on Pete's whim. Later Pete incorporated a quiet passage, in imitation of Cozy Cole, to provide a contrast to his atomic finale, and this helped considerably. 'It's all right,' Mick would say, puffing away in the darkness, 'he hasn't reached the quiet bit yet. Inspiration has descended, thank Christ.'

At concerts in theatres I had an additional job during 'Didn't He Ramble'. After walking off stage with my coffin, I had to climb hurriedly up the wall ladder to the electrician's platform and signal to him the exact beat on which to extinguish all the lights except for a spot on Pete. I used to enjoy this, but then I enjoyed everything to do with concerts.

After 'Didn't He Ramble' it was time for 'Frankie and Johnnie', or 'Harry Fallers' as Mick called it with reference to my trick of falling down at the point when Frankie shoots Johnnie. I had learned to do this with some expertise, and if the mood took me would hurl myself off quite a high bandstand. Although this looked rather dangerous, the only real hazard was that I was less adept at climbing back on to the stage, and if there were no convenient steps, I was sometimes reduced to running round through the pass-door and coming in half a chorus later.

If I chanced to land on the dance floor in such a position that it seemed possible to look up a girl's skirt, Mick would raise an inquiring eyebrow requiring either a thumbs up or down. We all have our obsessions, and Mick's was what he called 'a flash', a view of thigh and knicker. In the early days the wide skirts and top-like style of jiving were very productive of flashes, but during the trad boom, female jeans became *de rigueur* and a heavy elephantine jumping from foot to foot swept the jazz clubs. Flashes became very rare, and the conductor correspondingly desperate like a drug addict cut off from his supply. Due to his short sight, it was possible to tease him by pretending to see entirely imaginary flashes in the middle-distance. If we kept this up long enough he would finally ask Ian to lend him his glasses. That Mick was a genuine flash addict was reinforced by the fact that he didn't care what the girl looked like.

After 'Frankie and Johnnie' we finished off the show with a boring old tear-arse rabble rouser called 'Momma Don't Allow' in which vocal chori forbidding, on Momma's behalf, every instrument in turn alternated with solo chori from the instrument in question.

At the end of 'Momma Don't Allow' it was Mick's custom in dance halls to play an abbreviated version of 'The Queen', less to prove his conformism, although naturally most dance-hall managers insisted on the convention, more to convince the audience it was all over. Sometimes when in his Condonesque mood, the conductor would announce the anthem as 'Corky's Tune'. Corky was our name for the Queen. It dated back to my naval days. A friend of mine, a staunch republican, had always referred to the reigning Monarch as 'Korky the King'. He had chosen this name in imitation of 'Corky the Cat', an animal who appeared in a strip cartooon on the front of the *Beano*. Early in the band's history I had told Mick about the King being called Korky, and the name had stuck. When the Queen succeeded she also inherited this derisive pseudonym, but we dropped the 'K' in favour of a 'C' because alliteration no longer applied.

One Christmas the *New Statesman* published a satire on the *Radio Times* Christmas Day programme page. At three p.m. I was surprised to see 'Corky and her German Band', and at midnight 'Corky's Tune'. A footnote explained that 'Corky' was 'Jazz slang for H.M.', a rather wide attribution as, despite some general favour, the name was more or less confined to the Mulligan band. How the *Statesman* discovered about 'Corky' at all I never found out, unless Simon Watson Taylor had told John Raymond, then literary editor, in Finch's in the Fulham Road.

When I was in the Navy I found it strange and marvellous that whatever lay outside the portholes – foggy British dockyard, Norwegian fiord under a midnight sun, the Cap d'Azur at night – everything on the ship stayed exactly the same. In the Mulligan band the Volkswagen worked in the same way. Inside it we became a hydra. We worked on 'the myth'. We recreated the past and earmarked the present for future use.

The wagon itself contributed a great deal. To close the double door required calm and expertise in turning the handle.

Otherwise one of the two rods which moved upwards to engage the inner rim of the frame failed to connect. Miff Bell had a tendency to lose his temper if anything mechanical didn't work immediately, and it was he who most often fell foul of the doors. Cursing and swearing he would bang them open and shut, yanking the handle up and down, and eventually, led by Frank Parr, the most observant and priestlike of all the wagon *habitués*, a slow chant of 'normal doors' would begin, adding if anything to Miff's manic hysteria.

The interior of the wagon was of tin, and the heating only worked in the front. It had its own smell, difficult to define, but based on old newspaper and dog-ends. Frank's love of disorder and my neurotic neatness clashed spasmodically over the inside of the wagon. Driven mad by the knee-deep accumulation of rubbish, I would gather up armfuls of old Sunday papers, sandwich crusts, empty quart-bottles, dog-ends and cigarette packets and ram them into dustbins at the back of pubs or dance halls. I even bought a little dustpan and brush and several ashtrays with rubber suckers. When I'd got the wagon basically tidy, I would fold the blankets and 'Mummy's' fur coat along the back seat and stack the paperbacks in one corner. I even, although this was not a popular move, sprayed the interior with a scented atomizer. The rest of the band, although uncooperative, were amused and indifferent to my efforts, but Frank would eye them with aggressive distaste. Not only did he refuse to use the ashtrays, but worked on the suckers until they refused to grip, so that the ashtrays fell to the floor and were eventually lost.

The band instruments were for the most part tied on the roof rack. On a long journey an end of the rope inevitably worked loose and began to beat a syncopated, curiously regular, rhythm on the tin roof. This was known as 'the spade bongo player'. He became one of the phantoms who attended us at all times. Other demons lay dormant in the wagon itself. 'Maggie May', a Liverpool prostitute of violent erotic appetite and a gift for lyrical obscenity, occasionally possessed me. Miff Bell was an admirer of 'Maggie May'. He himself had been known to receive a 'Message for the day' from God. God was sparing with His messages however, although He was seldom ignored for long on our side. During violent storms Ian Christie spent a great deal of time banging on the tin roof and demanding to be struck dead. On the other hand, faced with an exceptionally beautiful view or even a striking effect of light, we would, after due consultation, give God a polite round of applause. He was not unique, however. Pretty girls passing in front of the wagon at traffic lights, or, in later days, zebra crossings, received the same accolade, and would blush, glare, or smile according to their nature.

Although Ian was the first to join in if God was in question, his hatred of cliché made him rather impatient at certain repetitive aspects of the myth. The ceremony of chanting the Jewish shop names while driving through Whitechapel, 'Jacobs, Cohen, Isaacs, Cohen, Fishberg, etc.', used to provoke an exasperated groan of 'how fucking boring', and the same was true of our passage through the first Welsh town after crossing the border, 'Evans, Jones, Jones, Davis, Evans, Morgan, etc.'

He also attempted to impose a personal censorship on stories or anecdotes which he felt had been repeated too often or too recently. 'Forbidden,' he would cry, and this gained him the nickname 'the Pope of the forbidden' although it did nothing to check our love of reiteration.

Ian was only referred to as 'The Pope' while actually in the act of forbidding, but his usual nickname, 'Bird', also evolved in the wagon. It had nothing to do with the late Charlie Parker, an artist whom at that time he rejected. It arose during a session of one of those games where you invent animals or birds which seem to fit the personality of different people. We were playing round the band and when it came to Ian somebody said he was definitely a bird, and added as a more exact description, 'A four-eyed Short-arse, which makes its nest in old *New*

Statesmans and flies through the air crying, "It's the system".'
This produced general laughter, although Ian's own response
had the staccato machine-gun corps quality with which he ac-
knowledged jokes at his own expense, but typically it was the
name 'Bird' which stuck.

Linguistic selection in the band always seemed to work on a
haphazard basis. At the same session I was described as a toad,
and for a time too this looked like replacing 'Fat' as my nickname, but it didn't. Ian on the other hand was always called
'Bird', despite the conductor's attempt to change it to 'The
Shrike' in acknowledgement of the thorny impaling of Ian's
verbal attacks.

14. A Bit of Fun

Jobs and towns melted into each other. There was no way of
placing events chronologically and the regularity of certain gigs
helped to destroy our sense of time. The annual engineers' ball
at Leeds University with its obligatory dinner jackets and acres
of chiffon and goose-flesh; the monthly appearance at 'The
Bodega', Manchester, on Saturday night followed on Sunday
by 'The Cavern', Liverpool; the eternal suburban 'milk round'
at the beginning of each week; an event had to appear pretty
weird to secure a place in our corporate memory for more than
a day of two. Furthermore, even when an incident earned its
niche in the myth, it became increasingly hard to place it.
Sometimes there was a clue. One night, for example, a young
girl and her brother at Leicester Jazz Club asked us back to a
party, but failed to prepare us for the adult set-up. Their
mother, a hard and desperate woman of a ravaged beauty, sat
by the fire talking to her lover who leant against the man-
telshelf. He was a swarthy man of extraordinary good looks but
so short that their faces were almost on a level. Meanwhile their
father, a doctor it would seem, roamed from room to room
knocking back glass after glass of neat gin and roaring with

laughter. When he appeared dressed in a white coat and brandishing a hypodermic syringe, Mick and I decided the time had come to go to bed and lock our doors – a precaution which proved justifiable as throughout the night he rattled the handles at regular intervals, muttering and chuckling. We would, of course, have remembered that night, but almost certainly forgotten when it happened. What enables me to date it within a month was that we had with us a boy called Johnnie, a regular at Cook's Ferry who happened to be in Leicester that night on business, had seen our name on a poster, come to the jazz club and rowed himself in on the party. When we entered the house, which was furnished in a style of opulent vulgarity based on Knole sofas and huge Chinese vases turned into lamp standards, he remarked that it was all very *Room at the Top*. I didn't know what he meant, and he explained that it was a new book about the rich in the north. As this was first published in March 1957, made a great stir, and would certainly have been brought to our attention by the Press within a day or two of the party at most, it's possible to say that we were threatened by the mad doctor in March 1957, but such clues are rare.

Of all the provincial cities we visited regularly it was Manchester which continued to supply forbidden stories on a lavish scale. It was here for example that Ian and Mick discovered the Caterers' Club, and full of enthusiasm took me there one grey afternoon after the pubs shut. It was a small room with a bar, originally a shop but with the window boarded up. It was lit by naked bulbs, the floor was bare boards, and on the wall was a hand-made poster which said, 'Try our cocktail, 1s. 6d.' The object of the club, according to the yellowing rules, was recreational and social, and designed to appeal to people in the small hotel and boarding-house business. In fact, the clientele were low-grade villains of a Dickensian aspect and the oldest whores in the world. We spent several happy hours listening to one of these: a toothless but cheerful lady called Margaret. She thought we were 'college students' and was proud to introduce us as such to her sisters in vice although we discovered that students, while respectable enough, occupied a comparatively humble position in her scale of social values.

'I've been with all sorts,' she told us. 'When I've got me teeth in and me make-up on like, well, you could take me anywhere. I've been to posh restaurants and clubs, with, well, you know — business people.'

Every time another old bag came in, Margaret greeted her warmly, but as soon as she was out of earshot told us, grinning and waving every time she saw her acquaintance looking in our direction, that she didn't keep herself clean and went with 'the lowest of the low for a dollar'. Margaret herself, she told us, only went with respectable people, sea captains and the like. She liked the club because they didn't let the blacks in. Now the Paramount Club, she told us, she wouldn't go there any more. They let them in there. Not long before she *had* gone in for a drink with a Polish seaman and he'd brought out a great wad of notes to pay. Well, that was foolish of him she agreed. Then he'd gone into the gents and not come out. Well, after a bit she'd asked the owner if he'd been in his gents lately. No, he'd said, why? Had she?

'Cheeky monkey,' said Margaret and went on with her story. She'd explained to the owner that her 'friend' had gone into the gents twenty minutes before and not come out. He'd gone to look and found him lying face down on the floor.

' 'Is wad of notes 'ad gone, of course,' said Margaret, and was about to drink when a new thought occurred to her.

' 'E were dead,' she added in a thrilling if unconvincing whisper.

Towards the end of the afternoon we were joined by a friend of Margaret's, an enormous man of formidable griminess wearing a neck scarf. Whether to take the piss out of us, or because he thought it genuinely funny, he pretended to be a homosexual. His imitation was of music-hall origin and consisted for the most part of wetting an extremely dirty finger every few seconds and applying it to his eyebrows while holding an imaginary mirror with his other hand.

He was obsessed with the meanness of the woman who lived in the room above him and to whom he had frequently lent 'cupfuls of shugger' and other household essentials, and to whom that morning he had applied for a 'bit of bacon fat'. What was extraordinary was the way he said 'bacon fat'. You could almost see a dirty frying pan with the fat in it. It was almost hallucinatory. Furthermore, he managed to introduce the phrase a surprising number of times into his recital.

'I said, "Luke, all I'm asking for is a bit o' bacon fat." She said, "I've got no bacon fat." Well, I could see 'er frying-pan on't gas cukor full o' bacon fat. I said, "What's that in't pan? 'Appen it's bacon fat." She said, "Aye, but that's all t' bacon fat I've got so fook off." I said, "I will and all and you can stuff yer bacon fat . . ." '

Round the corner from the Caterers' Club was an Indian restaurant where Mick and I often went for a meal. One evening, prior to our appearance at The Bodego, we were just finishing enormous platefuls of fried rice, Madras curry, chicken biriani, chutney, lime pickle and chapatis, when a Mancunian funeral party came in and occupied a large reserved table in the middle of the room. There was a nice old mum, obviously distressed by the loss of her husband, a burly middle-aged son and his wife who had a mouth like a contracted sphincter muscle, an unsympathetic daughter and her hen-pecked husband, a porcine grandson. They were served soup and half-way through a family row broke out. It began when the daughter-in-law asked the daughter to tell her husband to hold his knife properly. Within a moment there was a full-scale shout-up. Cries of, 'You always thought you were too good for him. Well you're nothing,' and 'Why don't you say something?' 'After all you're meant to be my husband,' were audible among the general confusion. At intervals the poor old mother tried to calm everybody down by pointing out that 'Dad's still warm in 'is grave', but nobody took any notice. There were too many old scores to settle, too many slights and insults to rake over. Finally both couples and the grandson rose and left at the same time, neither willing to acknowledge that it wasn't they who'd been insulted, and a minute or two later an Indian waiter came in, cleared away the soup plates and replaced them with enormous helpings of steak and chips. The old lady asked for the manager who turned out to be Irish and refused to refund the price of the steaks although he declared himself willing to let her off the peaches and custard which were to follow. She sat for a moment and then came over to our table.

'Would you fancy a couple of steaks each?' she asked us sadly. 'They're all paid for and it's a shame to let them go to waste.' After our huge meal, we were forced to refuse although, as Mick said, 'I'd have noshed the lot if I could have done, the poor old cow.' She quite understood, ate her own steak, paid and left.

Neither of these stories can be dated with any certainty. All I know is that they happened sometime between 1954 when the second band formed and 1958 because after that we left the rather squalid digs we had patronized in that area since we first played for Paddy and began to stay in an hotel the other end of town, an institution not noticeably more luxurious, but with several compensating features. We called it 'El Sordid's'.

It was quite a large hotel in an area on its way down. It had a reception desk, a dining-room with separate tables and a lounge with a television set. The proprietor was an elderly sad-faced man with the look of a Lancashire music-hall comedian. In homage to the U.S. airmen who were his main clientele, he wore a shirt outside his baggy grey trousers. On it was a sunset going down behind some palm trees.

You were allowed to lumber back a scrubber, but you were charged for it. If you were alone the bill was a pound for bed and breakfast. If you were with a girl it was twenty-five shil-

lings each, in effect a twenty-five per cent sin charge. There
was, furthermore, no truck with the usual polite fiction of Mr
and Mrs. Your bill was made out for 'one couple: B. & B.
... £2 10s.'

In Liverpool I stayed at home, but the band used a shabby
lodging house on Mount Pleasant. It was run by a family of
Liverpudlian Chinese and was later shut down after police ob-
servation. I went back there one night after The Cavern for a
drink with Mick, and found an excited family row in progress.
Two Chinese men were carrying out a radiogram they claimed
belonged to them. Several fights broke out in the hall with some
risk to a number of toddlers who were wandering about between the legs of the various factions, eating crisps. A woman
kept yelling, 'You've got a lovely wife and kiddies in a flat in
Birken'ead and you live over 'ere wid a prostitute!', but the
remark which knocked us out was when one of the Chinese men
shouted at another in a strong Scouse accent, 'Der trouble wid
youse is you're yeller!'

The Cavern, where we played on Sunday nights, has become
world famous as the womb of the Liverpool sound, but in those
days it was staunchly trad although just as packed and steamy.
The audience sat in front of the small stage on about twenty
rows of seats or jived at the back and sides of the long low cellar
under the sweating brick arches. When we came back from the
pub after the interval we could see clouds of steam billowing
out from the door at the top of the steep stone steps which led
down to the Cavern. It looked as if it must be on fire.

The girls in the audience had that dreamy, rather sad,
slightly scruffy look that Liverpool girls have. They were a
decided contrast to the Manchester girls of the previous night,
who were much smarter, more brisk and matter-of-fact, and
tended to have good if stereotyped legs and, less sym-
pathetically, a special mouth with thin lips curving tautly down
at the edges. I called this 'the Manchester mouth' and it was
surprising how often it reoccurred.

My father used to come to The Cavern after dinner with my Uncle Alan. He was usually a little high after his evening session in The Albert, and used to flirt mildly with the girls in the bandroom. He called them 'the band mice'. 'Mouse' as an expression for a girl had been widespread in the mid-fifties. Bruce Turner had been responsible for its popularity. 'Must have that mouse, Dad,' he used to say, but later it had given way to the word 'chick' which, in its turn, had been superseded by the still prevalent 'bird'. My father however remained faithful to 'mouse' until his death. He was very popular with the Liverpool mice because he was affectionate without being at all lecherous. A few weeks after he died we played Liverpool and a girl to whom he had always been warm and friendly asked me where he was. I told her, and her eyes filled with tears. Very sadly she said she could hardly believe it.

'Last time you were here,' she said quietly, 'it was raining, and I come in all wet, and he said me tits was smaller and must have got shrunk in the rain. I'm very sorry to think he's gone.'

My father didn't like The Cavern because it was so hot and crowded. About 1959 we moved to a much larger club. The Mardi Gras on Mount Pleasant, a few doors away from the Chinese Hotel. This was much bigger and quite plushy, and he liked it better, but I always preferred The Cavern. It had far more atmosphere.

Just before we transferred the management had begun to use a Beat group sometimes, instead of a local trad band during the intervals. In 1963 when the trad boom began to fade a little these took over the whole session. Among the other groups were 'The Beatles'.

The word 'scrubber' has cropped up quite frequently in this story, and perhaps the time has come to attempt a precise definition of what it means, or rather meant, for I understand that in the Beat world it has become debased and now means a prostitute. In our day this was not the case. A scrubber was a girl who slept with a jazzman but for her own satisfaction as much as his. Each scrubber had her own area, would turn up at the band's first job within her boundaries, sleep with the musician of her choice that night, travel on to the next job with him, and such jobs after that as lay within her province, and leave the band when it crossed the border into the next scrubber's territory. I don't mean to suggest that there was only one scrubber in each area, in fact many of them travelled in pairs, but that each individual was faithful in her fashion to one member in any given band. In her fashion, because many of them were very experimental sexually and would take part in gang bangs but only with the permission and participation of her regular partner.

Most scrubbers specialized in men who played a particular instrument. There were scrubbers for bass players, drummers, clarinettists, bandleaders, singers, and so on. Scrubbers were not distributed over the whole of the British Isles. In London and the towns within an eighty-mile radius there were lots of girls who did a turn, but no scrubbers in the full sense of the word because the bands usually travelled back to London the same night. Other areas, Scotland for example, were too imbued with the puritan tradition to tolerate the scrubber. In fact, scrubbers were mostly to be found in an area stretching from the West Coast to the East, but ending at a line drawn through the Potteries to the south and Newcastle-upon-Tyne in the north. It was the Alex Welsh Band who invented the name for this area. They called it 'The Scrubber Belt'.

Once in Barrow-in-Furness, Pete Appleby and I picked up two scrubbers and at their suggestion, drove out of town to a field above the sea. While on the job I heard Pete shriek with laughter and lifting my head discovered that a nearby furnace was blasting and the landscape for a moment or two was as bright as day. ' 'Ow bad,' Pete told the rest of the band later. 'I'm lying there feeling up this chick when it all 'appens, and suddenly I can see old Fat's arse going up and down like the clappers!'

The two most famous scrubbers of my time, who invariably cropped up in any conversation between jazzmen whenever they met, both came from Yorkshire. From Leeds, Jean Patterson set out each week-end in search of pleasure. In Bradford, Mucky Alice studied her *Melody Maker* to decide where to aim for after work on Fridays.

Jean Patterson, a big bonny girl with a friendly warm smile, was famous for her experimental temperament and her formidable breasts and was equally popular with both British and visiting American bands. Once she came round to pay us a social call in the bandroom at Sheffield City Hall. She had with her another girl, older than herself and very anonymous in appearance.

'Be careful what you say in front of my friend,' warned Jean. 'She's not like me. She doesn't like a bit of fun.'

A friend of mine on a recent trip to America wandered straight off the boat into a bar where a coloured trio were playing. Just after he'd bought his first beer, the leader made an announcement. 'Our next selection,' he said, 'is an original by our bass player. He entitles it "Theme for Jean Patterson".'

A month or two ago I invited an American blues singer to come and spend the day with us. As we live rather far out, I arranged that we should pick him up at his hotel, and at the agreed time knocked on his door. 'Come on in,' he said, 'I'm just up.' He was pulling on his undervest. Through the gap between his extended arm and torso I saw Jean Patterson zipping up her skirt. 'It's fucking Melly,' she said.

She looked marvellous, brown, relaxed and happy. She came to lunch and stayed until it was time for her to catch her train north. She radiated contentment and reaffirmed me in my belief that what you really want to do, provided it respects the identities of other people, is the basis of a workable morality.

Mucky Alice was not, as her name might suggest, unclean in

her person. In fact, like most scrubbers, she took some care and pride in how she looked, although an ambition to startle led to some rather strange ensembles. In fact the 'Mucky' came from two other young ladies from Bradford who, lips tight with disapproval, once spat out that they didn't know how 'you can go with Mucky Alice', and the adjective, like the 'dirty' in 'dirty week-end', had a moral rather than sanitary application. Alice had rather curious tastes. She was a masochist and liked being tied up. I usually had my fishing reel in the wagon so the tying-up was no problem. As a sadist, however, I'm afraid I was found wanting, and she complained that my bites and smacks erred towards the tentative. On the other hand we both liked fucking in difficult or bizarre circumstances. Top of the list came about during the interval in a small northern town hall. While I was working, Alice discovered a door which led through into the magistrates' court, and we did it in the dusty dark in front of the bench.

Alice and I had a fairly steady relationship over several years. The good thing about a proper scrubber, as opposed to a local one-night-stand, was that they never asked you what you did in the day; an infuriating question after a two-hundred-mile trip in the wagon, a three-hour session and the same distance to cover the next morning. Nor did they counter almost every remark with the phrase, 'you what?', pronounced, 'yer wah?' to indicate bored incomprehension. In fact they could talk our language. Alice was sexy and enjoyed sex. She was generous too and would stand her round or even lend me money if I was broke. I had heard recently that she was married and asked Jean Patterson the day she came to lunch if this was in fact true.

'Married?' she said, 'she's always married. Now who is it she's married to this week?'

15. An Unlikely Totem

I'd known Edward Montagu since my naval days when he'd been in the Irish Guards with Tim Whidborne. One morning in the winter of 1955 he rang me up with a request. He'd seen the band were giving a concert in Bournemouth the following Sunday. Would we like to look in at Beaulieu afterwards and play an hour or two for his house-party? He offered drinks and something to eat, and I said I'd put it to the band and see what they thought. Although it meant going ten miles out of our way, they said yes.

When we arrived at the palace, we were shown up to the drawing room in Edward's flat. There were about a dozen people including Ken Tynan, and I believe this was the occasion on which the Ian Christie 'Who's that hurray cunt over there?' myth originated. There was a table with every sort of drink on it near the fireplace, but this was for the guests. For the band there was a crate of brown ale and two plates of sandwiches. There was a certain amount of chuntering over this, but nothing was said at the time. We played for about an hour and a half and then drove home. Ken Tynan asked if he could have a lift, and managed to find room at the conductor's feet in the front of the wagon. No sooner had we driven off than Ian began a furious attack on Edward's meanness and bad manners in only offering the band beer when his guests could have what they wanted. Mick took the view that this was perfectly justifiable, and the resulting shout-up extended its territory to include all our usual political disagreements.

Mick was put down by the ferocity and logic of Bird's argument, but a week later he was to have his revenge. We were in Blackpool, and after the dance were invited as usual for a splendid meal of home-made cheese and potato pie at Ian's parents. His father had spent the evening at the local and was in an amiable if repetitive condition.

'My son,' he kept telling us, 'has been entertained by Lord Montagu in his own house.'

Ian, who had obviously told his dad because, like most of us, he told his parents anything he thought might interest them, was extremely put out. Mick was merciless. Assuming a bland and interested expression he turned round in his chair and said to old man Christie: 'Lord Montagu? Ian?'

'Yes,' said Ian's dad. 'My son. He's been as a guest in Lord Montagu's own place.'

He needed very little encouragement to repeat this information several times during the course of the evening.

Mick always used this devastating trick whenever a girl-friend or parent let drop, in innocent pride, that a member of the band had been swanking about anything. None of us were able to discover a counter-ploy, nor did we ever have an opportunity to repay him in kind – his pathological modesty and indeed constant self-deprecation saw to that.

It was because of our evening at Beaulieu that Lord Montagu asked us to appear at the first jazz festival he promoted in the summer of 1956. This was a comparatively small-scale venture: two local bands, the Dill Jones trio and us, providing an afternoon and evening session on the palace lawn. Several hundred people turned up and behaved with enthusiastic decorum. At the end of the last number Edward climbed up on the rostrum and promised, to ironic but friendly cries of 'Good old Monty', to hold a bigger and better festival the following year. There was no local opposition; on the contrary the pub and village shop were delighted with the extra business. We got to know Beaulieu pretty well over the next six years. For old time's sake we were booked every year, although in a justifiably and increasingly modest position on the bill. We watched the whole thing grow. The one day became two days. The low platform gave way to a huge antique roundabout with the musicians replacing the horses – 'Harmless amusement for all classes' read the refurbished circus baroque lettering round the perimeter of the awning.

A camping ground was available for those who brought their own tents. Beer and hot dog stalls sprang up around the edges of the great lawns. By night the palace was floodlit. Extra-festival attractions were tried out: a cricket match between musicians and Lord Montagu's eleven, a church service with music by members of the Dankworth band.

The success of Beaulieu pupped other jazz festivals and Montagu himself presented 'All-Night Carnivals of Jazz from Beaulieu' at large venues in the far north, but none of them managed to project the magic of the original, and from all over the country at first hundreds, later thousands, of people drove or hitch-hiked to listen to two days of jazz in this comparatively inaccessible corner of Hampshire.

Until 1960 there was never any trouble. Through Chris Barber the audience for traditional jazz was expanding steadily, and although perhaps its appreciation grew increasingly superficial, it was still based on the music. Beaulieu certainly had other facets, the mellow charm of its setting and a strong permissive atmosphere. In the late evening the extensive and well-shrubbed estate was athrob, and a policeman with fully developed voyeur tendencies, whose actual job was to see that no trouble developed at the festival, once told Mick that he found nothing in his whole life as rewarding as a discreet patrol round the grounds while the last band of the night was stomping it out under the stars.

But all this did nobody any harm, and for the first four years, although the increasing number of visitors, unable to leave until the festival was over, certainly put some strain on the small village at the palace gates, Beaulieu was for us something to look forward to as we travelled through cold foggy nights in the grim provinces.

In 1960, however, the trad boom was under way.

The reasons for the trad boom, indeed for any fad in pop music, are finally unsolvable. Trad had been around for some years, and Chris had won it a large audience and could, at that time, fill any concert hall in the country, but it was not a pop music exactly. Its audiences were young, but not particularly young. The majority were in their late teens, but many were in their early twenties. There was a proportion of art-school students, and a larger proportion who hoped to be taken for art-school students. These were inclined to dress rather beat and dance with no shoes on, and however rural a job, there was sure to be at least one such couple leaping about in front of the bandstand. They were known among the band as 'the local weirdies', but apart from them there was no trad uniform. It was the emergence of Acker Bilk which changed the whole scene.

Acker was born in a Somerset village, but had cut his jazz teeth in Bristol. He'd started to play clarinet in an Army detention cell in Egypt while serving a sentence for falling asleep on watch – a story which must have appeared in print as often as how Louis Armstrong learnt to play cornet in the Waifs' Home, New Orleans, or how Humphrey Lyttelton sneaked off from the Eton and Harrow Match at Lord's to buy his first trumpet in the Charing Cross Road.

In the mid-fifties Acker had run a band in Bristol, and I'd guested with him one cider-ridden evening. His music was very much based on Ken Colyer, and had the clumsiness and honesty which marked the genuine disciple.

Towards the end of the fifties, Acker had built up a solid following in Bristol, and thought the time had come to try his luck in London. He formed a band and then almost starved. Eventually, when the record companies, impressed by the success of the Sunshine-Barber recording of 'Petit Fleur', were recording every trad band in sight, he got his chance. This might well have come to nothing had he not been placed in the hands of a Mr Peter Leslie, a smooth and amusing P.R.O. who conceived the idea of promoting Bilk with a great deal of Victorian camp. It was he who decided on the 'Mr', on the heavy music-hall chairman prose on the record sleeves, on the striped waistcoats, and, above all, on the bowler hat. That this whole concept ran against Acker's rather earthy and rural personality may well be the reason it succeeded. 'The Alberts' and 'The Temperance Seven' had been pushing Victoriana for many years with only a limited impact, but when Mr Acker Bilk was created, his success was instantaneous.

At first sight he was an unlikely totem for a teenage religion. With his little beard and balding head, twinkling eyes and decided waddle, he looked more like a retired pirate than anything else. He revealed a basic if sympathetic sense of humour based on sending up his West Country Burr, the catch phrase, 'watch out', and the frequent interjection into his public pronouncements of a noise which can only be described as sounding like a vigorous yet watery fart. But none of this can explain his deification in the early months of 1960. As it was Acker became a password among the young, and the bowler hat, usually with his name daubed round the crown in whitewash, a cult object.

His more extreme followers wore, not only the bowler, but army boots, potato sacks, old fur coats cut down to look like stone-age waistcoats. This outfit became known as 'Rave Gear', an expression first coined by an eccentric jazz promoter called

'Uncle Bonny' who encouraged the wearing of it in his chain of southern clubs. On the whole, however, 'Rave Gear' was rare in clubs, and only came into its own at the festivals or at the gargantuan all-night raves which were held under the echoing dome of the Albert Hall or among the icy wastes of the Alexandra Palace.

Another mark of the raver was the C.N.D. symbol. Among the musicians there were some, myself among them, who were actively committed to the cause of nuclear disarmament, and the same was certainly true of a proportion of the trad fans, but I rather felt that for most of them the symbol was anti-authoritarian rather than anti-nuclear, not that I found this in any way unsympathetic.

What was infuriating about the trad fans *en masse* was their complete intolerance of any form of jazz which fell outside their own narrow predilection. Of course it can be argued that we too had been pretty biased in our early days, but in our favour we were fighting for a neglected music in the face of indifference and ridicule, and furthermore our idols were the great originals. The trad fans neither knew nor cared about Morton and Oliver, Bessie Smith or Bunk Johnson. It was exclusively British trad they raved about, and although it was the better bands who went to the top, any group, however abysmal, was sure of a respectful hearing as long as the overall sound was right. The basis of that sound, the instrument which provided the heartbeat of the trad Frankenstein monster, was that dullest and most constricting of all noises, a banjo played chung, chung, chung, chung, smack on the beat.

Some bands held out obstinately against banjo-mania. Humph, Al and Sandy, and later Bruce Turner, ploughed a lonely mainstream furrow. Alex Welsh, although he capitulated enough to use a banjo on the occasional number, remained faithful to the noise he wanted to make, a fierce but disciplined amalgamation of Condon-music and arranged Dixieland. They worked because there were enough clubs to give them a certain

amount of work, but they had a harder struggle than a great
number of vastly inferior bands. Not that the whole of British
trad was rubbish. There were some fine musicians in the
better bands, but by reducing the music to a formula, by breaking through into the pop world, by over-exposure and repetitive
gimmicks, trad signed its own death warrant. What seems odd
in retrospect was that many of the musicians involved had been
prepared to all but starve for the music in the days before the
break-through and yet, once the boom came, were willing to do
anything however idiotic in the name of commercialism.

It is, however, tempting but inaccurate to imagine that every
British trad band sounded identical, and that all of them wore
funny uniforms. There was certainly a basic trad noise and
several of the bands not only reproduced it exactly, but dressed
up as Confederate troops or Mississippi gamblers in order to do
so. There were exceptions however. Kenny Ball for example
dressed his band in ordinary suits, and although the recordings
which brought him fame were very pretty-pretty – 'traddy-
pop' was the word invented to describe this noise by its deni-
grators – at clubs and concerts Kenny could blow some exciting jazz. He himself had a formidable technique acquired
during his many years as a travelling dance-band musician, and
while far from contemptuous of money, he knew and loved
early Armstrong.

Chris Barber too scorned fancy dress, and though he may be
considered as playing John the Baptist to Acker's Saviour,
while the trad boom was actually at its height he was experimenting with rhythm and blues, and playing a fair amount of
arranged Ellington as well as his usual materia.

Still it was a monotonous and dreary time. The airwaves
were turgid with banjoes, programmes like 'Easy Beat' and
'Saturday Club' were clogged with trad, but at least these were
only intended to reflect popular taste not to direct it. More
lamentably, and much to the impotent chagrin of its producer,
Terry Henebery, 'Jazz Club' itself, until then a genuine

platform for every kind of jazz, received orders from above to limit itself exclusively to trad.

In fairness, I myself had nothing to complain about financially during the slow ascension of trad and its three-year omnipotence. The discovery by the B.B.C. that I could compére led initially to an occasional appearance on Jazz Club in this capacity and eventually to a more or less resident post. Furthermore as a trad band became obligatory on every pop programme, I was booked to compère a lunchtime potpourri called 'Bandbox' which lasted for well over a year, and later, after the Mulligan band had actually folded but before the trad bubble burst, a similar rush-hour mic-mac called 'Pop-along'. There were also occasional plum engagements for the Corporation like compèring a big jazz festival at the Albert Hall, and as a direct result of working regularly for the B.B.C., I was offered a fair amount of work as M.C. for commercial promoters both at jazz festivals and concerts. Whenever possible, Mick arranged it so that I was able to take advantage of these offers, which anyway frequently worked both ways. If a promoter wanted me as compère, he was often prepared to take Mick and the band on as part of the bill.

Considering that the Mulligan band played a long way outside the accepted trad idiom, they did a lot of broadcasts. Mick's personality was the reason for this. He remained modest and helpful without in any way crawling, and the producers, fed up with bandleaders on the make who were willing if necessary to kiss their rings and bandleaders who *had* made it doing the big-time, enjoyed working with him. He also thought to buy them a drink in the break between rehearsal and transmission, a social gesture which never seemed to occur to most of his colleagues.

Jimmy Grant, the producer of 'Saturday Club', was a great favourites of Mick's and mine. He cottoned on so completely to the Appleby legend. At broadcasts only Mick and I were handed scripts, and Pete, giving the excuse that he needed one to remember the order of the programme, but in fact because not to have a script of his own was an affront to his ego, used to ask if there was a spare one. Jimmy, Mick and I used to have a giggle about this, and eventually Jimmy arranged that when his secretary came down from the control box at the beginning of rehearsal with a script for Mick and me, she also gave one to Pete with his name written across the top. Jimmy's expression of blissful mischief as he watched, from behind the glass panel, Pete's pseudo-casual acceptance of this proof of his importance endeared him to us for ever.

We also continued to record. In 1958, for instance, Decca, finally convinced that my commercials were uncommercial, allowed me to make an L.P. of jazz and blues material. This was recorded live in the upper room of a public house called 'The Railway Arms' in West Hampstead in front of an invited audience. It was a very enjoyable evening, and some of the tracks, those recorded early on, were not too bad. Towards the end of the session everything got rather out of control. Among the public was a contingent from Finch's in the Fulham Road including a small blonde lady of indeterminate age who became extremely drunk. For one thing she demanded to sing. 'When can I do my song, Micky-Mick-Mick?' she kept on shouting in between takes. 'Micky-Mick-Mick' told her to shut her hole but to no effect. During the interval she invaded the bandroom where the company had provided a few bottles of the hard stuff for the Mulligan band and guests. Here the blonde lady decided to take her clothes off. While this was taking place, the man who had brought her was roaming the public rooms looking for her, and chanced to land up outside the door to the musicians' bar at the same moment that I was unsuccessfully trying to effect an entrance. I'd been for a pee, but didn't see why this should bar me from the free drinks, and yet although I banged and shouted, it was evident that someone was leaning against the door on the inside to stop me getting in. I walked across to the opposite wall and charged, but even though the door gave a little, it slammed shut again before I could take advantage of it. At this point the man, suspicious and rightly so that his girl-friend was somehow the cause of my difficulty, came to my assistance in what I imagined was a purely altruistic spirit. We charged together, the door flew open and there was the blonde lady flashing her tits. Mick somehow managed to blame me. 'Typical,' he said – he was on the verge of the 'how's your married life going' cycle. The girl, seeing her boy-friend, covered her breasts with her hands in the 'September Morn' position.

'You always spoil everything,' she told him petulantly.

He told her he was going home at once and was she coming? She said no, and on one of the tracks of the L.P., a song called 'Farewell to Storyville' which was recorded towards the end of the evening, and unwisely included audience participation, she can be heard joining in the chori half a tone sharp and half a beat in arrears.

We had to re-record several of the numbers we'd done in the latter half of the evening. We did this in the Decca studio proper and they dubbed in the atmosphere and applause later, but due to the difficulty of reassembling an actual audience, 'Farewell to Storyville' had to stand. It's a pretty rough old noise.

I made several E.P.s too during the late fifties, and the band recorded several L.P.s and E.P.s also, some with me on the vocals, some purely instrumental. My own records never sold very well, in fact I was usually a little in debt to the companies because my royalties never quite covered my advances. Recently however the issue of an L.P. called 'British Jazz in the Fifties', an anthology which included a couple of tracks by me, did surprisingly well, and clear of debt at last, I received a cheque the other day for three pounds fifteen.

As well as recording and broadcasting, I occasionally appeared on the box; in fact about once a year somebody would decide I was to become a television personality on one level or another. Unfortunately, or possibly fortunately, I come over on the telly as camp as Chloe and look drugged up to the eyeballs to boot, and after a single appearance I'd be dropped until I was rediscovered twelve months later. Still Mick and I had really little cause to complain at the way things went for us. We never really made the big time, but then to have done so, or even tried to do so, would have meant changing the whole band sound, which from Mick's point of view would have meant far too much work. He was lucky here to be able to count on unexpected support from Frank and Ian, not because they were afraid of rehearsal, quite the reverse, but because they detested the trad noise.

Once, during a sticky period financially which happened to correspond with the time Chris Barber had begun to make it, Mick actually flirted with the idea of seeking the flesh-pots. This came out during one of the drunken band discussions in the wagon on the way back to London. Everybody was putting forward different ways of increasing the band's earning power, solutions like more rehearsals, individual practising, new numbers, in fact all the suggestions guaranteed to put the conductor into a filthy temper. He was sitting in the front seat next to Appleby, saying nothing, but with his head sunk into the nylon fur collar of his pale grey shortie quilted mac, an unlikely garment he had bought because it was the first thing he'd been shown in a shop in Charing Cross Road when he'd been caught out in a cloud burst. Everybody's remarks were of course aimed at Mick although delivered in a rather serious detached way as though part of an abstract discussion. Eventually Mick got the needle.

'Only one way to make it these days,' he growled. 'That's to get a banjo. If you've got a banjo you're unassailable. Unassailable.'

A great cry of protest arose from the back of the wagon, but Mick wouldn't budge. As always when he was drunk and angry, a single idea took over. Whatever anybody else said, he countered it with the unassailability of the banjo. Furthermore, he finally insisted, he was going to get a banjo player. Of course none of us took him seriously, but Mick actually did get a banjo player, or at least a guitar player who said he was willing to play banjo.

His name was Bill Bramwell, and he was well known as a bass player too, and had played jazz all over the world since 1945, and had composed several TV jingles, but work was rather thin at that moment, and as he could manage to play with us and fit in most of his outside jobs as well, he decided to join us for a bit. He also looked on it as an opportunity to play some jazz. For the first week or two Bill did actually bring along the banjo he'd bought as his passport into the band, and even played it on a few numbers, but he soon dropped it, and later even took to amplifying his guitar. Mick didn't mind. His honour had been satisfied, and like the rest of us he much preferred guitar anyway.

Bill was a bit older than the rest of us. He came from the same generation of jazzmen as Lennie Felix and Dill Jones. He was less blasé then we were, and had managed to retain much more enthusiasm for playing. On listening to himself on play-back he would sometimes say how good he was. This, of course, was a great source of malicious delight to the conductor.

The very first week after he'd joined us we pulled up at a garage somewhere in South London on the way home from a job in Gillingham, and Bill told us that he'd thoroughly enjoyed the evening's session. 'You all love each other,' he explained, 'that's why you swing. You can't play jazz unless you love each other.' It was remarks like this which convinced Ian Christie that he and Bill were on different wave lengths and as time went on a considerable and mutual antipathy built up. Bill had recently married. He was Welsh working class himself, but his wife came from a county family in Devon who were also Roman Catholic and there'd been a grand wedding with Bill in a grey topper. Bill was rather impressed with his new relations and was always telling stories of what a marvellous old gentleman his father-in-law was. Squire of the manor and so on, but completely natural. Conservative and a bit crusty but very kind at heart. This also used to drive Ian mad.

Usually however they treated each other politely but distantly; but one night in the wagon a splendid explosion took place. Ian was in the back seat, Bill in the middle seat. Ian had said that what was really important was to be yourself. Whether the remark was aimed at Bill or not I can't remember, but Bill thought it was, and turning round mimicked Ian's accent.

'Be yourself,' he said, 'you've got to be yourself.'

Ian took no notice and went on talking, but every time he paused to draw breath, which was admittedly not often, Bill would say it again. Eventually Ian got the pin, and remembering that Bill had once told us that he had been to a psychoanalyst who used to knit while he was in session, began to reply in kind. Whenever Bill said anything Ian would mutter 'knit, knit, knit' in a manic frenzy. Eventually Bill and Ian faced each other over the back of the seat, and crimson with rage shouted in each other's face:

'Be yourself! Be yourself!'

'Knit, knit! Knit, knit, knit! Knit, knit, knit, knit!'

For Frank Parr on the other hand Bill Bramwell appeared to be a figure of fun. Because of the existence of an old blues singer called 'Bumble Bee Slim', he called Bill 'Bumble Bee Fat.' This name took into account not only Bill's comparative rotundity, but his habit of humming loudly to himself when taking a solo. Frank also removed any photograph of bald, plump, bespectacled men from the pages of the newspaper to take them home where he claimed to stick them in his 'Bill Bramwell Book'. Bill of course was bald, plump and bespectacled, and did bear a remarkable resemblance to most of the judges, business men, criminals, or anonymous figures Frank tore out for his collection. I've never actually examined 'The

Bill Bramwell Book' but knowing Frank I dare say it existed.

Bill was the only member of the band to outwit the conductor's financial one-upmanship. We were meant to be paid weekly, but as this meant sitting down during drinking and dart-playing time, and working out what we were owed in relation to what we'd had in subs, Mick did everything he could to avoid settling up, preferring to peel off a tenner from the wad of crumpled notes he kept stuffed in his back pocket with the inevitable query, 'Will this do for the mo, cock?'

As a result none of us knew exactly where we stood, and when eventually we did bully him into settling up, were likely to forget the five we'd had in the Working Men's Club during the interval at St Albans three weeks before, or the fifteen we'd taken on the way back from Nottingham. The conductor, with his photographic memory, never forgot and alleviated the boredom of paying out by making us feel guilty and dishonest. In my case he would rub more salt in the wound by calling me Maudie, a habit dating back to the extra fishcake, and implying that my mother's spirit watched over me at all times.

'Forgotten about the fistful when we stopped at that boozer outside Leicester, Maudie?' he'd say coldly. Maudie was also meant to be behind it when I had a good night at poker.

Bill Bramwell's counter-ploy was to never ask for settlement. On the contrary he made a point of accepting subs at all times, but deliberately confused the issue by asking for odd sums like three pounds ten, or twelve pounds and a cheque for another eight. In the end it was Mick who had to ask Bill if he'd like to straighten out and, as he said later, 'I can't remember what the bugger's had. I'm sure I was done.'

Getting paid was known as the eagle shitting. 'Can the eagle shit tonight?' somebody, usually Frank Parr, would ask. It was a great satisfaction to us all when Mick noticed that the little street off Piccadilly where his bank was situated was called Eagle Place.

Mick and I liked Bill Bramwell very much. He was kind and

funny. His humour depended on an exploitation of childishness which seemed very droll in relation to his rather adult and serious appearance. He was good at the sustained anecdote too, piling absurdity on absurdity until it was quite painful to go on laughing. To his disadvantage he snored very loudly. When in the Middlesborough area we used to stay with a clergyman and his wife. He was a nice and funny man with a wooden hand, or at least two, one for weekdays and a smarter one for Sundays, and he was, as he put it, 'Resident Rev.' at a reform school. He had run the jazz club in Newmarket before taking this post and that's how we'd got to know him. When we stayed with him in the small modern house provided by the detention school for its incumbent, there was plenty to drink, his wife cooked an enormous amount to eat, and we had a ball. During one of our visits we didn't go to bed until it was time for the Resident Rev. to conduct Holy Communion. When he came back for breakfast he was met by one of his children in a state of panic. 'Daddy,' said the little girl, 'there's a lion in one of the bedrooms!' It was Bill Bramwell snoring.

Bill left after a year or so to join an advertising firm on the musical side, but he still played occasionally with us – broadcasts, recording sessions and so on – when Mick felt we needed a fuller sound. He rowed me in on several commercials too, mostly advertising film designed for the African market, and we also did occasional prison concerts.

Mick was right about the unassailability of the banjo; without one we only got the crumbs that fell from the traddies' table. There was, however, one moment when we nearly made a film. In 1957 Ealing decided that a jazz band on the road would make a good subject for a picaresque comedy, and somebody had recommended the Mulligan band as a source on which to draw. As a result a director and a producer spent some time travelling about with us in the wagon. They were both called Mike.

The producing Mike was only with us for one tour, and managed to get his face slapped in Swansea by telling a young lady he could get her into pictures. He was rather drunk at the time. The directing Mike came with us on several tours. He was a nice, tall, curly-haired, enthusiastic, clumsy man, and afflicted with a bad stammer when excited. This usually happened when he recognized the potential of some northern scene, a shabby dance hall backed by slag heaps or a fish and chip shop reflected in a dirty canal. He'd never been north of Golders Green before, and these images had yet to be turned into clichés.

'T-t-t-t-terr-terribly visually exciting d-d-d-dear boy,' he would shout as he leapt about looking at such vistas through cupped hands.

We were all very impressed by the thought of being used as the basis for characters and camped it up like mad. As the film company provided a great deal of whisky this was even easier than it would otherwise have been. Staying in one hotel, Frank drank himself into being only fit for the human scrap heap in under five minutes and on to the floor in ten. Next morning we were all in the bar and he did it again. The fat bespectacled landlord came in at this point, stepped carefully over Parr's body and, without registering any surprise, wished him good morning.

That night we were booked to appear at a Lancashire seaside resort only thirty miles away. We not only contrived to be late, but indeed Frank didn't appear at all until the second half. There was a revolving stage and the conductor, who was at his most waggish, waited until Pete had begun his drum solo and then set it in motion. Pete was, of course, sober, and every time he appeared behind stage, would shout 'Drunken cunts!' at us before disappearing again into the light.

After the producer had seen enough, it was the turn of the writer, a Scottish novelist called James Kennaway. He had written a book about officers in a Highland regiment, but we were initially outside his terms of reference. To start with he hated us very much. In The Bodega, at the end of his first night with us on the road, he stood, his eyes full of angry tears, and beat his clenched fists against the wall.

'You're all shits!' he shouted. 'I hate you. I hate you.'

We didn't think he blew up a storm either to begin with, but by the time he left us to write his script, we were entirely reconciled. Actually it wasn't us that changed but him. He turned into a real raver.

James wasn't starry-eyed about us though, even by the end. He recognized our defensive cliquishness, our tendency to 'put it on' to impress him and others, the way we used funny voices for weeks at a time. Whether any of this would have got into the film I don't know. The company folded and it was never made.

We'd been offered fifty pounds each initially for allowing ourselves to be used as a basis for fiction. When we heard the film was off all of us, with one exception, took it for granted that we could kiss the money good-bye. The exception was Alan Duddington.

'Mick,' he suddenly announced in the wagon a good few months after most of us had forgotten the film had ever existed as a possibility. 'Could you ask if we could have the fifty pounds before Christmas? I'll need it to buy presents for my folk.' Shortly after this Alan left us and Gerry Salisbury replaced him.

Everybody in the band loved Gerry. He had married into the budgie and garden gnome belt, but his origins were Cockney-Italian, and he was in fact a cousin of Jo Lennard. He had been brought up in Covent Garden, and told some marvellous stories of his childhood. In particular I remember an incident in which a policeman, with whom the entire Salisbury family had been on bad terms for a whole year, was invited in at Christmas for what he imagined to be a peace-offering in the form of a seasonable drink. It had been well-laced with 'Jollops', a very strong laxative which, according to Jerry, worked instantly.

'He goes running down the stairs holding on to 'is ring to get to the outside toilet in time,' explained Gerry in his slow deep voice. 'And when 'e gets there, 'e discovers that the old man's been and gone and nailed up the door!'

But for Gerry his Chaucerian world was in the past, and by the time he joined the band he was living with his wife and baby daughter in his in-laws' semi out at Mill Hill.

Gerry's mind worked all right, but rather slowly, like a record player at the wrong speed. He realized this, and had developed a set of mannerisms to go with it. If asked a question he would stand absolutely still for a moment, and then he would turn his whole body towards his interrogator as though it were on a revolving platform for displaying sculpture, and subject him to a long and searching stare. Finally, when Gerry was ready, he would give a slight jerk, lift his eyebrows, and deliver his answer which was always pertinent and usually humorous.

Gerry's features were rather beautiful, and he had very long eyelashes, but his movements, and in particular the impression he gave that his head, neck and torso were not articulated, made him add up to a comic figure. With his completely deadpan face he reminded me of Buster Keaton, and indeed he had a real passion for early film comedies.

He used to share the driving with Aps, and when that gentleman decided he would like a break – this didn't happen very often as he was paid by the mile – an amusing little scene took place.

Pete would draw up in a layby and on the cue, 'Like ter drive for a bit, Ger?' both of them would throw open the two front doors of the van, and climb out. They would meet directly in front of the bonnet, small animated Aps and the slow-moving and stolid Gerry, and exchange a few words. These were, of course, inaudible for the rest of us in the back of the Volkswagen, but somehow the contrast between them suggested a music-hall exchange, and we called it their 'Wheeler and Woolsey Act'. Having finished what they had to say to each other, they completed their little walk. Pete would climb into the passenger seat and go to sleep, Gerry into the driving seat and start up the engine. It was a perfectly reasonable way of changing over, and much more sensible than clambering across each other's knees, but it always seemed faintly ridiculous.

Gerry's passion was coarse fishing, and he managed to interest Pete in this too. It made a change from their continuous rabbiting about second-hand cars on long journeys, although Pete soon reduced it, as he reduced everything else, to a formula. Every time we passed over or near a stretch of water, whether canal, river, pond, lake or reservoir, he would turn to Gerry and say: 'Must be a few in there, Ger.'

I confessed to Gerry that as a child I had been a keen trout fisherman, and he did his best to hook me on coarse fishing. We did spend several freezing days off on the banks of a small and muddy pond near Stanmore live-baiting for pike. I quite enjoyed these Spartan expeditions, but the final result of Gerry's propaganda was to rekindle my passion for trout. He refused to have anything to do with it, even in Scotland where it's very cheap.

'It's not a working man's sport,' he explained. He had retained from his Cockney childhood a fierce sense of class loyalty.

More than anyone else in the band, Gerry was a real musician. His thinking, so slow and earthbound in everyday life, became charged with originality once it turned to music. He was a good bass player, but what he should have been was a trumpet player. He used to play if Mick was ill, or would occasionally take a number if we had an especially long session, and his phrasing and the construction of his chori were absolutely delicious. The only trouble, the only tragedy really, was that he had no lip. Lip in a trumpet-player is the ability to go on playing without your mouth starting to jelly-up on you so that you can't blow. A lot of it, of course, comes from playing continuously; you develop a hard lip in the end as you can see from examining the extraordinary cushion of leather in photographs of Louis Armstrong, but Gerry had played a lot at one time and another, and it just didn't happen. After a couple of numbers he couldn't blow any more. Mick on the other hand had a lip of iron, and some ability to swing, but compared with Gerry he was very uninventive. It was very sad.

Gerry was not really so much an active figure in the band; he was more of a spectator, but his originality of vision, his stolid refusal to be shaken by anything, his eye for the absurd, provoked the rest of us into every form of mania and excess.

The abortive film project was the only chance we had of becoming national figures although we had a certain reputation as good copy. Patrick Campbell, the humorist, came with us to Oxford one night in 1957 and wrote a very funny piece about us in his column in the now defunct *Sunday Dispatch*. What especially pleased us about this was that he got several points poetically wrong. For example he misheard our expression, 'Put me in a snout' (i.e. Give me a cigarette) as 'Cut me in the snuff'. Also that particular night, the wagon picked up Gerry Salisbury and me at a pub called 'The Target' on Western Avenue. The reason for this was that we had been fishing unsuccessfully for pike in the pond in Stanmore. Gerry told the band that there was meant to be a huge pike in that pond which could take even full grown ducks. Frank Parr interjected at this point with a quote from some obscure poem. 'The wolf-jawed pike,' he intoned solemnly.

In Patrick Campbell's piece this came out as: ' . . . to pick up George Melly. . . . He told us that he had been fishing for Wolf Jaw, the monster pike in Stanmore Pond.'

From that day, 'Cut me in the snuff' became the way we did ask for a cigarette, at first humorously, but eventually as a matter of course, while Wolf Jaw, the monster pike of Stanmore Pond, joined the spade bongo player as one of our permanent phantoms.

I myself began, as the years went by, to appear quite frequently outside the band, not only on the radio, but as a solo compère and performer. One of the most profitable and enjoyable of these extra-Mulligan jobs was for Paddy McKiernan who organized for three years a show called 'Rhythm with the Stars', designed to expand the sales of the *Daily Express* in the north. The first year I compèred and sang a spot with Chris Barber. The second I just sang with Mick, but in my own spot and billed as a solo artist, the third year I compèred again and sang with Mick, but what seemed to me absolutely fabulous was what I got paid. A hundred pounds! I had never earned so much in my life in such a short period.

I discovered how to get rid of it, however. We played a different town every evening, and as I was usually in Paddy's company, I stayed at the same four-star hotels, ate at the best restaurants, and stood a great many very expensive rounds into the night.

The show consisted of a mixed bill, part jazz, part pop. The first year the star was Eddie Calvert. We opened in Manchester, the hall was packed with Chris Barber fans, and Eddie got the bird. He came down to the dressing room in a very bad temper and began to bawl out Paddy while he changed. Every time he swore, his father, who was sitting there in a cap, said, 'Now, now, Eddie,' in a mild voice.

In the middle of his diatribe he suddenly turned on me. 'It's all right for you,' he shouted, 'you're only an amateur.' After so long on the road I took exception to this, and told him I had been singing 'Frankie and Johnnie' – the number had gone down particularly well – for over eight years almost every night.

'Was that you falling down?' snapped Eddie. I said it was.

'You'll get cancer, you know,' he spat out, and returned to the attack.

But solo jobs were rare. For the most part we completed the fifties like somnambulists, always tired from the all-night poker sessions, often drunk, doing something we had once done for love out of habit. Jazz and the Mulligan band had a relationship like a failed marriage. We stuck together because we could see no alternative.

In Cleethorpes, on the way up to a Scottish tour, we chanced upon a figure who seemed to symbolize our condition. She was called 'Musical Marie' and was attempting, in a tent on the front, to beat the world record for non-stop piano playing. Before it was time for our first session we paid our sixpences and went in to see her. She'd been at it fifteen hours and had almost three more days to go.

She was a fat lady dressed in a powder-blue gown. She sat at the piano listlessly tinkling away. Her manager, a flamboyant middle-aged man, told us that she was in ordinary life a Manchester housewife.

'Every tune she plays,' he kept emphasizing, 'is a real melody.'

'What happens when she wants to piss?' Mick asked.

'She continues playing,' explained the manager, 'a screen is brought on to the stage, and she uses an Elsan behind it. She never stops playing for one moment. All recognizable tunes.'

The Elsan, he explained, was brought on and removed by a lady in Red Cross uniform. The manager himself fed her on glucose.

When the dance was over we passed the tent on the deserted front. Through the loud speakers we could hear Musical Marie playing her hesitant and stumbling notes into the small hours. She was still at it when we left next morning. I was interested enough to ring up Cleethorpes Town Hall from Scotland a few days later. I spoke to the Town Clerk.

'Oh, yes, she broke the record,' he told me, 'played for a

further 'alf 'our so there'd be no argument, and was then carried into t' Dolphin 'otel in a state of collapse.'

In 1960 the trad boom at its height, and a riot occurred at Beaulieu. It wasn't a vicious riot. It was stupid. The traddies in rave gear booing the Dankworth Band. A young man clumbing up the outside of the palace in the floodlights waving a bowler hat from the battlements. Cheers and scuffles. Then, when the television transmission was going on and Acker playing, the crowd surged forward and began to climb the scaffolding supporting the arc-lights. The few police and the official stewards struggled with them, and the B.B.C. went off the air.

Gerald Lascelles shouted at a young man to climb down.

'Say please,' said the young man.

'Please,' said Gerald.

'No,' said the young man.

Somewhere in the audience was a boy who'd killed a taxi-driver and come to Beaulieu on the money. The papers, of course, had a field day.

The next year there wasn't a riot. Inside the grounds there were lots of police with dogs but there was no need for them. Modern jazz and traditional took place at different sessions. Anita O'Day, in a lace dress so tight she had difficulty climbing up the steps to the roundabout, sang 'Sweet Georgia Brown' while the dancers silhouetted against the floodlit wall jumped for joy in the warm night. It was very beautiful.

The trouble was that there were too many people for the village to absorb, not enough lavatories, too few litter bins. Local feeling rose high, and at midnight Edward Montagu told the Press that this was the last festival he would hold at Beaulieu. Trad jazz had outgrown its most typical and happiest occasion.

16. What Has Happened to the Chaps?

During my first year and a half at Tregunter Road I was sexually a freewheeler. One night in a club I watched a coloured
girl doing a snake charming act. When she'd finished and had
dressed, and was on her way out of the place, I left the girl I'd
brought with me, rushed up to her and kissed her on the mouth.
I persuaded her to come over to the bar, bought her a drink and
she gave me her telephone number. The girl I'd left so abruptly
didn't say anything but a few days later, following another act
of aggressive and quite unnecessary sexual insult on my part,
we broke up.

I didn't do anything about the snake charmer for some time,
but one evening I found her name, Cerise Johnson, and her
telephone number in my wallet. I rang her up and asked her
over. We went out to dinner, back to Tregunter Road, and
eventually to bed. I liked her very much – she had an extraordinary line in hot chat – but the next day we went away on
tour.

A week or two later it was Christmas and I felt I'd had the
whole Christmas thing, so on the way home from a family
supper at my sister's flat I rang her up again, picked her up

from the Bayswater Hotel she had a room in, and took her home in a taxi. This time she stayed two days. We saw each other regularly after that and gradually slipped into an affair.

The first intimation of trouble happened the first time I took her to Cook's Ferry Inn. She had a row with a band – I didn't hear it actually happen – and threw her shoe in the canal. I put this down to having drunk too many whiskies, bought a new pair of shoes and made Cerise apologize.

But it was only the beginning. Cerise was often violent and for the next two years I was seldom without scratches on my face. Before one lot had healed properly there was a new display.

At the beginning of our relationship I was frequently in the wrong. I tried to treat her in the casual way I'd treated my other girl friends and she wouldn't have it, but later on her attacks were without any basis in reality. It was usually somebody else she went for – a girl she imagined had tried to date me, someone she claimed had insulted her on the grounds of colour. She was extremely strong, and I felt it necessary to intervene, thereby adding fuel to her obsessive suspicions. After the initial outbreak she could usually be persuaded to leave, but once home she'd work herself up into a rage again. This time it was me she went for. She fought like a tiger and was far stronger than I am. Although we usually finished with Cerise riding me, bleeding and bruised, in bed, there was nothing much in it for anybody else. The jazz world is prejudiced to a fault in favour of the coloured race, but they found Cerise a bit much. She'd soon had rows with most of my men friends – girls were of course out of the question – and as Simon refused for a time to allow her in the flat (she'd threatened him with a broken milk bottle and tried to set some spades on us in the middle of Notting Vale during the riots) we found ourselves living more or less in isolation in a flat she'd taken in West Kensington. We went to the theatre and to night clubs, we saw her friends, mostly coloured cabaret artistes, but apart from the band and Wally, the whole of my social life went by the board.

Why didn't I leave her? Fear mostly, but also I felt a great affection for her. She could be wounded as well as wound. Although even in the flat, and with no outside stimuli to provoke her, she could suddenly appear possessed and, screaming hysterical nonsense, attack me with such violence that on several occasions I was frightened for my life, ninety per cent of the time she was gentle, loving, erotic and protective. To leave the flat, however, was to court almost certain disaster.

One night we went to a party at the Fawkes' in Swiss Cottage: a big house, lots to eat and drink; Jimmy Rushing was the guest of honour. Mick was there. So was Pam. Although Wally had seen Cerise in action several times, he knew how much I admired and liked Jimmy and decided to risk it. Within half an hour it had started. I'd gone to the lavatory and when I came back I found Cerise screaming at the foot of the stairs. She claimed that the French *au pair* girl – a plain girl who had by this time fled prudently up to her room – had been making eyes at me.

'Anaemic white shit!' Cerise was yelling. Wally was blocking the staircase. Sandy Fawkes and several other guests were trying to persuade her she'd been mistaken. This she managed to twist so as to accuse them of colour prejudice. What made this especially absurd in retrospect was that one of the people so accused was Max Jones, the jazz critic, who if he believed in God, which he doesn't, would be convinced He was black.

After some minutes, still screaming with rage, she threw open the door of the sitting-room and rushed full-tilt into the rock-like figure of Jimmy Rushing who was sitting playing the piano. He immediately played the opening phrase of 'Shoo fly don't bother me'. She called him a white man's nigger. He took no notice at all.

There was one man at the party who had never met Cerise

before, and seeing her surrounded by a large group of Caucasians, he waded in on her side. This was all she needed. Her fantasy had a believer. She went outside into the front garden and began to collect a pile of stones and rocks which she intended to throw at the windows. Pam Mulligan went out after her to try and talk her out of it. I'd had enough and decided to opt out. She'd promised not to make a scene. I'd told Sandy and Wally I'd guarantee this time it would be all right. I felt absolutely miserable. I poured myself out a tumbler of gin and drank it down neat in one swallow. Then I went over to Jimmy Rushing at the piano and asked him to play a blues. He did and I began to sing with the tears streaming down my face. As the gin hit me I slid, still singing, towards the floor and passed out. Mick Mulligan picked me up, according to Wally, as tenderly as if I'd been a sick child, carried me through into the kitchen and put me on the couch. He was arranging a blanket over me when Pam came in from the garden.

'I've managed to calm her down,' she said, 'she wants to take George home.'

The next moment personified, according to Wally again, the whole difference between Mick's attitude to men and women. After all the tender care he'd displayed towards me, he turned to Pam and said: 'Why don't you keep your fucking hooter out of it?'

But Pam had succeeded in calming Cerise, who came back into the house, picked me up off the sofa, threw me over her shoulder like a sack, and marched out.

The strange thing about Cerise was that she took it for granted that I fucked in the provinces. She didn't seem to care either. Once I caught crabs – she spotted one when she was going down – but she didn't seem a bit put out. I nervously insisted that you could catch them off a lavatory seat or from dirty sheets. She just smiled and said I shouldn't go with such dirty girls. I said I hoped she hadn't caught them from me.

'Crabs don't bite me never. Me blood too rich,' she explained. Furthermore, she wouldn't let me buy any ointment. She insisted on searching them out herself.

'I likes to crack 'em between me nails,' she told me.

It was only in London she expected complete fidelity. She once did a week's cabaret in Manchester and told me she'd be back on the Monday. On the Sunday night I went out with my sister Andrée. She drove me back and said she'd come in for a drink. The door to Simon's basement flat is round the side of the house in a dark dustbin-haunted alley down some steep steps. As Andrée and I were walking down this passage laughing and chatting, and I was feeling for my key, Cerise spoke from the shadows.

'Who's that white pussy you got there?' I told her it was Andrée whom she knew well. 'That's O.K. then,' she said. 'You in luck it weren't no white pussy you tipping home with,' and she replaced the heavy iron dustbin lid she'd been holding at the ready.

Simon didn't bar Cerise from the flat for long and we sometimes stayed at her place, sometimes mine. One afternoon Cerise was cleaning the flat as I was expected back that evening. Simon was putting on his B.O.A.C. uniform to go to London airport. The bell rang. It was Victoria back from Rome with nowhere to stay. She asked Simon if she could stay there.

Simon told me later that he drove his scooter out to the airport trembling with nerves. He was convinced Cerise would murder Victoria. She didn't though. When I came in after the job she told me coldly that my wife was asleep on the divan in the sitting-room. I went in to say hello, and Victoria kissed me affectionately. Cerise and I went to bed.

'She must go in the morning,' she said not unreasonably, 'I'm your woman. How she think she tip in here after three year and give you tongue sandwich?'

Next morning I told Victoria she'd have to find somewhere

else. Cerise was quite calm if unfriendly until she'd gone. Then she let fly.

I didn't contradict her. I was so relieved that nothing terrible had happened. Victoria found a modelling job and a basement flat in Chelsea. Cerise and I lived together much as before for another five months.

Then suddenly she told me she'd decided to go and work on the Continent. She'd been offered a job in Paris, fares paid, and decided to take it. I went to the airport to see her off. I stood on the roof of the new Queen's Building and watched her walk – she walked beautifully – towards the plane. I couldn't believe she was going. After two years I was sad, but my strongest feeling was relief.

I went over to spend a week with her in Paris shortly afterwards. I'd promised. It was all right, but we both knew it was over.

I came back to London and within the month Victoria and I said, well, it might work this time.

It didn't work at all. Within a month of being together again we both knew it. There were concrete reasons of course, things either of us could point to as to why it didn't work, but the real reason was that we didn't add up. We weren't a couple.

We moved first to a basement flat in Swan Walk. Here we got on very badly. Then, both of us imagining that if we had something solid there was a chance to build up a relationship again, we bought a house on Hampstead Heath. It didn't do any good either, but as it was bigger, we got on better. There were even days when it all looked possible. We'd go to the pictures and come back arm in arm, we'd have a nice dinner together at Wheelers, but nothing came of it. We started to lead our own lives. It wasn't hell or anything like it. More a cushioned limbo.

Appleby had left the band to join Donegan and was replaced, after a week or two, by a plump funny manic-depressive from Bristol called Fat John Cox. He was a dandy with little feet for whom nothing ever went right. He was married to a beautiful German wife he'd met in Cologne. He called her 'Missus'. He called the conductor 'Leader'. He moaned and complained about everything in his strong Bristol accent. He looked, like a lot of fat men, rather lesbian. He was interested in sadomasochistic fetishism and eating. He sometimes tried to go on a diet, would hold out for a day, and then go to a pie stall and eat six pies.

We ran through an exceptional number of bass players in 1960–61. The most memorable was called Cliff – small, bespectacled, with a fine crop of acne. We nicknamed him 'Weasel'. He was much younger than us and got everything wrong. He was Ian's particular *bête noire* on two counts. The first day he joined the band, he observed in his whiny transpontine voice that it was surprising there should be three public school boys in the band. Mick – Merchant Taylors, me – Stowe, himself – Alleyns College. The Bird's face was a real joy at that moment. On the other hand he offended Ian's feeling for the good life by getting everything wrong. Favourite fish – cod; in a restaurant he'd order a drambuie with his soup.

Ian and I went fishing whenever we had a chance. I got better at it, much to Frank Parr's annoyance. He used to enjoy it when I came back in the evening with nothing to show for it 'Caught anything?' he'd ask with an infuriating smile on his face. The first time I was able to say yes and produce a pound grayling was a sweet moment. I began to welcome Scottish tours.

Mick and Frank played golf together. Mick usually won and Frank would lose his temper and attack the putting green. This very much offended Mick's sense of propriety as did Frank's habit of playing stripped to the waist on fine days so as to expose himself to 'the currant bun' or 'big fellow' as he called the sun. Eventually, despite his pleasure both at winning from

Frank and making him lose his temper into the bargain, Mick wouldn't play with him any more.

We did a tour of Ireland in 1961. I neglected to do any Flook strip and got back to find an angry Wally biting his nails and five days backlog. This was the only time this happened.

That Easter my father died. He was sixty-one. His funeral was the last occasion Victoria put in an official appearance as my wife.

Later that summer the editress of *Queen* magazine sent for me and said that Colin McInnes had suggested that I might write something for them. Colin was a keen Flook fan and had written a laudatory article in the *Twentieth Century*. I did a piece for them called 'A Week-end in the Jazz World'. In it I wrote: 'On the road. Ten years of it. I seem to have spent a lifetime looking out of grimy windows in digs at backyards in the rain. Weeds, rotting iron, collapsing outhouses.'

That article was in fact the key to my release. Out of it came other reviews and pieces, my Flook money had gone up and Wally and I were doing a weekly cartoon for the *Spectator*. I was also compèring 'Jazz Club' regularly, and I suddenly realized I could make enough to pack it in. It took me a week or two to raise the courage to tell Mick. I did it one evening in a pub.

'I was thinking of doing the same,' he said.

He had recently bought a house on the Sussex coast. Pam and the children were down there the whole time. He kept on the flat in Lisle Street as a *pied-à-terre*, but most nights he used to drive the extra eighty miles home. He was thinking, he told me, of buying an off-licence in that part of the world. He had begun to yearn for a home life, regular hours, fewer hangovers. We decided that 1 January 1962 would be the day to disband.

The band were divided. Ian had begun to write a jazz column in the *Sunday Telegraph*. He thought he might make out as a writer too. Bix could always get along. Fat John decided to form his own band. Frank was the most pessimistic. In July of that year, the last Beaulieu.

On the river-boat shuffle, or 'Floating Festival' as it was called in the high noon of the trad boom, I sang, as had become accepted custom, an obscene Liverpool ballad called 'The Lobster Song'. In Margate we went to the flea circus. 'This little lady is Madame Frou Frou. And this is Hercules, the strongest flea in the world.'

Steaming slowly back through the pool of London in the dusk, I reflected nostalgically on other years. The time Simon Watson Taylor brought John Raymond and he, charmed by the high spirits and physical beauty of all the young people, said that for the first time he understood the point of the Welfare State.

The band's last autumn. In the Colony Room early in October I met Diana; she was also married. We spent the afternoon together, I was meant to be taking Victoria to the newly opened 'Establishment Club'. I rang her up and she said did I mind but she'd been asked out by somebody else. I said no. I took Diana. Afterwards we went and made love on the heath. We knew that day we were going to get married.

Three days later I went in to Victoria's bedroom to tell her. Before I'd got it out, she told me she was leaving. She'd fallen in love with somebody else. I gave her my reciprocal piece of information. She asked who it was. I told her.

'But she's quite pretty!' she said.

A few weeks later Victoria left in her Floride and Diana moved in with her two children and a Victorian bassinette.

Many people think it was Diana who persuaded me to stop touring. I had in fact decided three months before I'd met her. Diana came to all the jobs we could manage during the band's last three months. At the Anarchists' Ball at Fulham Town Hall, Mick said to me while we were going out of a pub together: 'You've got yourself a good one there, cock.' I thought he was being sarcastic on the 'another good chap lost' level. 'No, cock,' he said, 'I mean it.'

That Christmas Eve we played The Bodega. Frank Parr fell off the stage and pulled down a huge Christmas tree on top of him. That was the last real moment in the official history of the band. The final job, a B.B.C. show called 'Trad Tavern', proved to be a remarkably unemotional evening.

Actually, although the band no longer existed, we played together a lot over the next year. The trad boom was still on and I agreed with Mick to do a week-end a month and the odd job near town. Indeed so elastically did the conductor interpret his terms of reference that at one moment it was like being on the road and I had to put my foot down.

Diana and I bought a mini-van and she learnt to drive. I loved that year. She'd hardly been out of London, and it was all new for her. She turned it on for me too.

As well as band work I compèred a big festival for Paddy in Blackpool, and a three-day stint in Cleethorpes.

At the Albert Hall around Easter 1963, Diz Disley, Rolf Harris and myself were linkmen for a B.B.C. spectacular of 'Jazz 'n Pop'. The jazz bands got a lot of applause, but the stars of the evening were 'The Beatles', a group I'd only just heard of. The bell had begun to toll for trad.

Over the last two years trad has died. Clubs closed. Managements turned over to Beat groups. Only the toughest bands survived. The Mulligan band, unaware of it at the time, did its last job. In '64 I hardly sang at all – a few cabarets, the festivals at Redcar and Cleethorpes were about my lot. We love these jazz festivals. It's great to see the old faces milling about in the private bar tent. Humph, Sandy and Al, Jim Bray and Alex Welsh. It's like the instant vision of a whole life which is meant to flash before the eyes of the drowning.

At the time of writing rhythm and blues is taking over from Beat. This is nearer allied to trad and several of the bands have made the jump. What is good about rhythm and blues is that it has meant almost every month one or more Negro blues singers come over on tour. We went to Croydon recently. A young, serious audience, and several figures from the past: Jimmy Asman and Derrick Stewart-Baxter.

Lately there have been some signs too of trad reviving on a small scale. I have sung recently in a South London pub and a rugger club out at Osterley. The audiences were enthusiastic. The atmosphere fresh again. It seemed to be for love not money.

Do I regret anything? Only this. I'm vain enough to find it hard to walk up the queue outside the Marquee on my way to listen to Howling Wolf, and to be completely unrecognized by several hundred blues fans. Wally Fawkes went through the same thing some time before me. He was a great figure in the revivalist days, second only to Humph. You get over it, he told me. I'm beginning to already.

When I started this book the trad boom was still on. Certain statements at the beginning are now inaccurate, but I'll let them rest. In the middle there are one or two references to the beat boom. That too is dying. If I was to aim at up-to-the-minute accuracy I should have to correct the proofs right up to publication date.

What has happened to the chaps?

Mick has his off-licence and grocery. He comes up to see me once a month with a booze order. He is still my manager. His character too has altered. He washes and shaves every morning. He works long hours to make his business a success. He has decided the time has come to 'pull his finger out', and yet his charm is as irresistible as ever. Under his white coat beats the same anarchic heart.

Ian, after a period as a photographer and a stint in a P.R.O. office, is now a feature writer on the *Express*.

Fat John is doing lounge work. He has a trio in various clubs.

Appleby is still with Donegan. He turned up to see me not long ago in an American car that filled the street.

Frank is general manager for the Acker Bilk organization.

Gerry Salisbury plays on Sunday mornings at a jam session in a pub in Kentish Town. He also works for a car firm.

What is marvellous is that once again I can listen to jazz. Sinclair Traill asked me if I would like to review blues records for him. 'We pay, of course,' he told me. Needless to say, he doesn't, but it's very exciting to get a packet of records every month.

But what about the raving and the birds? Don't I miss that bit, some people ask and more people think.

No. I read a book recently by a man now dead called Verrier Elwin. He was a marvellous old man who spent most of his life in India. He wrote this:

Today, and for many years past, my old loves have been concentrated on my beloved wife, in whom I have found the essence of them all. I am a better lover now for those experiences.

More about Penguins and Pelicans

Penguinews, which appears every month, contains details of all the new books issued by Penguins as they are published. From time to time it is supplemented by our stock list, which is our list of almost 5,000 titles.

A specimen copy of *Penguinews* will be sent to you free on request. Please write to Dept EP, Penguin Books Ltd, Harmondsworth, Middlesex, for your copy.

In the U.S.A.: For a complete list of books available from Penguins in the United States write to Dept CS, Penguin Books, 625 Madison Avenue, New York, New York 10022.

In Canada: For a complete list of books available from Penguins in Canada write to Penguin Books Canada Ltd, 2801 John Street, Markham, Ontario L3R 1B4.

'Rommel?' 'Gunner Who?'

Spike Milligan

Some comments on the second volume of Mr Milligan's reminiscences of World War II:

'Alters our whole conception of the Desert War' – A. J. P. T*y**r

'I resign' – Field Marshal Earl M*ntg*m*ry

'We deplore the absence of an index' – *The Times Literary Supplement*

'Gunner Who?' – Rommel

Also published in Penguins:

Adolf Hitler: My Part in his Downfall

Monty: His Part in My Victory

Puckoon

Small Dreams of a Scorpion

Transports of Delight

William McGonagall: The Truth at Last
(with Jack Hobbs)

New Penguin Fiction and Non-Fiction

Changing Places
David Lodge

'Not since *Lucky Jim* has such a funny book about academic life come my way' – *Sunday Times*

Rumpole of the Bailey
John Mortimer

Horace Rumpole, sixty-eight next birthday, with an unsurpassed knowledge of Blood and Typewriters, a penchant for quoting from the *Oxford Book of English Verse*, and a habit of referring to his judge as 'the old darling' . . .

Rumpole now takes up his pen in the pious hope of making a bob or two. In doing so he opens up some less well-charted corners of British justice.

The Seventh Gate
Peter Greave

'The story of an adventurous, action-packed, emotion-filled life, full of twists and turns, disasters and escapes, comedy and suffering, so enthralling that at times I felt it had to be fiction' – *Sunday Times*

'One of the most remarkable books about life in India ever to have been written' – *Daily Telegraph*

The Life of Noël Coward
Cole Lesley

'*The Life of Noël Coward* is – to borrow Coward's own description of his life – "fabulously enjoyable": a graceful and glistening piece of biography, reading which is like a holiday in a rented Rolls' – Kenneth Tynan in the *Observer*

'Funny, sad, witty, bawdy and totally unputdownable, it sheds new light on its many splendoured subject and enshrines for all time several decades of social history. I loved it!' – Peta Fordham in *The Times*